D1294241

The
GUITAR
in
AMERICA

The GUITAR *in* AMERICA

Victorian Era to Jazz Age

Jeffrey J. Noonan

UNIVERSITY PRESS OF MISSISSIPPI
JACKSON

AMERICAN MADE MUSIC SERIES
Advisory Board

David Evans, General Editor
Barry Jean Ancelet
Edward A. Berlin
Joyce J. Bolden
Rob Bowman
Susan C. Cook
Curtis Ellison
William Ferris
Michael Harris
John Edward Hasse
Kip Lornell
Frank McArthur
Bill Malone
Eddie S. Meadows
Manuel H. Peña
David Sanjek
Wayne D. Shirley
Robert Walser

ML
1015
.G9
N66
2008
JAZZ

www.upress.state.ms.us

The University Press of Mississippi is a member of the Association of American University Presses.

Unless noted otherwise, illustrations reproduced in this book have been drawn from BMG magazines held at the Library of Congress.

Copyright © 2008 by University Press of Mississippi
All rights reserved
Manufactured in the United States of America

First printing 2008

∞

Library of Congress Cataloging-in-Publication Data

Noonan, Jeffrey.
    The guitar in America : Victorian era to jazz age / Jeffrey J. Noonan.
        p. cm. — (American made music series)
    Includes bibliographical references (p.   ), discography (p.   ), and index.
    ISBN-13: 978-1-934110-18-8 (cloth : alk. paper)
    ISBN-10: 1-934110-18-3 (cloth : alk. paper) 1. Guitar—United States—History.
2. Guitarists—United States. 3. Guitar music—United States—History and criticism.
I. Title.
    ML1015.G9N66   2008
    787.870973—dc22   2007021095

British Library Cataloging-in-Publication Data available

B2350623

⤙ CONTENTS ⤚

CONTENTS

⋘ ACKNOWLEDGMENTS ⋙

This book began as my doctoral dissertation and I reiterate the thanks and acknowledgments I offered in the opening pages of that document several years ago. Craig Monson, principal reader on that project, has continued to go above and beyond his official duties, offering sound professional advice and pointed criticism of my ideas and writing. I do not exaggerate when I say that without his help this book would not have deserved to see the light of day.

My initial research took place in and with the cooperation of numerous libraries and I thank these institutions and their staffs for their assistance. These libraries include the Music Division of the Library of Congress, Kent Library of Southeast Missouri State University, the Newberry Library, and the New York Public Library for the Performing Arts. Much of my research, writing, and revising took place in the Gaylord Music Library of Washington University and I thank Music Librarian Brad Short and his staff for their pleasant and professional assistance.

In the early stages of my research, Peter Danner and Thomas Heck, two of this country's most respected scholars of the classical guitar, offered critical commentary and collegial encouragement. I thank them for both. The College of Liberal Arts at Southeast Missouri State University supported several research trips and I thank Emeritus Dean Martin Jones, Associate Dean Gary Miller of the Holland School for Visual and Performing Arts, and the Committee for Faculty Development for their financial assistance and professional interest. My colleagues at Southeast Missouri State University deserve my thanks for allowing me to occasionally bend their ears and for their encouraging questions. These folks include Steve Hendricks and Brandon Christensen in the Department of Music and Marc Strauss in the Department of Theater and Dance.

As I began work on turning my dissertation into a book, I had the good fortune to meet two gentlemen whose collections of instruments, books, and ephemera related to the banjo in America are surpassed only by their knowledge of the subject. Eli Kaufman and Jim Bollman graciously opened their homes and their collections to me, sharing not only their spectacular holdings but their encyclopedic knowledge of the period, the music, and the personalities. As a guitarist, I suppose I can provide little in return that real banjo experts like Eli and Jim want, but I offer them my sincere thanks. I include Madeleine Kaufman in that thanks, too.

In the rewriting process, I imposed on friends and colleagues to read bits and pieces of this book. Warren Anderson, a fine banjoist and professor of anthropology at Southeast Missouri State University, encouraged me to "tell the story." I thank him for his scholarly suggestions, professional example, and our weekly lunches. Tim Brookes, an author cited in this book, played a major role in the direction of parts of my dissertation. More recently, he found the time to read enough of my book manuscript to immediately pinpoint a beginner's errors. His professional critique has improved the book immensely. I only hope the revision comes up to his expectations. Robert Ferguson, a friend and scholar, not only shared his unpublished research with me but also read an early draft of this book with an eye to grammatical, bibliographic, and factual detail that overwhelmed me. As I incorporated his suggestions, I sometimes wondered if perhaps Bob should have written this book.

Thanks, too, to Craig Gill, Anne Stascavage, Will Rigby, and the staff at University Press of Mississippi for their encouragement and hard work. I sincerely appreciate the Press taking this project on and hope that my part in the process has met their expectations. Thanks, as well, to the Press's anonymous reader whose comments perfectly balanced scholarly criticism with collegial encouragement.

I offer a general "thank you" to other friends, colleagues, and family who supported the completion of this book. And while I wish I could shift the blame, any errors—factual, grammatical, and otherwise—in the following pages are my responsibility. I dedicate this book to Nancy Bristol and our blended/extended family—Erin and Brian, Brendan and Sarah, and Joe. Their hard work and well-deserved successes in their respective fields continue to impress and inspire me, as I try to keep up with them. Nancy's contribution to this book transcends her toleration of my paper trails, hours in the library, and absent-minded disregard for the day-to-day. Her patience, good humor, and encouragement allowed it to happen. Love you all.

The
GUITAR
in
AMERICA

⤙ INTRODUCTION ⤚

In the second half of the twentieth century, the guitar became America's instrument. In the hands of innovators like Les Paul, Charlie Christian, Merle Travis, Jimi Hendrix, and a host of other players, the instrument helped define—and was in turn defined by—America's music: country, blues, jazz, and rock in all its varieties. These players and their music did not develop in a vacuum. They had predecessors, they were heirs to traditions; and, if we do our homework or our fieldwork, we can find their roots, discovering stylistic bloodlines. In Maybelle Carter's "Wildwood Flower" we hear the hillbilly roots of honky-tonk, country and western, and Chet Atkins's popularized Nashville Sound. In Robert Johnson's plaintive singing and playing we hear B.B. King, Buddy Guy, and a multitude of other bluesmen and women. In the bluesy jazz lines of Eddie Lang or Lonnie Johnson, we hear premonitions of the steady work of Freddie Green with Count Basie or Barney Kessel in the studio as well as the sophisticated jazz stylings of Wes Montgomery, Joe Pass, Jim Hall, and others. None of these musical examples really surprises us; each makes sense, musically and historically, in light of what we know followed.

This history of the guitar in America is really a documentation of musical genres, a history built principally on recorded performance. The guitar's ubiquitous use in America's recorded popular music has dictated how its players and fans understand its origins and its story. Contemporary players and fans look to the past for the roots of their own music, tracing the guitar's stylistic history in this country backward from the most recent performances on CDs or MP3 files to its earliest manifestations on LPs, 78s, or cylinders. In this telling, the guitar's recorded sounds echo the various musical dialects of America's popular musics. And the histories of the guitar based on these recordings has consistently described the instrument as a tool of the folk, its repertoire an oral tradition, its heroes and heroines unschooled troubadours who used their instruments, as Woody Guthrie used his, to fight fascism, as well as racism, sexism, colonialism, and commercialism. In this history, the guitar, an equal opportunity instrument, was a social and cultural leveler.

Until recently, guitar fans (and even some scholars) consistently projected such a late-twentieth-century interpretation of the guitar's place and role back into the nineteenth century. They often glossed over the years before the 1920s, assuming that the nineteenth-century guitar functioned as the steel-string "acoustic guitar" (that is, the non-electric guitar) did in the late twentieth century. In this view, the guitar has always been an instrument of the "folk" in America, its music transmitted orally, its function to accompany "folk songs," its associations primarily with blues-playing blacks, rural string bands, and cowboys.[1] This anachronistic view regularly projects late-twentieth-century approaches to the instrument—including steel stringing, a plectrum technique, and a lack of formal notation, among others—onto earlier players and their repertoire.

The advent of the electric guitar in the late 1920s and early 1930s established the direction of the instrument in this country for the rest of the century; as significantly, the electric guitar assumed an iconic role in American musical culture. Steve Waksman's recent study of the electric guitar reflects this approach, drawing on Jacques Attali's work to interpret the instrument as a tool of the cultural outsider whose noise challenges the status quo. In this story of the guitar in America, informal and accessible performance trumps formal and elite concerts, oral transmission negates standardized notation, and loose, improvised structures dominate formally composed works; the guitar becomes America's instrument from the bottom up, helping the outsider tell his or her story. This history of the guitar expands the instrument's connection to the "folk," linking it to musical stories of repression and resilience (in blues and country music) and more recently rebellion and transgression (in rock and its various offshoots). Studies of American popular music regularly emphasize this transgressive character of the guitar, celebrating its role in breaking down musical and social barriers, emphasizing the iconic and the mythological.[2] Indeed, the language of popular histories of the guitar regularly utilizes the mythological. Players are described as heroes while stories of training or performances range from the apocryphal to fantastic. These mythologies resonate with many deeply held beliefs about America, its people, and their music.

Yet, while mythologies illustrate the values and beliefs of communities and peoples, they more often transcend history than tell it. In recent years, scholars have offered new evaluations of America's musical history, describing a variegated culture of great complexity. These evaluations include discussions of America's cultural hierarchies, a sophisticated appreciation of technology's role in American musical culture, consideration of the significant influence of commerce on American music-making, and recognition of the increasing fragmentation of America's musical audiences/consumers. If the guitar has played any role in America's musical story, then it both participates in and reflects the complexity of America's musical culture. And when the guitar is examined in light of these new approaches to America's musical history, its story broadens, adding depth to the one-dimensional mythology.

A little-known part of this broader and deeper history of the guitar in America spans the late nineteenth century and early years of the twentieth and features a cast of amateur and professional players who recognized the guitar not as a tool of the folk, but as a cultivated instrument with roots in Europe's courts and salons. These guitarists studied the instrument formally, played music from published scores, and attempted to follow the technical guidelines of recognized masters. Although they certainly accompanied themselves or others in song, many of these players studied and performed formally composed solo pieces. These guitarists seldom shared the platform with large orchestras or traditional chamber ensembles, but the best appeared in formal concert settings while the less accomplished performed in the parlor, sharing the limelight with the piano, harp, flute, violin and other refined, classical instruments. While most of these guitarists played a standard repertoire, some of them composed and arranged, modeling their creations on the works of European musicians.

This musical world is a far cry from that of the hillbilly strummer or the blues picker. While not necessarily a better musical world than that of America's traditional musicians, it clearly is a different musical world, consciously connected to Europe, built on the formalities of composition, and manifested in recital and concert halls. This world has seldom been considered by historians of the guitar in America, most of whom appear unaware of it.

The following narrative considers this musical world and offers a different perspective on the guitar in America. Drawing on the work of other scholars, it first traces early descriptions of the guitar in the British colonies through its use in the middle-class parlors of nineteenth-century America. Following a discussion of its eclipse in the shadow of the mid-century minstrel banjo and mass-produced piano, the story considers the guitar's revival at the end of the century in the "plectral orchestras" of the Banjo, Mandolin and Guitar (BMG) movement. This movement was led by manufacturers and inventors who created new instruments like the banjeaurine, the guitar-neck banjo, the mandola, and the mando-cello. They rethought the guitar, too, offering America not just a larger, steel-strung guitar, but new hybrid instruments making the guitar more like the banjo, the mandolin, or the harp.

By the late 1920s and early 1930s, the nineteenth-century homogeneity of America's musical culture had broken down. Performers were categorized by (and occasionally vilified for) the type of music they performed, while marketing specialists identified consumers by reinforcing divisions of race, class, geography, and education. The American guitar reflected these divisions as manufacturers introduced new versions of the instrument and players created new techniques for the emerging popular musics of the period. America's community of guitarists reflected the country's musical divisiveness as popular players took up the oversized, hybrid f-hole guitars designed and manufactured in America, while more traditional players emulated Europe's emerging generation of classical guitarists, playing a standardized European repertoire on European instruments. Later sections of this study consider the guitar in the 1920s and early 1930s, examining how the fracturing community of players and fans reflected the growing chasms within America's wider musical community.

The story of America's other guitar-driven musics stands on an aural tradition, but despite the fact that the BMG movement's heyday corresponded with the invention and development of sound recordings, its most important players left few recorded examples and remain largely unknown today except to specialists. The movement's story has been preserved rather in promotional periodicals devoted to the three "plectral" instruments. In addition to advertising products—instruments, sheet music, and accessories—the BMG magazines explained techniques, published compositions, documented important performances, and recorded biographies. These journals offer a window on the aesthetic, commercial, and social worlds in which many of America's guitarists operated and serve as the basis of the history of the guitar told in this book.

In offering this revised "pre-history" of the guitar in America, I want to suggest that the BMG movement offers important insights into America's musical history. While its aesthetic and musical values—based on written music and focused on elite music-making—did not survive the new century, its commercial values and procedures remain with us today. The BMG community of players, teachers, and fans strove to create a place for itself in America's musical culture somewhere between the elite and the popular. But it never earned the attention, much less the respect, of America's elite musical audiences nor has it been recognized as having an influence on America's popular and folk musics. This failure to reconcile the popular and the elite, coupled with the recognition that commerce and advertising played significant roles in America's musical world, resonates even a century later. The following pages offer a revised history of the guitar in America—retold to include its stint in the BMG orchestras—and confirm that even before it became an iconic electric instrument, the guitar and its players stood as important markers for the history of music in America.

Chapter One

THE GUITAR IN AMERICA TO 1880

Histories of musical instruments, with rare exceptions, document their organological evolution, repertoires, or significant and innovative performers. In most cases, the histories of the guitar in America favor the organological approach, primarily because the physical instruments themselves have weathered the past two hundred years better than the music and reputations of American guitar composers and players. These studies focus primarily on the guitar's design and construction, with particular emphasis on brand names and instrument types. Prices for historic and "collectable" American guitars soared in the late twentieth century, contributing to an interest in old instruments as much for their investment value as for their musical or historical importance. As a result, specific nineteenth-century instrument brands or manufacturing companies are far better known than America's nineteenth-century players, composers, or compositions for the instrument.[1]

While the number of serious bibliographical and historical studies has increased over the past quarter century, scholarly documentation of the guitar's early history in America remains fragmentary.[2] To date, the best survey of the guitar in early-nineteenth-century America appears as an introductory chapter of Philip Gura's recent book about Christian Frederick Martin and his storied guitars.[3] Gura's opening chapter offers welcome relief from many of the earlier, anachronistic reports about the guitar in America. The later chapters of his book document significant manufacturing and marketing developments of the mid-nineteenth century, but Gura also weaves information about numerous individuals—teachers, performers, luthiers, and publishers, among others—into his narrative. His book is a timely and valuable resource about the guitar in nineteenth-century America.

The following historical survey offers a slightly different approach from that of Gura, growing out of a consideration of several important developments in America's nineteenth-century musical culture. First, as Gura's account of C. F. Martin's career corroborates, America's musical life balances unsteadily on the twin supports of art and commerce. This uneasy partnering, identified in the early twentieth century by Oscar Sonneck and highlighted in Richard Crawford's influential studies nearly one hundred years later, permeates the entirety of America's musical history, including that of the guitar.[4] Second, the history of the arts in nineteenth-century America documents a widening gap between cultivated fine art and disposable popular art.[5] This "highbrow/lowbrow" split describes a trajectory of cultural development that includes the history of the guitar in America. Lastly, while these cultural divisions manifested themselves prominently late in the nineteenth century, America's musical culture during that period was far more homogenous than conflicted. Musical activity ranged from the extremes of imported European operatic and symphonic works to home-grown bawdy songs and unrefined dance tunes, but the tonal language, musical forms, instruments, and other aspects of musical expression remained remark-ably consistent. America's musical culture at this time flowed along a shared continuum of language and tools, its differences residing principally in thematic content and performance context. This continuity of musical tools and language has played an important role in the guitar's American history, too.

THE EARLY YEARS—THE GUITAR IN COLONIAL AND FEDERALIST AMERICA

Neither music nor any of the other arts figures prominently in the earliest his-tories of the Americas, stories of exploration and conquest. Yet the explorers and first settlers of the New World certainly brought music with them, using it in religious, military, and governmental rituals as well as for entertainment. By the seventeenth century, when New World exploration expanded dramati-cally, the five-course guitar had become an integral part of Spanish, French, and Italian musical life, played by noble amateurs and virtuoso professionals. Composer/performers published collections of guitar solos and duos as well as instructions for accompaniment from a figured bass. Italy and Spain pro-duced player/composers well into the nineteenth century, musical emissaries who carried the instrument and its music to London, Paris, Vienna, Prague, and other northern musical centers. In all likelihood, early forms of the gui-tar came to this continent, too, with both French and Spanish explorers and colonists. In his engaging survey of the guitar in America, Tim Brookes sug-gests several individuals who may well have been among America's first guitar-ists. These include a Spanish soldier stationed in St. Augustine, Florida, in the 1570s as well as slightly earlier French settlers in the same area.[6]

Despite these beginnings, however, French and Spanish cultural influences remained on the periphery of America's mainstream. Northern European countries—Great Britain, of course, but also Germany—came to dominate mainstream America's musical tastes. Although musicians of northern Europe knew and played the guitar from the seventeenth to the nineteenth centuries, the instrument held greater significance in southern Europe's musical world. And despite its popularity in northern Europe, the guitar remained an exotic and foreign instrument there, an attitude eventually embraced by America's musical mainstream, too.

Nonetheless, the instrument was played publicly in colonial and Federalist America by professionals as a formal concert instrument and privately by amateurs as part of home entertainments. In addition, contemporaneous documents confirm occasional associations of the guitar with such eminent colonial figures as Benjamin Franklin. O. G. Sonneck's *Early Concert Life in America 1731–1800* documents recital and concert appearances of guitarists in America before 1800 not only as accompanists, but also as soloists, performing sonatas, caprices, and other unidentified works. Typically, a group of musicians would present a variety of vocal and instrumental music in these performances, and a guitarist might participate in several works, sometimes singing or playing other instruments, too. These notices occurred primarily in periodicals and newspapers from larger cultural centers of the era, including Charleston, Philadelphia, and New York.[7]

In the early nineteenth century the guitar was promoted, taught, and studied in this country in much the same way as other serious, cultivated European instruments. American guitar instructors (like other teaching musicians) touted their European roots and taught their instrument based on formal techniques—including written notation—imported from Europe. The popularity of the guitar in European courts and homes served as a useful advertising gambit for these teachers. As early as 1787, an advertisement for a concert in which a Mr. Capron played both guitar and cello concludes with a plug for Capron as a guitar teacher: "Mr. Capron respectfully informs the public that he instructs ladies and gentlemen in the art of singing and of playing on the Spanish and English guitars, recording the most approved method of the first masters of Europe. . . . The guitar, from the late improvement which it has received, being so portable and so easily kept in order, is considered not only as a desirable but as a fashionable instrument."[8] Capron's advertisement touts an expected and valorized European influence on guitar pedagogy in the early years of the United States. Capron, like many immigrant music masters in America, offered instruction in several musical areas. Additionally, he links his guitar instruction with vocal instruction, not at all surprising since the guitar has a long history as a subtle and appropriate accompaniment to the voice. Capron's advertisement for music lessons remains tantalizingly vague, however, for he reveals nothing about his specific pedagogical approach to the guitar.[9]

Printed instruction books for a transitional five-string guitar first appeared in Europe in the 1770s and methods for the six-string instrument proliferated in the first half of the nineteenth century. Teachers produced guitar method books in America as early as 1820, most based on European models. American-published tutors include J. Siegling's *Complete Instructor for the Spanish and English Guitar* (1820), Otto Torp's *New and Improved Method for the Spanish Guitar* (1828, 1834) and James Ballard's *Elements of Guitar-Playing* (1838). Most homegrown American methods of the era have been justifiably criticized for vague instructions and watered-down repertoires, but Ballard's *Elements* stands out for its effective imitation of formal European methods.[10]

Henri Capron's earlier reference to two guitars—Spanish and English—points up an important organological distinction about the guitar in eighteenth- and nineteenth-century America. The American guitar was an import whose design and construction derived directly from European models. In America, as in Europe, the gut-strung "Spanish guitar" eventually became the standard instrument, but the wire-strung "English guittar," taught by Capron and others, enjoyed considerable popularity in England beginning in the 1750s and found its way to the colonies, as evidenced in extant method books in American collections. One scholar has argued that nearly all American references to the guitar prior to the 1820s—including those tying Washington, Jefferson and Franklin to the guitar—point not to the gut-strung Spanish guitar but to the wire-strung English guittar. These two distinct instruments share no characteristics other than the fact that each has plucked or strummed strings stretched across a wooden body and a fretted neck. The eighteenth-century English guitar (or guittar) bears striking similarities to the earlier cittern, but their tunings, techniques, and repertoires differ significantly. While the Spanish guitar appears to have been played by professionals (like Capron) as well as some amateurs, the English guittar remained a diversion of upper-crust amateurs. The latter's popularity waned early in the nineteenth century in England and America, and the "English" guittar exerted no apparent influence on the "Spanish" guitar.[11]

The earliest luthiers in nineteenth-century America were European immigrants who built guitars modeled on the instrument recently evolved from the eighteenth-century baroque guitar.[12] In the late eighteenth century, continental European luthiers modified the double-strung, five-course baroque guitar by dropping the doubled strings and adding a lower bass string. Notation for this new guitar evolved as well, as composers and players abandoned various tablature and *alfabeto* chord systems to adopt a transposing treble clef.[13] Henri Capron's advertisement cited above may have referred to the mechanization of the English guittar, which acquired keyed hammers at this time, but may also point to the physical and notational changes affecting the Spanish guitar.

By the time the guitar achieved early popularity in America in the 1830s, it had become the "Spanish guitar," carrying six gut or silk strings across a figure-8-shaped body to a headstock with either violin-style tuning pegs or mechanical, geared tuning machines. Many of the earliest nineteenth-century guitars reflect their direct heritage from the baroque instrument with small, shallow bodies and upper and lower bouts of almost equal dimensions.[14] The fingerboards of the earliest new guitars, like those of baroque guitars, lay in the same plane as the soundboard, with the highest frets glued directly onto the soundboard. Frets, which had been tied around the neck and fingerboard of baroque guitars, became inlaid wood, bone, or metal on the newer "classical" guitar. Fingerboards thickened and lengthened, eventually extending onto the soundboard, beyond where the neck joined the guitar's body. Bridges of baroque guitars were, like those of the earlier lute, "tie-ons"—essentially low, wooden bars with holes drilled through to accommodate strings knotted and looped around the bridge. In the early nineteenth century, luthiers in Europe and America increased the height of the bridge, adding a bone or wooden saddle to lift the strings higher above the soundboard, delivering greater impulses from the vibrating strings to the guitar's body. In time, the lower bout widened and guitars took on their characteristic shape with narrower "shoulders" (upper bout) and wider "hips" (lower bout). While European luthiers continued a tradition of delicate and often ostentatious decoration on guitars designed for upper-crust tastes and performances, American builders responded to harsher climatic, economic, and social conditions by simplifying their instruments and making the guitar accessible (aesthetically and economically) to a broad swath of American society. By mid-century, American luthiers were building a distinctively American guitar that was simple, sturdy, and moderately priced. Such an instrument suited the climate, could be quickly and easily built in large workshops or factories, and could be priced to fit most any middle-class budget. As late as the end of the nineteenth century, American players and teachers still discouraged the importation of European guitars because the instruments could not withstand the rigors of the North American climate.[15]

THE GUITAR IN ANTEBELLUM AMERICA

Much of Peter Danner's research establishes the guitar's importance in the nineteenth century as an instrument of the American middle-class amateur. He describes several periods of popularity for the guitar in the century, the first between 1835 and 1850, and concludes that this popularity derived from the guitar's role in the lower-middle-class parlors of men and (especially) women aspiring to better things: "[T]he place of the guitar in 19th-century American life was not among the itinerant workers or the rural poor; nor was it an instrument of upper-class society. Rather the guitar was to be found within the middle class, particularly among those who could not yet afford a piano (the true symbol of Victorian propriety), or who were just beyond the pioneer stage and not yet settled enough to make one practical."[16] Young women in freed and middle-class African American families also utilized the guitar, like the piano, in social events in the home: "It is rarely that the Visitor in the different families where there are 2 or 3 ladies will not find one or more of them competent to perform on the pianoforte, guitar, or some other appropriate musical instrument; and these, with singing and conversation . . . constitute the amusements of their evenings at home."[17]

The guitar's repertoire at this time mimicked the piano's, consisting primarily of simple solos or songs, many based on or derived from popular Italian opera tunes. Music publishers provided this repertoire to pianists and guitarists in printed reductions and arrangements for home performance. Publishers often offered the same songs with different accompaniments, for piano or for guitar. A number of Stephen Foster's songs, for example, were published in this manner. And, as Richard Crawford demonstrates, although such a repertoire achieved notoriety in theatre or operatic performance, it achieved currency as printed sheet music purchased for home performance.[18]

A recent study of early American guitar tutors documents at least seventy-five titles published between 1816 and 1900. Most of these books were produced by established commercial publishers and their numbers point to a lively competition for the public's dollars. This number also reflects a perceived need—if not an actual demand—for formal and systematic guitar instruction using notation. Even the authors of method books promoted to "those who study without a master" recognized the need for musical literacy and presented the rudiments of standard musical notation before offering lessons and repertoire in the same notation.[19]

Until recently, most popular histories of the guitar in America have passed over the intersection of the guitar and musical notation. But if the guitar truly participated in America's musical world in the nineteenth century, notation played a significant role in the instrument's history. Crawford asserts that notation played a critical role in the development of America's musical culture, explaining that in the nineteenth century, the difference between the classical and popular spheres "lies in notation, the authority it carries and the spirit in which it is interpreted." In fact, nineteenth-century Americans understood much of the power and value of music to lie in its formal aspects, including notation. By the middle of the century the lines between "popular" music and "classical" music had been drawn and American meliorists, led by minister-turned-music critic John Sullivan Dwight, promoted the latter for its moral and aesthetic superiority. For Dwight and his followers, instrumental music, especially that of the German symphonists, offered a transcendent musical and aesthetic experience. And although their instrument seldom reached Dwight's elevated gaze, guitarists participated in this musical transcendence when they learned and performed sonatas, fantasies, variation sets, and operatic potpourris by European masters Fernando Sor, Mauro Giuliani, Johann Kaspar Mertz, and others. Even lesser musical lights, including American guitarists such as Winslow Hayden, William O. Bateman, and James Flint, conceived of and transmitted their music in formal notation.[20]

In addition to the burst of publishing activity and consequent parlor performances in the 1830s, the same period witnessed a significant increase in professional guitar activity in the United States. Recent research documents an upsurge in concert appearances of European and South American visitors and immigrants before the Civil War, many patterning their touring and performances on those of successful European stars such as Jenny Lind and Ole Bull. Foremost among these was the Spaniard A. F. Huerta (1804–1875), who first performed in New York in the 1820s. Concerts featuring professional touring guitarists such as Huerta paralleled those of other touring virtuosi, offering a variety of solo and ensemble instrumental and vocal numbers. The touring soloist largely presented his own compositions and arrangements, allowing him to display a highly developed technique.

Besides Huerta, other prominent performers included John B. Coupa, Leopold de Janon, and James Dorn (1809–after 1859). While their New York concerts appear to have caused little stir, each of these men had some influence on the later history of the guitar in America. Coupa became a business partner to the immigrant luthier C. F. Martin; de Janon may have been related to the Columbian-American guitarist Charles de Janon (1834–1911); and Dorn was the uncle of the American guitarist Charles Dorn (1839–1909). The younger Dorn and de Janon established themselves as respected figures in America's guitar-playing community at the close of the nineteenth century.[21]

Americans craved musical instruction and the second half of the nineteenth century witnessed a steady stream of formal guitar tutors, both American and European. Of the European instruction books available in this country, Matteo Carcassi's (1836) dominated the market in a variety of editions from several American publishers. A number of American methods appearing in the second of half of the century incorporated ideas or exercises from Carcassi.[22] While publishers of some of these methods promoted and distributed them nationally, many were probably produced for local or regional consumption by individual teacher/authors and their students. James Ballard's 1838 tutor has been noted as the best of the antebellum American methods and Justin Holland's *Comprehensive Method for the Guitar* (1874) deserves the same recognition among late-nineteenth-century tutors. Holland reinforced the guitar's connection to Europe's elite musical culture with a brief history of the modern guitar, emphasizing its eighteenth-century connection to German and Austrian courts. He insisted that beginners give themselves over to the serious work of learning the "elements of music" and "a systematic fingering." Openly acknowledging his debt to Europe's masters, Holland noted that he had based his method on numerous standard works, all foreign.[23]

Holland was not alone in encouraging guitarists to learn to read music. Antonio Lopes expressed the sympathies of numerous American teachers and players of the nineteenth century when he advised: "Learning the Guitar (or any other Instrument) by ear or figures, is loss of time and money, for what is learned to-day may be forgotten tomorrow. In learning by NOTE you have the advantage of constant Progress."[24] Despite such advice, the guitar was undoubtedly also taught and played in this country by ear, and some teachers published guitar tutors touted as "Simplified Methods," utilizing tablature systems as an alternative to staff notation. Despite evidence of such oral and tablature transmission, however, standard musical notation appears to have been the principal means of preserving and transmitting instructional materials and repertoire for the guitar throughout the nineteenth century. Reports of informal performances suggest, in fact, that much of the popular repertoire transmitted orally—songs and simple solos—first appeared in standard notation and only entered the oral chain after distribution as print music. This information points up the fact that although the guitar was a popular instrument through the nineteenth century, it was not a "folk" or "traditional" instrument like the fiddle. Rural dance ensembles consisted principally of melody instruments, especially the fiddle. As numerous studies confirm, the guitar joined such ensembles only very late in the nineteenth century or early in the twentieth.[25]

THE GUITAR AT MID-CENTURY

Several scholars have suggested that the popularity of the guitar waned in America from the 1850s until about 1880, blaming the upheaval of the Civil War among other causes. But more recent research documents a marked increase in the number of guitar tutors published in this country in the three decades between 1850 and 1880, suggesting that the guitar's popularity may have actually increased or at least held steady. While the precise answer remains elusive, following mid-century the guitar felt pressure on two cultural and economic fronts. On one hand, the cultivated piano exerted significant pressure on the guitar from above while, at the same time, the lower-class banjo encroached from below.[26]

Mass production, combined with an expanding rail system, made the piano more readily available to American families who might once have only dreamed of owning such an instrument. In his entertaining history of the piano, Arthur Loesser traces not only the development of the American upright piano from its European models, but the significant impact of mass production based on the assembly of complete instruments from independently produced parts. He also documents how Joseph P. Hale's creative approach to branding contributed to the successful marketing of inexpensive, mass-produced pianos to local dealers across the country. In the mid-1860s, Hale sold approximately 500 instruments a year; by 1876, he sold ten times that number. Even less expensive pianos carried a cachet of upper-class respectability and "wider and wider groups of less-moneyed people . . . were encouraged to develop aspirations and pretenses toward fancier things." In 1867, an article in the *Atlantic Monthly* observed that "almost every couple that sets up housekeeping on a respectable scale considers a piano only less indispensable than a kitchen range." The piano's physical *gravitas* and concert-hall associations trumped the guitar's ancient history and cultivated repertoire. A guitar in the parlor indicated an interest in music, but a piano, even an inexpensive piano, confirmed both a serious interest in music and the financial wherewithal to support middle-class aspirations. As new rail lines made manufactured goods more readily available across the country, affordable upright pianos by Hale and others promised America's aspiring classes upper-crust cultivation more decisively and more quickly than the guitar.[27]

From an entirely different direction but at nearly the same time, the banjo caught the attention of middle America, challenging the guitar's role as the country's preeminent plucked instrument. The banjo's popularity grew from the near-universal popularity of the minstrel show. The change from guitar to banjo was, however, more than the replacement of one popular plucked instrument with another. The choice of the banjo over the guitar reflected the development of a new and different type of entertainment that flourished in the public sphere. At the same time, this displacement of the guitar by the banjo illustrates how these instruments played roles in America's nineteenth-century highbrow/lowbrow cultural division. Despite concert appearances of touring professionals like Huerta and Coupa, guitar performance in early-nineteenth-century America centered on the parlor, featuring popular and light classical works in "private" music-making. Such private popular music "treasured reserve and sentiment, was without ostentation, and could be performed by the competent amateur." This was the sphere of the guitar. On the other hand, the banjo's popularity grew directly out of its use in an eminently public sphere, the theatre. Public music of this era featured "noise, excess, unrestrained emotionalism, and showy professionalism," all inappropriate for the refined entertainments of the sequestered world of the middle-class nuclear family.[28] To challenge the guitar's standing in middle-class parlors, the banjo had to shed such theatrical associations.

The banjo came to white, middle-class America from the black slave through the rough world of itinerant white entertainers. Its early repertoire consisted principally of minstrel or plantation songs and rustic dances, generally transmitted orally or in tablature notations. And although these pieces eventually found their way into print and into the parlor, it was with piano or guitar rather than banjo accompaniment. By the 1850s, their technical level had improved to the point that professional banjo players engaged in public tournaments with instruments and cash as prizes, sometimes even playing arranged classical pieces. But until the late decades of the nineteenth century, the banjo maintained stronger associations with the public stage and a minstrel repertoire than with the home parlor and refined music. In their efforts to domesticate their instrument, banjoists looked to the guitar, adopting a similar notational system and repertoire as well as the guitar's right-hand technique, fretting system, and performance locale.[29]

While the banjo never shed its role as both musical prop and racial marker in the minstrel show, after mid-century players expanded its repertoire, arranging refined songs and dances from the European tradition. This drift away from the blackface caricatures of Ethiopian songs and dances toward a more respectable repertoire began in the minstrel shows themselves as performers and promoters aimed their shows at a family audience. Karen Linn asserts that the late-nineteenth-century goal of elevating the banjo depended more on the "intellectual and moral reform of the banjo" than on a more refined repertoire. "The 'elevated' banjoists still played popular music, but in a very different context. The journey from barroom to parlor and minstrel stage to recital hall implies a change of class orientation and social values." Such change had to occur not just within the banjo players' ranks but also among promoters of America's refined musical traditions, who were loath to admit that the banjo was even a musical instrument. The banjo appeared but once in John Sullivan Dwight's *Journal*, when he wholeheartedly endorsed the damning evaluation of an international panel of adjudicators: "We admire the frankness with which the [panel's] report dismisses some productions as of bad tendency in Art. For instance: 'The Banjos, being esteemed barbarous, are passed by our body as unworthy of notice and beneath the dignity of Art.'"[30]

Although Dwight held the banjo and its music in low regard, promoters of the elevated banjo followed his aesthetic lead, describing music as a force capable of enlightening intellects and uplifting morals. They discussed music as a science and called for its teaching as both a melodic art and a harmonic science.[31] Philip Gura and James Bollman identify a number of banjoists who contributed to banjo's cultural makeover in the 1850s and 1860s, but credit Frank Converse with uniting formal notation and a new right-hand technique in his influential tutors from 1865. Although Converse had begun his musical studies as a pianist, it appears that the guitar served as a more significant influence on his approach to the banjo. Converse promoted a transposing treble clef notation as well as a three-finger plucking technique, both derived from the guitar. The cover of his 1872 method book, *The Banjo and How to Play It*, reinforced the connection as well by depicting a young player holding his banjo much as a classical guitarist would support his instrument. Gura and Bollman also document that by the mid-1850s, advocates for the banjo began to eye the guitar as a competitor, taking on its repertoire and creating hybrid instruments with a banjo's body and a guitar's stringing and fingerboard or a banjo with a guitar's braced wooden soundboard.[32]

Reflecting the value of notation for America's musical culture, proponents of the refined banjo argued that "Simplified" (tablature) methods had been the principle impediment to the banjo's acceptance as a real musical instrument. The availability of properly composed music in standard notation opened the door for the banjo's admittance into a refined musical world.

> What held the banjo back for so many years and prevented its recognition as a musical instrument was principally the . . . simpleton's method. As long as there was no good music printed for the instrument there was nothing to attract the notice of musicians who had never heard a good banjo, and as many of the so-called "simple method" players had no ear for music whatever, and as the average intelligence of many of them was not far above that of the idiot, there is no wonder that it took some time for the comparatively few good players and teachers to conquer these disadvantages. Now we have good music and instruction books for the banjo, and good instruments as well. The same line which divides the "fiddler" from the "violinist"—the street player from the solo artist of the concert room—divides the "simple method banjo player" . . . from the player of today.[33]

Through the 1870s, banjo advocates argued and lobbied for its recognition as an elite instrument. By the 1880s, the instrument's increased popularity, growing technical sophistication, and falling production costs made the banjo the basis of an emerging industry and cultural movement. With this emergence of the banjo, industry leaders like S. S. Stewart and others argued more and more forcefully for the guitar's replacement by their product, basing their arguments on two points. They claimed, first, that the banjo had reached the apogee of its development in the hands of white, progressive manufacturers and players. This argument rested on the denial of the African and African American roots of the instrument and on the mechanical refinement of the banjo's technology in workshops and factories run by whites. Second, they insisted that the banjo could and should replace the guitar in its role as the music world's most refined plucked instrument. This argument grew out of the technical similarities between the two instruments but stood even more on the characterization of the guitar as old-fashioned, overly difficult to play, foreign, and decadent.

To Stewart and his contemporaries, the lack of a verifiable history of the banjo in black America supported their promotion of the banjo as a white invention. Because whites made significant technological contributions to the evolution of the banjo, nineteenth-century authorities insisted on identifying it as both Caucasian and progressive, an instrument suited to the modern world and for use in the parlor and in the recital hall by white men and women.

Many of these same authorities identified the guitar as the preferred instrument of black musicians, usually using this association to denigrate the guitar. Banjo advocates painted the guitar as a favorite of America's own undesirables, devaluing it through association with the black underclass. Such a business tactic had been used before in eighteenth-century England, when the harpsichord builder Kirkman attacked the "common guitar's" (English guittar) rising popularity among refined Londoners by giving inexpensive instruments and quick lessons to "girls in milliners' shops and to ballad singers in the streets." Respectable ladies, "ashamed of their frivolous and vulgar taste," quickly abandoned the guitar in favor of the safe and respectable harpsichord.[34]

Despite these efforts, however, until late in the nineteenth century the cachet of the parlor and recital hall resided more with the guitar than the banjo. Additionally, specific techniques, repertoire, and social functions of the banjo and guitar differed significantly. Because both instruments were gut-strung and quiet, they might interchangeably share the musical role of accompanying the voice, but the guitar's wider range, which includes a true bass register, gives it a decided advantage in this role. While sharing a similar left-hand technique of depressing strings on a fingerboard to play pitches or chords, each instrument had a different system of intonation. The guitar's fretting system made it a tempered instrument, appropriate for counterpoint and chords in tonal pieces. The unfretted banjo, on the other hand, was better suited to doubling the voice or offering rhythmic ostinati under a melody in more modally-inflected folk music. In addition to fingerboard arrangements, right-hand techniques differed dramatically for banjo and guitar until well after mid-century. Guitarists, of course, could strum their instrument rhythmically, but the right-hand technique promoted in tutors and in printed nineteenth-century guitar repertoire generally promoted a three-finger (thumb, index, and middle) plucking of strings. Such a technique favored single-line melodies, arpeggiated or block chords, and multi-voice textures. Banjoists, on the other hand, usually played their instruments

with a rhythmic strumming limited to thumb and index finger, generally identified as "stroke playing." The guitar had clear associations with a notated repertoire and formal, even refined, performances. The banjo repertoire existed
primarily in the oral tradition, associated with stylized and sometimes virtuosic,
but unrefined minstrel performances.

In the final decades of the nineteenth century, the banjo and its technique underwent changes that made it more like the refined guitar. The banjo
acquired frets, allowing the banjoist to play pitches and more importantly,
chords accurately within a tonal, equally-tempered harmonic system. "Guitar-
style" playing—a controlled, upward picking of individual strings—super-
ceded stroke playing and became the standard right-hand banjo technique.
Composers, arrangers, and publishers presented banjo music to the American
musical public in the form of method books, ensemble scores, musical anthologies, and individual solo works, all in treble clef notation. This notated banjo
repertoire reflected the guitar's—songs with arranged and notated accompaniment; arrangements and variations of popular themes from shows and operas;
and characteristic dances. While advocates such as S. S. Stewart never overtly
suggested that the banjo become more like the guitar, their drive to achieve
respect for it and its players necessitated associating the banjo with the guitar
as well as encouraging banjoists to emulate guitarists in technique and repertoire. Stewart still saw fit to attack the guitar, claiming it to be difficult to play
and unsatisfying to its players. Stewart asserted that the guitar "is a very soft
and agreeable accompaniment to the banjo, but it must and will ever play 'second-
fiddle' to the banjo."[35]

By 1880, the scene had been set for the guitar to play a new role in
America's musical culture. It retained a cachet of European cultivation derived
from its association with Old World nobility, yet served to accompany informal music-making across America. While it could be easily taught by rote
and its tunes passed along orally, most of the guitar's repertoire continued to
be transmitted in formal, standardized notation. Recognized as a less expensive stand-in for the piano, the guitar offered lower-middle-class Americans
access to the uplifting influence of music's meliorating powers. Yet the instrument also acquired negative associations in the late nineteenth century. White,
Protestant America considered the guitar an emotional, unpredictable instrument, associating it with Roman Catholic Spanish and Italian immigrants.
And in a curious turnaround, African Americans appear to have preferred the
guitar to the banjo, too. While the guitar remained a modestly priced instrument, the banjo's increased technical complexity made the modern instrument
relatively expensive, out of the reach of many black musicians. Perhaps more
significantly, the banjo continued to be associated with the minstrel show's caricature of black culture, an association unlikely to endear the instrument to the

African American community. Starting in the 1880s, America's Anglo banjoists aggressively attempted to usurp the guitar's place in America's polite musical life by adopting its repertoire and techniques, eventually joining with guitarists in newly created chamber ensembles.

Over the next fifty years, these conflicts and contradictions played out in America's musical culture, contributing to both the development and the fragmentation of the country's musical life. And the guitar—redefined and reconfigured—sounded new musics, assumed new roles, and represented new cultural values, all of which remain with us today.

Chapter Two

INTERLUDE

The BMG Movement—The Sources

B eginning in the early 1880s, the guitar entered a new period of popularity, this time in the carefully orchestrated company of the banjo and, eventually, the mandolin. Highlighting the similarity of playing techniques, instrument manufacturers and music publishers created a fictional family of plucked instruments, identifying them as the "trio" or "plectral" instruments. By the early years of the twentieth century, these businessmen identified themselves, their customers, and others devoted to the plectral instruments as the banjo, mandolin, and guitar (BMG) movement.[1]

Although dedicated in principle to musical instruments and music-making, the BMG movement—reflecting the values of America's musical culture—was as devoted to commercial interests, fully participating in the numerous late-nineteenth-century developments in America's approach to both music and business. Among the important commercial changes that played a significant role in the BMG movement were industrialized mass production, newly invented advertising techniques, and a burgeoning magazine publishing industry. These three developments were inextricably linked in American business's search for and creation of national mass markets.

The American guitar has been profoundly influenced by these developments, becoming in the late nineteenth century not only a mass-produced and nationally distributed item but also the subject of national advertising campaigns carried to consumers on the pages of inexpensive magazines. Leaders of the BMG movement created magazines dedicated to the promotion of instruments and sheet music, overflowing with articles, editorials, instructional columns, and especially advertisements. These periodicals document a fifty-year period of significant musical and commercial activity around the trio instruments, outlining the movement's history and confirming its commitment to America's mainstream musical and commercial values.[2]

The BMG movement grew out of the activities of northeastern manufacturers and publishers, remaining rooted in that region's metropolitan areas. The earliest BMG magazines came from Philadelphia, Boston, and New York, but in the 1890s periodicals sprouted up in the Midwest and on the West Coast. The heyday of the BMG movement extended from the late 1890s to about 1920, although BMG magazines first appeared in the early 1880s and continued to be published into the 1930s. Many of these magazines were short-lived, in some cases surviving less than a year; others ran for decades, persisting through numerous business cycles, new owners, and relocations. Several of these long-running magazines are relatively well-known to historians of the banjo, mandolin, and guitar, in part because they have survived in nearly complete runs in public and private collections. These include *S. S. Stewart's Banjo and Guitar Journal* (Philadelphia), *Cadenza* (Kansas City, New York and Boston), *The F.O.G. Journal* (Cleveland), and *Crescendo* (Boston and Hartford). Others surviving in fragmentary form, sometimes in libraries but more often in private collections, include *The Musical Enterprise* (Philadelphia), *Gatcomb's Musical Gazette* (Boston), *The Chicago Trio* (Chicago), *The Musical Tempo* (Philadelphia), *The Major* (Saginaw, Michigan), *The Allegro* (Dwight, Illinois), *The Reveille* (San Francisco), *The Studio Journal* (Philadelphia), *Griffith's* (Philadelphia), and the *Serenader* (Sioux City, Iowa).

The significance of these magazines in the history of the guitar in late-nineteenth-century America rests on three points. First, despite the fact that these publications spanned approximately fifty years and were spread across the country, collectively they convey a remarkably consistent message and perspective. Even when publishers, editors, and columnists regularly attacked each other in their journals, the magazines reflect a consensus that confirms the unity of the BMG community, including its use and vision of the guitar. Second, members of the BMG community regularly described its mission in artistic and pedagogical terms, but the magazines confirm that the BMG movement was business-driven. As a result, the guitar, its music, and its use were judged as much by commercial considerations as by artistic or aesthetic. Third, although late in the twentieth century the guitar became an instrument of the social outsider, these magazines confirm that during the BMG era the guitar was a middle-class instrument used to instill and reinforce the cultural and musical values of America's mainstream. These values include not just the primacy of commercial concerns and the importance of the banjo and mandolin, but also cultural jingoism, a faith in progressive ideals, musical literacy, privileging of European musical forms and styles, and secondary, supporting roles for women.

The BMG magazines offer later readers a contemporaneous record of the movement, its instruments, and its values based on musical and textual documents. So much of the guitar's story in America has been derived from second- or third-hand observation and interpretation of oral accounts or recorded examples; the documentation residing in the BMG periodicals offers a unique resource written by and for the people actively engaged in playing, teaching, and selling the guitar.

This is not to say that the BMG magazines can be read as objective and dispassionate reports. In his survey of *Cadenza*, Peter Danner cautioned that contributors to that magazine were not writing musicology but biased and often impassioned journalism. The same can be said about all of the BMG periodicals. Each promoted specific musical products, sometimes blatantly, other times subtly. At the same time, the BMG magazines shared a worldview not only with each other, but with the hundreds of other commercial magazines published in this era.[3]

In the late nineteenth century, America's mainstream magazines told people how to live, reinforcing "middle-class values against the dangerous classes (blacks and immigrants) on one side and decadent classes on the other." These magazines also "helped readers understand how things worked," offering rational and scientific explanations of the natural world and newly invented products. Lastly, they explained how society operated, providing "readers a sense of athomeness in the distanced and puzzling world that capitalism had made."[4] BMG magazines followed this model, using stories, editorials, illustrations, and advertisements to offer readers a world peopled by middle-class Caucasian men and women who used new, "scientific" musical products in comprehensible and comfortable social relationships.

The first of the BMG magazines, *S. S. Stewart's Banjo & Guitar Journal*, was created to promote a company that utilized mass-production technologies to manufacture musical instruments, musical accessories, and sheet music. Samuel Swaim Stewart (1855–1898) employed new techniques of advertising and promotion in his venture, and his success grew initially from his ability to identify and manipulate a middle-class market. Just as importantly, refining the manufacturing process allowed Stewart to produce a variety of banjo models marketed for a range of prices.[5] Like other successful businessmen of the era, Stewart eventually rationalized his manufacturing, promotion, and distribution systems, uniting them under one roof. All other BMG publishers emulated Stewart, responding to the new consumer culture with increasingly sophisticated mass production, advertising methodologies, and distribution systems for products and information. Nearly all BMG magazines had links to some sort of large-scale commercial operation that produced and promoted instruments, sheet music, or both.

Mass production meant that everything from processed foods to home furnishings—including musical instruments—could be made more quickly, more efficiently, and more cheaply outside the home. And by the late nineteenth century, large American factories turned out banjos, guitars, and mandolins, often assembled in discrete stages from components produced elsewhere.[6] Once considered luxuries available chiefly to families of means, mass-produced items were now offered to the middle class in better quality, in greater quantity, and for less money. Some of these mass-produced items—especially musical instruments—retained their upper-class cachet and served as markers of the achievements and aspirations of the middle class.

Manufacturers coupled these new production methods with changes in distribution and pricing, creating a new relationship between buyer and seller in which first the department store and then the magazine reframed "shopping as a luxurious and eminently pleasurable pursuit." Like department store displays, magazines showed readers—through stories and articles as well as advertisements—an accessible and achievable world. The department store and the new magazine "joined in one package, or booklet, the commercial world of goods and sales with the world of private musing and romantic fantasy."[7]

Late-nineteenth-century magazine publishers, like department store owners and managers, characterized their promotion of products as an educational service for readers, presenting themselves as partners in an educational venture with manufacturers and distributors. *Cadenza* and *Crescendo*, two of the most successful of the BMG magazines, had close ties to the American Guild of Banjoists, Mandolinists and Guitarists (established in 1900), whose membership included not only amateur players, independent teachers, and performers but also important and influential trade members. Guild leadership regularly praised these magazines for preaching and "constantly spreading our doctrines to every civilized part of the world." Just as regularly, the magazine editors returned the compliments, recognizing manufacturers and publishers as educational partners to the magazines.[8]

While most BMG magazines included obvious instructional material describing playing techniques, some also offered advice ranging from how to form ensembles to decorating a teaching studio. More subtly, stories and articles used advertisers' products, promoting specific "product categories, along with the general sense that shopping choices and consumption itself were important."[9] Buyer and seller met in advertisements, and magazines allowed this meeting to take place in the home. In a world of wage earners and homemakers—roles for Victorian men and women that developed new meanings through the nineteenth century—the home became the locus of identities determined largely by items brought into the home and by leisure time activities.[10] While the BMG magazines lionized the professional musician, their target audience was the amateur with time and money on his or her hands. BMG editors and contributors worked to create identities for these amateurs, identities that revolved around musical products and activities. They recognized that the amateur music-making they promoted competed directly with other new leisure activities like photography and bicycling. In one BMG article from the late 1890s, a writer set the banjo against numerous (but, he hoped, passing) fads, including the bicycle, photography, ping pong, the mandolin, and clog dancing. Articles and editorials lamented the attractions of these other activities, offering teachers and ensemble leaders strategies to attract and maintain students and players.[11]

The BMG magazines participated fully in America's new consumer world, not only inventing an identity (plectral players) for their readers, but also creating and sustaining a musical/commercial world in which this identity had meaning (the BMG community). Aligning themselves with America's nineteenth-century meliorists, leaders of the BMG movement sold music in their magazines as a force that offered entertainment and edification both in and out of the home. The magazines defined music-making as a cultured activity that could be enjoyed by any middle-class person. Articles and reviews in these journals touted the skills, culture, and intelligence of ensemble and club members, showing readers an accessible world of elevated achievement and enjoyable society. Readers might easily infer that participation in BMG activities could lift players into the middle class. Halftone prints of amateur and semiprofessional banjo, mandolin, and guitar players pictured them most often in groups—well-groomed, well-dressed, and well-mannered. Their stolid demeanors conveyed the seriousness with which they pursued their musical studies and implied intelligence capable of grasping the intricacies of music notation and performance. For example, in 1888 *Gatcomb's Musical Gazette* acknowledged the receipt of a photograph of a music-making family from Kansas, noting that "They are a remarkably fine looking family, and judging from their refined and intelligent faces, their music must be a corresponding nature."[12] *Cadenza* featured portraits and biographies of players and teachers in every issue, most detailing personality traits as well as musical skills. The benefits of playing music and the visual clues of intelligence and enlightenment extended even to children working in vaudeville: "The portraiture of these musically gifted lads and lassies in their picturesque semi-sailor costumes and white shoes is an attractive one, and the ensemble speaks for itself as to their intelligence and ability, while still retaining the true boy and girl spirit."[13]

Stories of lives saved or love found through music painted musicians (especially single amateurs) as noble and desirable. *Stewart's* documented a heroic banjo player who saved a young girl in a theater fire, while other stories and poems in *Cadenza* recounted how the musical skills of young women attracted eligible men, including nobility.[14] Such images offered single men and women a romantic impetus to become proficient musicians in hopes of attracting a

A refined family ensemble, the Fox Sisters of Sandusky, Ohio. (*American Music Journal*)

mate while presenting the married a cultured pastime that would enrich and ennoble their home and children. The banjo, guitar, and mandolin appeared in advertisements and promotions as easy-to-use products that brought to their possessor musical and intellectual achievement, access to the opposite sex, and an elevated social status.

While the BMG magazines shared these attitudes and approaches to music and business, each had its own character, determined to a great extent by its founder. In some cases, biographical details are difficult to ascertain, but often the personal stories of BMG publishers and editors appeared in the magazines, testaments to the commercial opportunities available through America's musical arts. The following pages highlight some of the magazines and the individuals behind them.

Stewart's Banjo and Guitar Journal (1882–1903) the first American periodical devoted to the guitar and related instruments, set the standards by which all other banjo, mandolin, and guitar magazines were measured. For twenty years, Samuel Swaim Stewart's *Journal* dominated the BMG publishing world, inspiring admiration, imitation, and competition, to which Stewart responded with magnanimity, derision, or active hostility.

As the *Journal*'s founder, publisher, editor, principal contributor, and namesake, S. S. Stewart proselytized unceasingly for his chosen instrument, becoming

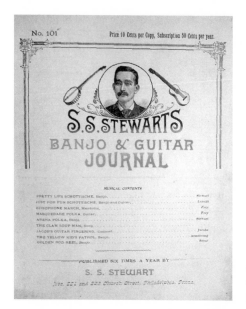

Covers of *S. S. Stewart's Banjo & Guitar Journal* featured a portrait of its namesake.

America's most visible proponent of the banjo as a refined instrument for the middle and upper classes. In the course of the magazine's run, Stewart challenged other manufacturers and publishers to match his standards, encouraged and promoted young players and composers until they crossed him, excoriated apostates who abandoned his mission, aggressively attacked anyone who dared belittle the banjo or his products, and promoted his chosen instrument as equal to (if not, on occasion, superior to) the violin and piano. Stewart utilized the guitar in his promotion of the banjo, presenting it positively when it served his purpose, but just as often belittling it as old-fashioned, dangerously sensual, and low-class. In these attacks, Stewart articulated a new attitude toward the guitar that not only found its way into other BMG magazines but also became the basis for a new approach to the instrument, eventually helping to open the way for the important changes in the construction and use of the guitar that occurred later in the twentieth century.

Born in Philadelphia in 1855, Stewart learned the violin, piano, organ, and flute as a boy. He encountered the banjo as a youth, studying with George Dobson, a member of the family of American virtuoso banjoists who flourished in the second half of the nineteenth century. Once introduced to the banjo, Stewart devoted his life to it. He opened a banjo school in Philadelphia in 1878 and shortly after began building instruments. Within a few years, the Stewart workshop had become a factory, utilizing the most modern industrial techniques to mass-produce a quality product. When he turned to music publishing, Stewart incorporated the latest technologies in that field, as well.

Although the third-person biography he wrote smacks of regal affectation, he could justifiably claim in 1897 that

> Stewart ... literally worked day and night to win success. ... If there are any records, books, treatises, etc. published that give a comprehensive account of the banjo and its history, they are the books and writings of S.S. Stewart, and it is since the advent of Stewart that the various "jobbers" in the musical lines have undertaken to copy the Stewart Banjo; ... Stewart, to-day, holds first place as banjo maker throughout the world ... [S]o it may be said of the music publishing business—Stewart was about the first man to enter that line of business, and he has built up the largest banjo publishing business in this country.[15]

He established *Stewart's Banjo and Guitar Journal* in 1882 as a promotional arm of his company, controlling all aspects of the magazine until his death in 1898.

Besides being the first BMG magazine, *Stewart's* exemplified the most important characteristics of nearly all of these periodicals. First, the magazine functioned principally as a promotional tool for the publisher's commercial ventures. Second, despite its overtly commercial purposes, the magazine's philosophical underpinnings rested on the late-nineteenth-century appreciation of music as both a science and an uplifting, enlightening force in society. Third, its focus was not the guitar, but the banjo. Stewart united the guitar and banjo in his title and masthead—a graphic example of his crusade to elevate the banjo to the status of the refined guitar. Despite equal billing in its title, however, the guitar clearly played a subservient role in the magazine's letterpress. Lastly, *Stewart's* promoted the banjo as the legitimate equal of any orchestral or solo instrument, capable of producing high-class music and worthy of the respect and attention of musicians and aficionados alike.

Confirming the American penchant for blending art and commerce, Stewart identified his *Journal* as an advertising tool for his business, unequivocally asserting that "no effort has ever been made to misrepresent the fact that the Journal is published *principally as an advertising medium for our business*."[16] He intended that the *Journal* put his name and product in the public eye and educate those it reached to the superiority of S. S. Stewart's banjos and print music. In the first few years of publication, Stewart accepted paid advertisements from other music publishers and manufacturers, but by 1890 he had put an end to that magnanimous practice.

Stewart's commitment to music-making and the power of music was wholehearted, but his determination to prosper as a businessman at all costs proved as powerful. Anything Stewart published in his magazine, from hysterical rants against other manufacturers to lists of BMG teachers from the English-speaking world, served his own commercial ends. In Stewart's model, musical and commercial interests never separated. Stewart and his cohorts created, developed, and promoted instruments, ensembles, and music, offering new musical experiences and opportunities but also enticing a targeted readership to spend its money. His promotions and aggression paid off, for Stewart eventually "oversaw an extensive mercantile empire," selling "great quantities of banjos, instrument parts, strings, instruction books, sheet music and advertising."[17]

Stewart had the BMG magazine market to himself for five years, but his banjo factory was only one of many throughout New England. New York was home to the Dobson brothers, several of whom marketed banjos, but Boston manufacturers offered the Philadelphian especially stiff competition. Banjos by Bostonians Albert C. Fairbanks, William A. Cole, John C. Haynes, and others compared favorably to Stewart's in sound, materials, workmanship, and price, offering consumers a wide variety of alternatives to Stewart's instruments. His peers recognized the important role Stewart's *Journal* played in promoting his instruments, and several competitors, contributors, and even protégés eventually followed his lead, each producing a BMG periodical.[18]

L. B. Gatcomb, the first of these imitators, had been building banjos for nearly ten years before turning to magazine publishing. Gatcomb—like Stewart a self-made entrepreneur—respected the Philadelphian's successful model and slavishly followed Stewart's lead. Each magazine represented both an instrument manufacturer and publishing house. Each promoted a strong personal identification of the company products and publications with a name and face; early issues of the *Gatcomb's Musical Gazette*, like *Stewart's*, featured a portrait of its publisher embedded in the graphic design of the magazine's cover. And, while each magazine claimed equal consideration of the three plectral instruments, both focused principally on the banjo as a serious and legitimate musical instrument. Despite his claims of welcoming honest competition, Stewart could not abide direct competition and regularly attacked Gatcomb's instruments and periodical.

Lincoln B. Gatcomb, a native of rural Maine, was born a year earlier than his Philadelphia rival, in 1854. He left the family farm on his father's death in 1869 and apprenticed as a stair-builder in Boston. By 1875, Gatcomb was constructing banjos as a hobby and in 1880 went into business with George L. Lansing, a Boston-based banjoist and teacher. In 1885, Gatcomb established a factory to build banjos and (unlike Stewart) guitars. He incorporated his business and expanded into music publishing in 1887, the same year his *Gazette* first appeared.

Unlike Stewart, Gatcomb did not edit his own publication, but hired men who performed and taught in the Boston area. His first editor, the guitarist B. E. Shattuck, taught in Gatcomb's offices. Shattuck, like most BMG teachers of the era, composed and arranged solo and ensemble works, and several of his guitar pieces appeared late in the first decade of the new century in the later

BMG magazine *Cadenza*. L. H. Galeucia, Gatcomb's second editor, performed with the very popular Boston Ideal Banjo, Mandolin and Guitar Club, a professional quintet. The first issue of the *Gazette* featured this Club and noted that "Mr. L.H. Galeucia is a fine Guitar and Banjo performer, and the press notices in reference to him are very flattering. His work with the club is mainly with the Guitar, where he is invaluable."[19] Despite its apparent success, publication of the *Gazette* ceased in 1899 when Gatcomb shifted to a new business interest: piano building.

Although it did not appear until nearly ten years after the first BMG magazine had begun creating a national market, *The New York Musical Era* (1890–1891) represents periodicals of an earlier era. More closely akin to regional, mid-nineteenth-century magazines than to its more widely distributed competitors, the *Era* focused primarily on musical news and promotions of interest to New York players, teachers, and students. Its anachronistic approach is not at all surprising, since the *Era* was published by one of the five Dobson brothers, generally credited with first putting the banjo on the elevated path into middle-class parlors some forty years earlier.

Members of the Dobson family had established themselves as banjo authorities in New York in the 1850s and maintained a significant presence in the banjo world, especially in Boston and New York, for the next half century. Five brothers—Henry Clay (1832–1908), Charles Edgar (1839–1910), George Clifton (1842–1890), Frank Prescott, and Edward Clarendon (1858–1919)—made their marks throughout New England as banjo performers, teachers, manufacturers, and publishers. Their performances as a quintet created a sensation, but their various business arrangements—always featuring the Dobson name—often led to intense and confusing commercial rivalries. While not the first to play the banjo in the "guitar style" or to perform elevated music on it, they popularized both. All brothers taught the banjo, and four of the five held patents for various technological innovations for the instrument. And, although he referred to other Dobson publications in its pages, C. Edgar Dobson's *New York Musical Era* represents the family's only surviving contribution to BMG periodical literature.[20]

Specific biographical information for C. Edgar Dobson remains sketchy. Gura and Bollman cite a mid-nineteenth-century source describing the two oldest Dobson brothers' early and aggressive promotional efforts in New York in the late 1850s. One resident of New York recalled their posters plastered all over the city, "presenting several square feet of mustache, digit, and banjo" that "stared into the eyes of visitors and residents from every dead wall." C. Edgar offered a selective and brief family biography in the *Era*, but provided only hyperbolic information of dubious reliability about himself: "C. Edgar Dobson, being the youngest, has accomplished more in shorter time than any other member of the family, he being a manufacturer, teacher, publisher and performer. He started in business for himself in a humble manner in 1883, and has gradually advanced, until to-day he stands without an equal. He has patented the famous 'Echo' banjo, and performed at all the principal theatres, and has the honor of being the editor of the New York Musical Era." Dobson's self-promoting hyperbole appeared throughout the *Era* and often seemed designed as much to irritate his brothers as to boost his own image. He regularly reported his brothers' visits to the magazine offices as well as their musical activities, but blanket statements of estrangement and disaffection appeared almost as often: "Charles Edgar Dobson has no acquaintance or business relations with any people bearing his surname and professing to be teachers of the banjo."[21]

C. Edgar remained a musical presence in New York into the next century, but the BMG community generally considered him a relic of an earlier day. In 1910, an obituary from the *New York Herald* described Dobson as "pioneer in the minstrel show business" who toured the United States and Europe as a performer in and manager of minstrel troupes. A business associate observed that in 1859 Dobson had established the first music studio in New York to offer banjo instruction and that he had composed "many fine pieces for the banjo, but published only a few of them, as they were too difficult for ordinary use." The *Cadenza's* brief but respectful obituary cited these sources and identified Dobson as a member of the "old guard," but made no mention of *The New York Musical Era* by name.[22]

While Dobson's activities remained very localized, two short-lived BMG magazines, *The Elite Banjoist* (1890–91) and *The Chicago Trio* (1897–98), document an effort by their creator, John E. Henning, to expand his local musical activities—primarily performing and teaching—into national publishing and instrument sales. Like other BMG publishers, Henning both modeled his ventures on S. S. Stewart's accomplishments and strove to differentiate his own musical products from Stewart's. But Henning also had the unenviable task of disentangling himself from an active role in Stewart's commercial and publishing empire. Beginning in 1885, J. E. Henning and his wife, guitarist Meta Bischoff-Henning, appeared regularly in *S. S. Stewart's Banjo and Guitar Journal*, not just as virtuoso performers and well-qualified teachers, but also as Stewart's designated representatives in the upper Midwest. Originally an endorser and distributor of Stewart's instruments, Henning declared independence in 1890 by marketing his own instruments and music.

Born in 1855 in Lockport, New York, to parents who "were both prominent musicians in their day," Henning went on the road and "at twelve years of age he was doing song and dance and guitar solos with a small company in the gold and silver mining regions of the far West." He eventually mastered "the piano, violin, guitar and banjo, and also became an expert performer on the xylophone, mandolin and other instruments." Stewart characteristically took credit for this musical polymath's conversion to the banjo, claiming that the acquisition of an S. S. Stewart instrument led to Henning's exclusive focus on the banjo. Henning eventually settled in Emporia, Kansas, achieving considerable success as a teacher and performer. He relocated to Chicago in 1885 to open a banjo and guitar school from which he promoted Stewart banjos and sold subscriptions to *Stewart's Journal*. The following year, Henning married nineteen-year-old Meta Bischoff, daughter of an immigrant guitarist, Wilhelm Bischoff. She played banjo as well as guitar and the Hennings toured as a duo after their wedding, appearing in private recitals on the east coast before returning to Chicago to resume performing and teaching.[23]

Like his predecessors, Henning promised to serve all members of the BMG fraternity, but cited his special interest in elevating the banjo. By 1897 when he published his second magazine, Henning had added a line of guitars and mandolins to the Henning banjos, promoting all three in his magazine with illustrated full-page ads. Given his earlier business negotiations with Stewart and the fact that Henning never described a manufacturing facility, his instruments were, in all likelihood, built for him by an independent manufacturer. Neither of Henning's publishing ventures survived more than about six months, but The Henning Music Company remained a peripatetic player on the Chicago music scene through the 1890s.[24]

Unlike *Stewart's*, Clarence Partee's *Cadenza* (1894–1924) primarily promoted sheet music rather than a musical instrument line. Subscribers enthusiastically encouraged support for *Cadenza* because "its columns are not restricted to the mention of any certain make of instruments," a point Partee himself played up in editorials. As a result, the magazine enjoyed widespread popularity, offering readers a broad range of opinions and attitudes corresponding to a large and varied cast of contributors.[25]

Like many professional members of the BMG community, Clarence L. Partee (d. 1915) received his earliest notices in *Stewart's Journal*, announcing concerts he, his wife, and brother gave in Kansas City, Missouri. Partee created *Cadenza* there in 1894, proclaiming his magazine "Devoted to the Interests of Banjo, Mandolin and Guitar Players." Like nearly all who attempted to imitate or compete with Stewart, Partee eventually fell afoul of the Philadelphian and for several years the two editors exchanged barbs in their periodicals. *Cadenza* quickly became as significant a presence in the BMG community as *Stewart's*, growing from sixteen to twenty-four pages; by late 1896 Partee's publication had grown to thirty-two pages and by the turn of the century was running to nearly fifty pages.[26]

In 1900, Partee moved his publishing operation from Kansas City to New York City.[27] Despite the popularity of the plectral instruments in the far West and upper Midwest, New England remained the center of the BMG movement, with large contingents of teachers, players, and ensembles in and around Philadelphia, New York, and Boston. Partee's relocation put him and his magazine in the center of the BMG action and marked a radical change for *Cadenza* and its publisher. These changes included new content, like regular columns devoted to the violin and the piano, which reflected Partee's intention to raise the cultural standards of his "western" magazine. *Cadenza* became a much more cosmopolitan magazine, offering more articles by and about eastern players, featuring covers with stylishly dressed girls and ladies, and even sponsoring concerts in some of New York's finest concert halls.

In 1907, *Cadenza* moved to Boston when Partee sold the magazine to Walter Jacobs (b. 1868), a BMG teacher, composer, and publisher. Jacobs, an Oberlin, Ohio, native, taught himself piano, discovering the guitar at thirteen and "becoming infatuated with the instrument." He began teaching guitar in his teens and apparently taught in Paris for a year. Jacobs qualified for the bar in Texas and held public office there before he was twenty but by 1894, he had established himself in Boston as a BMG teacher and publisher. Jacobs flourished in Boston and, by the time he took over *Cadenza*, "his catalogue of Mandolin, Banjo, Guitar, Band and Orchestra music [ran] into the thousands." When *Cadenza* ceased independent publication in 1924, Jacobs controlled a thriving enterprise that included three other musical periodicals.[28]

Like most of his predecessors and competitors in BMG publication, Partee played all three plectral instruments but considered himself primarily a banjoist. Also like the others, he saw the banjo as an instrument maligned by the mainstream music world and in need of champions to elevate it to the same status as the piano and violin. Not surprisingly, early issues of *Cadenza* focused on the banjo. But in the thirty-year history of *Cadenza*, its two publishers offered readers a wide variety of materials, sometimes only peripherally related to the plectral instruments. *Cadenza*'s subtitle and subject matter changed with time, adding voice, violin, harp, and piano to its list.[29] Pianists, violinists, and vocalists received their own "divisions," written by experts in those areas. In another attempt to broaden readership, Partee published potboiling serial love stories about BMG musicians who triumphed in love through their musical art. Jacobs also effected numerous changes when he assumed *Cadenza* from Partee, including one run of articles on playing ragtime piano and another listing scene-by-scene musical recommendations for professional movie accompanists.

While some of these changes of focus and subject matter clearly reflected a more commercial or popular flavor, most reinforced the BMG community's desire to be recognized as part of America's elite musical culture. *Cadenza* and the other BMG magazines that straddled the nineteenth and twentieth centuries continued the crusade of elevating the banjo, begun by Stewart and his contemporaries twenty years earlier. But the explosion of interest in the mandolin forced the new generation of BMG leaders to change tactics. By bringing the harp, violin, piano, and voice into their magazines, BMG publishers and editors created associations and illusions of musical sophistication for magazines, instruments, and players. More significantly, through the teens and twenties, the BMG leadership created plectral instruments and ensembles that mirrored those of the elite musical mainstream, a move that had a major impact on how the guitar functioned in the BMG community.

F. O. Gutman (d. 1915) established the *FOG Journal* (1899–1904) as a promotional tool for his music business. Unlike many other BMG publishers, however, Gutman produced his magazine primarily in the interests of the mandolin, not the banjo, and primarily to promote his teaching and publications, not his instruments. Until its last few issues, the journal had no full-page advertisements for FOG instruments, and even then only the mandolin and guitar were featured under the FOG moniker. Banjos did appear in small, generic advertisements for FOG instruments, but this magazine stands out among the BMG periodicals for the limited letterpress devoted to the banjo. More importantly, Gutman's magazine offers a glimpse into the workings of a regional teacher, wholeheartedly committed to the business of music. Throughout the run of *FOG*, Gutman enthusiastically and unapologetically proselytized for music teaching as a business, offering articles on such practical items as collecting fees and retaining students. Late in the run, he even marketed signs announcing payment policies for use in private music studios.[30]

Precise biographical details for Gutman remain sketchy, but as a young man in the 1880s he heard the touring Spanish Students. Inspired, he secured lessons with one or more of the Students, learning to play the *bandurria*, a Spanish instrument that resembles the mandolin. Gutman formed an ensemble that performed in costume, mimicking the Spanish Students. The *bandurria* never caught on in America, but the Students—with the help of mandolin-playing imitators—inspired a craze for the mandolin. Gutman taught himself to play mandolin and guitar, eventually establishing himself in the mid-1890s in Cleveland as a teacher and publisher. He directed a number of BMG ensembles there, including several all-women's groups. Prior to launching his own magazine in 1901, Gutman advertised regularly in *Cadenza*, promoting both his music and his instruments. Reflecting his interest in the mandolin, these advertisements identified Gutman as "Publisher of the largest and most complete catalogue of mandolin music in the world," and by 1898 he had a catalogue of a hundred ensemble pieces with parts for violin, cello, flute, and piano in addition to the standard plucked instruments. *Cadenza*'s "Trade Notes" column also observed that Gutman had begun marketing mandolins and guitars in 1898.[31]

A portrait of F. O. Gutman floating above the Ladies Euterpean Club, an ensemble he directed in Cleveland in the 1890s prior to the publication of his magazine. (*Cadenza*)

Gutman expended considerable energy and letterpress in his new journal promoting a series of conventions for BMG teachers and players. While one promotion emphasized the recreational aspects of the conventions, another article confirmed that Gutman hoped to create a fraternity of plectral teachers and players to "advance the standard of their profession for their own cause." Gutman's call for organization promoted a number of familiar themes: equality of the plucked instruments with the standard instruments and voice; advancement/elevation of the BMG instruments; fraternal bonhomie; and financial rewards for everyone.[32]

Gutman's attempt to unite the BMG community stands in marked contrast to the aggressive thrusts and parries of other BMG journalists like Stewart, Gatcomb, and Henning. Yet his efforts to create a unifying national BMG organization actually led to a direct confrontation with east coast BMG activists. When Gutman created the "National Qualified Teachers' League of Mandolin, Banjo and Guitar" in 1902, he did so in direct competition with the "American Guild of Banjoists, Mandolinists and Guitarists," founded in 1900 by Clarence Partee and others. Just as Partee's *Cadenza* became the official organ of the Guild, so did Gutman's *FOG Journal* function for his League. Gutman's League and Partee's

Guild shared much the same mission, the identification and promotion of qualified BMG teachers. Unlike the Guild, which created an examination system for admission, Gutman's League certified a teacher based on "a good reputation," recommendations from two League members, and five years prior teaching experience. The League's more subjective qualifications—a function of connections as much as musical skills—probably contributed to its remaining a regional organization, with membership clustered in the upper Midwest. Certainly, many of the League's initial members were Gutman's students or associates.[33]

In early 1904, editorials in *FOG* announced not only the cancellation of the next League convention but also discounted membership fees. Later that spring, the magazine itself disappeared. A little over a year later, a new Gutman publication, *The American Music Journal* (1905–7), emanated from Cleveland. Its subtitle, *Official Organ of the National Qualified Teachers' League*, confirmed that Gutman's crusade and organization had survived the hiatus. In an effort to play up its independent status, however, Gutman removed his name from the publication's title and no individual editor or publisher was ever identified in its pages. Despite this charade, Gutman remained the power behind both the League and its official organ, and the new *Journal* reflected his more ambitious goals for the League. He intended the League to be an influential organization representing music teachers to the public and to the national government. Moreover, he expanded the reach of the League in the pages of this reconstituted *Journal*, giving most over to articles and advertising for brass band, piano, and vocal interests.[34]

Despite the broadening scope of Gutman's periodical, articles in its Mandolin Orchestra Department maintained the goal of raising the standards for BMG teachers, players, and students. Through its run, *American Music Journal* offered teaching suggestions, in-depth articles on the new harp-guitar, and ramblingly romantic histories of the guitar. Of particular interest to the student of the BMG movement, the *Journal* featured a series of photographic portraits coupled with brief biographies of musical notables. These included a number of BMG figures, including guitarists Giulia Pelzer, Ethel Lucretia Olcott, Gertrude Miller, and Regina Bischoff, as well as composers and publishers like Myron A. Bickford, H. F. Odell, C. E. Pomeroy, and R. M. Tyrrell. Unfortunately, *The American Music Journal* was little more successful than *FOG*, and shuttered in late 1907. Despite his expansive vision, Gutman's influence remained local or, at best, regional, and his League disappeared with his magazines. Gutman's name also disappeared from the pages of the BMG periodicals with the demise of the League's official organ. Eight years after his second magazine ceased publication, Gutman received his last notice in a BMG journal: "Just as the CRESCENDO goes to press, we learn that F. O. Gutman committed suicide early in Sept. by shooting himself. Mr. Gutman was formerly editor of the American Music Magazine, at one time devoted exclusively to promoting the interests of the mandolin, banjo and guitar. He was also a publisher of a large catalog of music for the three instruments. Some time ago he melted his plates and sold them for junk and sold his stock of music for old paper. During his musical life he did much to promote the interests of the plectral instruments."[35]

Herbert Forrest Odell's *Crescendo* (1908–34) first appeared in the same month that Walter Jacobs moved his newly acquired *Cadenza* from New York to Boston. A report in *Crescendo*'s first issue implied that Odell had intended to purchase *Cadenza* from its founder, Clarence Partee, but had been outmaneuvered by Jacobs.[36] Odell quickly founded *Crescendo* as an aggressive competitor to *Cadenza*, wresting the title of "Official Organ of the American Guild of Banjoists, Mandolinists and Guitarists" from Jacobs's periodical. The right to speak to and for the Guild represented a significant business advantage for Odell's new periodical, providing immediate access to an informed and committed readership, and a proven market for musical products. These two magazines jockeyed for position within the BMG community and the Guild, regularly launching editorial attacks and counterattacks and exchanging the Guild imprimatur several times during the years they ran concurrently.

Crescendo entered the marketplace with the content, layout, advertisements, and attitude of a mature magazine. Not surprisingly, the periodical *Crescendo* most resembled was its principal competitor, *Cadenza*, which Odell, despite his antipathy for its new owner, recognized as a successful model for his own new journal. Although Odell's first issue ran only sixteen pages, it featured nearly all the components of a flourishing BMG magazine: large advertisements from influential firms such as the Gibson Mandolin-Guitar Company and Oliver Ditson Publishing, reports and photographs from the recent Guild convention, an article about new instruments in the mandolin orchestra, a list of recent concert programs, a promotional list of prominent BMG teachers, a "puff" column for advertisers entitled "Trade Notes," an editorial analyzing the business climate for the BMG industry, and musical numbers, including mandolin/guitar duos and guitar solos. *Cadenza*'s July 1908 issue ran to nearly twice the number of pages as *Crescendo*'s initial offering, yet offered little more than a greater number of advertisements and a decidedly different point of view regarding developments in the Guild. From its beginnings, *Crescendo* exerted a significant influence within the BMG community, in large part because it faithfully followed *Cadenza*'s model.

Unlike many BMG editors and publishers, Herbert Forrest Odell (1872–1926) came from a professional music family. His father, I. H. Odell, an active bandleader in Boston, had played in Patrick Gilmore's band, written several instrumental methods, and served as the first president of the BMG Guild.[37]

An early biographical sketch of H. F. Odell noted that he had been in business with his father since 1892, identifying the younger Odell as "Soloist, Teacher, Director, Dealer, Arranger, Composer, Harmonist, Publisher, Secretary-Treasurer of the American Guild and one of its organizers, Author, Member of Conservatory Faculty and Music Critic, Composer of several operas, and member of the Board of Government of Handel and Haydn Society."[38] Odell's early training in New England included study of the violin, piano, organ, and voice. In 1895 he discovered the mandolin and traveled to Paris to study his new instrument with the virtuoso Jean Pietrapertosa.[39] Besides his work with mandolin orchestras, Odell had an active career with other sorts of ensembles, directing his own military band and concert orchestra as well as a number of choral ensembles. A devotee of comic opera, he composed and produced several in Boston, which a biographer noted as being "among the greatest of his works." Odell's composing and arranging appears to have had a commercial bent from its beginnings. When he founded *Crescendo* in 1908, he was already an established arranger with works issued by his own publishing firm as well as by the Gibson Mandolin-Guitar Company and Oliver Ditson Company, among others. Odell represented the ideal American BMG figure, with musical training in the United States and abroad as well as significant experience in the music business as a performer, director, arranger, and publisher. *Crescendo's* early success and long-term viability rested, in large part, on its founder's expertise as both a musician and a businessman.

A principal point of contention between *Cadenza* and *Crescendo* and between various factions within the Guild concerned notational systems for banjo and mandolin. Debate roiled around two issues: the notation of banjo music in A (transposing) or C (non-transposing) and, more significantly, the use of standard orchestral clefs or a set of Universal (transposing) treble clefs for the various instruments in the mandolin orchestra. To a later reader these intense arguments appear to be overwrought posturing about inconsequential arcana, but behind the public debate about tradition, pedagogy, and musical literacy, BMG manufacturers and publishers were locked in a battle for market control. Most BMG players were unlikely to learn more than one notational system and publishers understood that their success relied on reaching the predominantly amateur market with pieces in an accessible notation. Those pushing Universal Notation clearly hoped to force established publishers from the field. Supporters of Standard Notation battled to maintain their catalogs as stable foundations on which to build their growing business.[40]

As the last significant BMG periodical of the era that began with *Stewart's Journal* in 1882, *Crescendo* stood as the mature voice of a well-established industry. It broke no new ground as a periodical but represented a comfortable status quo. Leaders of the BMG community and its supporting businesses, as well as the editors and contributors to *Crescendo,* proselytized on behalf of the plectral instruments in an effort to spread their use and to control market share in America's musical life. Despite the ongoing promotion of the BMG instruments, *Crescendo's* pages reflected significantly less concern with justifying and elevating the instruments than had been displayed in the earlier periodicals. The instruments and the industry that produced and supported them had achieved a solid position in America's musical and business worlds. Many within the BMG community recognized that the simultaneous publication of two successful periodicals—*Cadenza* and *Crescendo*—speaking to and for the businessmen, professional performers, teachers, and amateur players confirmed that the industry and its instruments had arrived in America's musical mainstream.

With Odell's death in 1926, *Crescendo* eventually passed into the hands of Walter Kaye Bauer (1899–1997), a multi-instrumentalist whose primary instrument was the mandolin. Bauer, an active contributor, moved the magazine to Hartford, Connecticut, when he assumed control of *Crescendo* late in 1929. Bauer began his performing career as a child actor and remained active in musical circles until well into his 90s, teaching mandolin, banjo, and guitar as well as leading The Bauer Banjo Band in the 1950s. Besides publishing several method books, Bauer claimed to have produced over four thousand compositions and arrangements. His articles for *Crescendo* conveyed an indefatigable energy coupled with a willingness to speak his mind. Bauer called loudly and often for a more refined, classical repertoire for the mandolin ensembles he championed, arguing that a better class of music made good business sense.[41]

As will be seen in later chapters, *Crescendo* stands as an important witness to seismic changes in the guitar's role in American music. Through the late 1920s until its demise in 1934, *Crescendo* offered reports on the electrical amplification of plucked instruments as well as the early American performances of Spanish guitarist Andres Segovia. Either of these developments alone would have had significant impact on the BMG movement, but together they signaled the beginning of its end.

Other periodicals carried on the BMG tradition through the 1930s and later. The few scattered issues of the *Serenader* that survive from the early 1930s indicate that it maintained the values of an earlier era, eschewing jazz and other popular music of the day. In the mid-1930s, mandolinist Giuseppe Pettine took up the banner of the American Guild of Banjoists, Mandolinists and Guitarists in *Fretted Instrument News*, carrying it well into the 1940s. Even *Etude*, the juggernaut of piano and vocal pedagogy, offered articles in the 1930s and 1940s on BMG topics. But the golden age of the BMG movement had passed.

The story of the guitar that follows focuses on that golden age, roughly the half century between 1880 and 1930, and stands on the accounts from the BMG magazines of that era. It makes no pretensions of being a history in the broadest sense, inclusive of all influences, considering all points of view, attentive to all personalities and styles. Rather, it brings to light the values, the characters, and the music of this forgotten generation of guitarists, a troupe of composers, performers, pedagogues, and businesspeople who helped shape the future of America's relationship to the guitar.

THE GUITAR IN THE BMG MOVEMENT
1880–1900

The BMG movement instigated by S. S. Stewart grew out of the two great themes of his life—unstinting devotion to the banjo and an unrelenting desire to make money. Given this dedication to the banjo and to business, later readers should recognize that the guitar's appearance in *S. S. Stewart's Banjo and Guitar Journal* served principally to support the publisher's goals. Stewart himself implied as much when guitarists requested more articles about their instrument in his magazine. He reminded them that his periodical was "published on the one hand as an advertising medium for our business; and on the other hand from pure love for the instrument we represent—the banjo." A later editor soft-pedaled *Stewart's* early disregard of the guitar, noting that "the reason of this seeming neglect of their favorite instrument lay . . . not in any partiality of Mr. Stewart for the banjo, but to a scarcity of writers for the guitar."[1]

Nonetheless, when Stewart used the guitar, he did so as a means of elevating the status of the banjo, encouraging readers and customers to associate his banjos with the cultivated guitar and its musical traditions. Most overtly, Stewart displayed the instruments as equals on his magazine cover, bracketing his portrait. Stewart reinforced this pictorial balance with musical numbers published in his *Journal*, offering readers not just banjo solos or duets, but also banjo/guitar duets in which the refined guitar supported the solo banjo with an unobtrusive accompaniment.

In Stewart's view, the road to refinement and upper-class acceptance ran from the public theaters where the banjo served as a raucous class and racial marker to the refined middle- and upper-class parlor. And although the piano dominated the parlor, the guitar remained entirely at home in this refined musical sanctum. Changes to the banjo and its repertoire—a right-hand technique mimicking the guitar's, a similar treble-clef notation, and eventually fixed frets—brought the instruments closer together, allowing Stewart to promote the banjo through the 1880s as an entirely appropriate replacement of the guitar in the parlor. He did not suggest a change in repertoire or a change in performance style appropriate to the parlor, merely a change in instrument, asserting that "the guitar is capable of no higher class music than is the banjo. In fact it is not as perfect an instrument as a properly constructed banjo, nor is it capable of the variety of musical effects." In recognizing the parlor as a step up the musical social ladder on the way to the concert stage, Stewart allowed that if certain "society ladies" would take it seriously, their playing of the banjo had considerable potential in elevating the instrument. Unsurprisingly, these ladies disappointed Stewart, but he made the best of it, admitting that their interest was a step in the right direction: "The banjo is now in what may be termed an intermediate state of development. It has partly risen from its standard as a 'negro minstrel instrument,' and got in a manner introduced among a better class of people [*sic*]. When it became known that 'society ladies' had taken up the banjo we looked upon that as only one small step in advancement. If these ladies had the talent and perseverance as a class, to learn to play a banjo *well*; they would do much to give it a musical status . . ." And ever mindful of the business side of music, in the same issue of the *Journal* Stewart advised teachers that "the guitar and banjo make the best combination of instruments for a single teacher to work as a business."[2]

Despite the occasional positive statement, Stewart more often used the guitar as a foil for the banjo, denigrating it as vulgar, difficult to play, and less musically expressive than the banjo. The guitar's vulgarity derived from the spread-legged sitting position advocated by most guitar methods and nearly all American and European guitarists. Stewart claimed that its thick strings, wide fingerboard, and awkward chord shapes made the guitar nearly impossible to play well. And, he asserted, even if one could actually manipulate the instrument, its raised frets prevented expressive playing. Stewart also used the guitar's association with Spain and its use by African Americans to point up its primitive and sensual nature. During the Spanish-American War especially, the *Journal* presented editorial asides, articles, and poems designed to undermine the guitar. In another case, Stewart archly noted a correspondent's "wandering eulogy of the guitar as an 'exponent of sexual love,' " hardly a subject welcome in the late Victorian parlor. In a poem, thoughts of the "sweet guitar" led directly to Spain's sinking of the Maine in Havana, and Stewart himself ascribed the Spanish penchant for the "continual playing of frivolously sensuous airs on the mandolin and guitar" to Iberian indolence.[3]

Despite his overwhelmingly negative attitude toward the guitar, in the early 1890s Stewart recognized the talent of guitar virtuoso Luis T. Romero. Unsurprisingly, Stewart still insisted that any success of the guitar in America rested in its association with the banjo.[4] From this point on, however, *Stewart's*

Journal presented a more positive approach to the guitar, linking it to the banjo (and eventually the mandolin) as harmonic and rhythmic support in mixed ensembles.

> The mandolin and guitar are growing in popularity and increasing in use, along with the banjo, one instrument assisting the other. Twenty years ago the mandolin was almost entirely unknown in this country and the guitar seemed to have fallen into disuse as a concert instrument, but from the time the banjo came into popular use, the guitar began to renew its youth, then the mandolin came upon the scene, and now the three instruments are smilingly going along together. This is a musical world, sure enough. On the "long winter evenings," what man or woman is not glad to have one or more of these instruments as a friend or companion?[5]

In short, Stewart offered his readership and his imitators a conflicted relationship with the guitar—part grudging respect, part progressive disdain, and part a desire for joint efforts. While his columns may well have reflected the relative status of the guitar with the other plucked instruments in late Victorian America, there can be no doubt that Stewart consciously and conspicuously attempted to define and control these relationships on the pages of his magazine. To a great extent, this conflicted approach to the guitar dominated America's late Victorian BMG magazines well into the twentieth century.

Like Stewart, his Boston competitor Lincoln Gatcomb also played the banjo and recognized the great popularity of this instrument. The first issue of *Gatcomb's Gazette* opened with a brief article about each of the three plectral instruments, but the interests of the publisher remained clear. The article about the banjo received pride of place, observing that the banjo was the "most popular instrument in refined society," "strictly an American instrument" and "our favorite instrument."[6] As in *Stewart's*, when compared to the banjo the guitar often came off badly: "although in considerable repute at our time in France and England as a solo instrument, its limited capacity is said to have brought it into disfavor, except as an instrument of accompaniment, and the fact that it does not compare to-day as a solo instrument with the banjo."[7]

Despite a clear preference for the banjo, *Gatcomb's* never adopted the aggressively negative slant toward the guitar seen in many of S. S. Stewart's comments. This friendlier editorial slant may well have been a reflection of Gatcomb's early editors, guitarists B. E. Shattuck and L. H. Galeucia. Short blurbs as well as longer articles about the guitar in *Gatcomb's* reflected this more positive appreciation of the instrument.

> Who has not heard the soft rich tones of this beautiful instrument? Wherever or whenever it is played, it exerts a charm which is irresistible. The greatest writers of poetry and prose have accorded it their praises and gratitude. The minstrel of old has

endorsed it to us by his serenades to his fair lady under her balcony, and hardly any novelist would write of Spain without mentioning the "twang of the soft Guitar." As an accompaniment to the voice it is without an equal; its tone is beautiful and plaintive, and also full and strong when desired, while the deep resonance and power of the bass renders it the instrument above all others to use as an accompaniment to the Banjo or Mandolin.[8]

Of course, the last sentence of the citation confirms that the editors of *Gatcomb's*, like Stewart before and most other contributors to the BMG literature after, placed the guitar in a subservient role to the banjo and mandolin. For them, its principal value lay in its full sound and lower range, making it especially appropriate to accompany the higher-pitched banjo and mandolin.

Variations on this romantic description of the guitar appeared again and again in late Victorian American musical literature. Such descriptions mirrored the goals of many mid-century guitar tutors (some still in use later in the century), written to teach guitar students to accompany songs.[9] In *Stewart's Journal*, the guitar's Iberian roots surfaced numerous times, contributing to the appreciation of the instrument as exotic, sensual, and dangerous as well as expressive and charming. Here *Gatcomb's* added another layer of exoticism to the guitar in its imagined history, with references to guitars played by "the minstrels of old" or troubadours. This was one of the first— but not the last—BMG references linking the guitar with the poetry and music of medieval Europe. Curiously, *Gatcomb's* appreciation of the guitar made no reference to the actual history of the guitar and the earlier nineteenth-century players so often highlighted in guitar histories from other BMG magazines.

As other competitors took up the cause of the banjo, they touched on the status of the guitar in their journals. Despite his firm commitment to the banjo, in 1890 C. Edgar Dobson observed in his *New York Musical Era* that "guitar playing is now the rage in the best society circles." Dobson also placed the guitar (usually in the company of the banjo) in the hands of society girls and at wedding celebrations: "An orchestra composed of mandolins, banjos and guitars, with sometimes a violinist as leader, is now considered the proper musical caper at weddings. A sort of sixteenth century arrangement." Later that same year, Dobson observed that a concert at Chickering Hall featuring the mandolin and guitar drew an audience of nearly 1,200 people.[10]

Both of John Henning's Chicago-based magazines featured the guitar in a variety of ways and presented it more regularly in a positive light than did Stewart or Gatcomb. *The Elite Banjoist* devoted considerable letterpress to the guitar, including this introduction from the first issue:

The Guitar as well as the Banjo and Mandolin is gaining in popularity. The Guitar is almost an absolute necessity in Banjo and Mandolin Clubs, and for the proper rendering of Mandolin Music is indispensable. It is the most independent instrument of all, as it produces as complete harmony and melody when played alone as the piano. While not so brilliant as the banjo, nor capable of as rapid execution as the Mandolin, yet there is a sweet fascination about it, that is very pleasing when in the hands of an expert. It has been the favorite instrument of the lover in all ages, and its sweet tone will ever be a source of pleasure and satisfaction to all who cultivate it.[11]

Henning noted that the guitar's technical challenges required an expert to realize its full potential but, unlike Stewart and others, he resisted using such technical demands as a reason to attack the guitar and thereby boost the banjo. Although he still relegated the guitar principally to accompanying roles, Henning avoided the active and implicit negative attitudes of his publishing predecessors.

Henning's more favorable attitude toward the guitar may have stemmed in part from his wife's influence. Meta Bischoff-Henning's documented contributions to her husband's periodicals were limited, but one might surmise that, as an accomplished guitarist with a repertoire that included works by both early classical and mid-century romantic player/composers, she demanded respect for and encouraged a positive promotion of her primary instrument. At the same time, Henning's approach to the elevation of the banjo, especially in *The Chicago Trio*, differed from that of the earlier publishers. Many banjo advocates, especially Stewart, promoted the banjo as a legitimate instrument in part by setting it in competition with other instruments, like the guitar or the violin. Henning sidestepped comparisons of the banjo and guitar, also noting that "the banjo can never hope to attain any great success as a competitor of the violin, nor can it hope to receive anything but ridicule in its efforts in that direction." He remained much more even-tempered about the banjo's place in elevated music-making than other BMG apologists, philosophically reflecting that "the banjo will come along in due time; . . . our instruments are fast gaining a foothold that will place them on the top round of success, for they are the people's choice."[12]

An advertisement in *The Elite Banjoist*'s first issue announced that the next one would be a "Banner Number for Guitarists," featuring "special Guitar Music" as well as biographies and portraits of eminent guitarists. The second issue did, indeed, offer two works for solo guitar as well as two biographies. The first—a translation of a personal letter from Zani de Ferranti's (1802–1878) granddaughter to a young Wisconsin guitarist, Emma Miller—offers a detailed account of the Italian virtuoso's career. The second biography documents the life of Henning's late father-in-law, guitarist Wilhelm Frederick Bischoff (1844–1888). Born in Germany, Bischoff immigrated as a boy with his family to Chicago, where he spent most of his professional life. He moved to New York at age eighteen to devote himself to the study of the guitar, studying with Charles de Janon, the celebrated Colombian American performer, composer, and teacher. Bischoff married in New York and fathered his only child, Meta, there in 1867. He returned to Chicago with his family in 1868 and concertized with one of his three brothers through the 1870s and 1880s. This article attributes Bischoff's death to an illness contracted while touring.[13]

In his first magazine, Henning compared his late father-in-law to Europe's finest guitarist/composers and later described him as "without a doubt the most wonderful guitarist who ever lived. He was known far and wide as the inspired guitarist." Despite his enthusiasm, Henning's estimation of his late father-in-law's skills and reputation do not stand up to close scrutiny. Bischoff's compositions were known, but outside of Henning's magazines his name seldom comes up in either contemporaneous literature or in historical studies. The examples of Bischoff's compositional technique offered in these periodicals stand several steps above those by Henning himself, but only advertising hyperbole bolstered by family pride permit Bischoff's works to be compared to those of Sor, Mertz, and other European guitar masters.[14]

These early magazines dealt with more than biography, of course. A variety of technical, historical, and aesthetic points surfaced again and again in articles, editorials, and letters about the guitar in the BMG literature well into the twentieth century. Among the points of contention that arose in magazines from the 1880s and 1890s, four remained hot topics for years to come: right-hand fingering techniques, supporting the guitar when playing, the use of steel strings on the guitar, and the creation of new, hybrid instruments.

American guitarists stroked the strings of their instruments with their right-hand fingertips, most often using the fleshy part of the finger and avoiding the fingernail. Most of them supported their right hands by bracing the little finger on the face of the instrument. As a result, right-hand technique generally used only the thumb, index, and middle fingers (*pim*), seldom calling for the ring finger (*a*).[15] Readers familiar with the development of classical guitar technique recognize this immediately as the right-hand technique most commonly promoted in early-nineteenth-century guitar instruction books. In this matter, American guitar technique clearly lagged behind that in Europe where mid- and late-century players and pedagogues experimented with an unsupported hand position and more complex finger alternations. Right-hand guitar technique in America through the 1880s and 1890s rested firmly on the precepts of Europe's early-century guitar masters, especially Matteo Carcassi.

Experts might wish for a more detailed discussion of the niceties of these technical matters at this point, and the BMG magazines certainly offer considerable fodder for examination. But three broader points appear more significant in the story of the guitar in America at the turn of the century. First, right-hand guitar technique in this period clearly did not include the use of a plectrum. While technical articles for the mandolin in the BMG magazines often offered long disquisitions about control, angles of attack, and stroke direction of the plectrum, no such articles appeared for the guitar. By the late 1920s, however, plectrum technique was an essential part of much American guitar playing, especially in popular musics. Any serious examination of the guitar in this era must look for the impetus for this significant technical change.[16]

Second, the out-of-date technical approach to the guitarist's right hand favored by American guitarists placed them at a serious disadvantage in respect to European players. Technical innovation, often driven by compositional experimentation, encourages the creation of musical works to match new techniques. As we shall see, in the late 1920s America's guitar community proved able to appreciate neither the new European techniques for the guitar nor the new music and aesthetic that developed simultaneously. This inability contributed directly to significant changes that occurred to the guitar and its music in the first half of the twentieth century in this country.

Lastly, the predominance of the banjo in the BMG community distorted debate about guitar technique in the magazines. When right-hand finger patterns for the guitar were discussed, columnists very often attributed them to new developments in banjo technique. The earliest discussion of right-hand fingerings for the guitar in BMG periodicals appeared early in 1895 in *Stewart's Journal* when Dominga Lynch, a young Philadelphian who had studied in France, responded to a reader's question about several tricky measures in a specific piece. She endorsed what came to be known as the "usual way" with the thumb striking the three bass strings and alternating index and middle fingers the trebles. In a serial article surely inspired by Lynch's comments, George Gregory, best known in the pages of *Stewart's* as a banjoist, encouraged guitarists to play scales using "the modern method of fingering now advocated for the banjo"—alternation of the thumb and index finger (*pipi*).[17] Although used for centuries on lutes and guitars, this thumb/index alternation appeared revolutionary to banjoists and Gregory's comment implies his ignorance of the historical precedents. Banjoists like Gregory, Stewart, and others wished to demonstrate the advanced state of their instrument and regularly suggested that contemporary guitarists update their techniques with "progressive" skills from banjo playing. These letters and articles confirm that despite claims of unanimity and equality by the BMG leadership, the distinctions between banjoists and guitarists (and their techniques)—so prevalent earlier in the century—remained significant, even later in the nineteenth century. One correspondent identified them as two distinct systems and suggested that melding banjo and guitar right-hand techniques would make the instruments more accessible for his students:

> Could not the present system of right hand banjo fingering be successfully applied to the guitar in order to avoid learning two systems in performing on these instruments? The present system of banjo fingering is conceded to be the most rapid as well as the smoothest in the world. . . . I find guitar fingerings stated in various ways from one finger continuously on a string, to alternating the first and second fingers on several strings, but with thumb always continuously on the bass. This strikes me as being slow and awkward after having played the banjo. Now my question in another form is this: Would the following system of guitar right-hand fingering be correct, and would I be justified in teaching it to my pupils, especially those contemplating the study of the banjo also?[18]

Despite its longer history, codified pedagogy, and refined repertoire, the guitar remained a second-class instrument in the BMG community, relegated to a supporting role by banjoists who insisted on their instrument's musical, technical, and aesthetic superiority.

Attacks on the guitar and promotion of the banjo also created a new playing position for guitarists. Most guitar pedagogues of the nineteenth century followed Matteo Carcassi's lead, recommending that the guitarist play with a low stool under the left foot and the guitar resting on the left thigh. In fact, American BMG magazines of the 1880s generally recognized the "Carcassi" position as the norm. But in an attack designed to promote his instruments, S. S. Stewart decried the standard position. "The guitar, as a ladies' instrument, when compared with the banjo, is decidedly vulgar. The position of holding the guitar (its manner of construction compelling its rest upon the left leg) covering the pelvis, when compared with the graceful picture of a young lady holding the banjo upon the right thigh is decidedly constrastive [sic], and the contrast is all in favor of the banjo. There is nothing graceful about a young lady playing a guitar." While some illustrations depict banjo players with crossed legs, the refined banjo technique endorsed by Stewart required players of either sex to keep both feet on the floor. In the last years of the century, outward appearance in performance, especially amateur performance, conveyed the moral, aesthetic, and intellectual state of the performer. A relaxed, elegant sitting position for the banjo bolstered Stewart's argument for its refined nature and cultured use in the parlor or on the concert platform.[19]

Guitarists apparently picked up on Stewart's concerns quickly. Several months after Stewart's attack, an excerpt from Denver's *Rocky Mountain News*, quoted at length in *Stewart's Journal*, noted that "performers on the guitar do not hold the instrument now as formerly." They utilized a new upright position, described

MANNER OF HOLDING THE GUITAR

Illustration of conventional sitting position from Matteo Carcassi's *Complete Method for Guitar* (Philadelphia, 1894). (collection of the author)

as "a great advantage over the awkward position which has been taught in the past and is especially graceful for ladies."[20]

The following year an article with an illustration appeared in *Cadenza*, clarifying this new sitting position. J. W. Freeman, identified simply as "Guitarist, Denver, Colo.," acknowledged banjoists as the models for this new, "correct" manner of holding the guitar. Both feet rest on the floor, the lower bout of the guitar rests on the right thigh and the player holds the guitar steeply angled with its neck pulled back toward the left shoulder. The right arm secures the guitar by exerting downward pressure. Like a cellist, the guitarist in this position holds his left hand quite high, nearly even with his face.

Freeman contended that the new sitting position prevented the player from looking at his left hand on the fingerboard of the guitar, freeing him to engage the gaze of his audience: "The ideal position, then, is one which enables the performer to keep his eye on his audience." He concluded by proclaiming the new technique to be "the only really graceful position," the only one allowing the player to realize the full "capabilities of the instrument" and "especially adapted for the use of ladies."[21]

C. L. Partee, editor of *Cadenza*, enthusiastically embraced this new sitting position, agreeing on all counts with Freeman. In fact, Partee dedicated more than two full columns to this technical advance, asserting the unsubstantiated but impressive "fact" that it increased the playing ability of a guitarist by a full fifty percent. Partee continued his argument along similarly tortured lines, asserting that although it improved the player's overall competence, this sitting position primarily benefited the listening public, allowing a guitarist to come before his

Illustration of new, progressive sitting position. (*Cadenza*)

public making a "presentable appearance" rather than a twisted, humped-over image.

More significantly, unlike other BMG apologists who endorsed the "progressive" nature of this sitting position, Partee expanded his comments to attack the European technical tradition. In the same article, he dismissed Sor, Carcassi, and others as at least fifty years out of date and not "infallible." While American guitar pedagogues never supplanted Sor and his contemporaries as technical touchstones, Partee's assertion, supported by the new American sitting position, was a bold declaration of independence from European influences—an independence inspired by the American banjo.[22]

This divisive discussion persisted for decades, especially in the pages of the *Cadenza*. While some guitarists spoke against it, most endorsed the new sitting position, citing its progressive nature and its graceful appearance. Even as late as 1927 Vahdah Olcott-Bickford continued to endorse the "progressive" position, warning a former student to be wary of the techniques, including the use of a footstool, promoted by the new school of European guitarists led by Andres Segovia and Miguel Llobet.[23]

Like the debate about banjo-inspired right-hand techniques, the controversy about how guitarists held their instrument reinforced two important principles of the BMG movement — primacy of the banjo as the more progressive and evolved instrument, and the inevitable superiority of America's musical culture based on progressive ideals and a vibrant commercialism. While the guitar had initially served as a model for the aspiring banjo, the BMG leadership valorized the banjo and its techniques, in part by denigrating the guitar and its traditions and in part by pushing guitarists to adopt banjo techniques. In doing so, they encouraged American guitarists to reject their traditions and

Gertrude Miller demonstrating that the new sitting position is, in fact, appropriate for ladies. (*American Music Journal*)

to distance themselves from Europe. As will be seen in later chapters, this sort of musical jingoism played a role in the creation of a new American guitar.

An even more inflammatory and divisive practice, the use of steel strings on the guitar, not only touched on guitar technique, musical aesthetics, and business practices but also inspired debate about race and class values. Precise information about their introduction and early use on guitars in North America remains sketchy, but by the last two decades of the nineteenth century, steel strings appeared regularly on guitars in America. Some BMG publishers attempted to remain above the debate, but most found themselves drawn into it at some point. An editorial reply to a reader's inquiry in *Gatcomb's* typically endorsed the use of gut strings, but allowed that steel strings might serve a purpose on the guitar. Yet, "we have always discountenanced the use of wire strings for the guitar . . . [because] their continued use proves to be an injury to both instrument and fingers, and the guitar looses [*sic*] its identity and becomes merely an imitation of the zither, and a poor one at that." Nonetheless, many of the early BMG publishers who sold musical merchandise marketed both gut and steel strings for the guitar side by side in their magazines. S. S. Stewart, who supported the use of gut on both banjo and guitar, regularly promoted his guitar string sets in the same box advertisement, offering gut for eighty cents and steel sets for a nickel less. Curiously, neither contributors nor corresponding readers ever noted the incongruity of publisher/merchants like Stewart strenuously endorsing gut strings while marketing steel strings. As in nearly all aspects of the BMG magazines, business interests remained as significant an influence as aesthetics in the promotion of gut or steel strings.[24]

More important than the advertisements, however, were the many inches of letterpress devoted to this debate. Throughout the BMG era, no other subject concerning the guitar generated such impassioned prose. Supporters of steel strings cited their greater volume, more dependable tuning, and greater durability, among other points. Stewart's advertisement cited above confirms another popular argument for steel strings: their affordability. Although the retail prices of steel and gut sets might have differed by only a few cents, steel strings were a bargain, since they lasted far longer than gut strings.[25]

On the surface, this argument appears technical, but it actually reflected some of the more pressing questions about America's musical culture in the final decades of the nineteenth century. Proponents of gut strings often responded to endorsements of steel strings with vitriolic attacks and hysterical warnings that lumped steel strings with simplified (tablature) notational systems, open tunings (like the "Spanish" tuning), a right-hand plectrum technique, and music of questionable value played by America's minorities. "The publishers [of a recent simplified method] are making a strong appeal to favor, and I have no doubt, will do considerable toward elevating the instrument on the downward journey, especially among that class of plunkers whose ideal *guitarist* is a negro armed with a steel-strung jangle-trap, tuned more or less Spanish, and which he manipulates with the second finger of his left hand, and a mandolin pick. I have three reasons for writing this: First, I am disgusted; Second, I love the guitar; Third, I despise *fakirs*."[26]

While such screeds focus on the guitar, they illustrate the highbrow/lowbrow cultural skirmishes of the era, which pitted elite, formal, and Eurocentric music and music-making against generally accessible, informal, and Americanized popular music and performance. Such outbursts also point to the guitar as a marker of the lower classes, a role the guitar played more and more as the cultural and aesthetic gulf widened in America. Unsurprisingly, official representatives of the BMG community generally stood together on this point, discouraging steel-strung guitars, noting that their metallic sound did not blend well, especially with the gut-strung banjo.[27]

Despite the active promotion of steel strings, several BMG writers argued that the construction of many guitars, especially the better and more refined instruments, could not sustain the tension of steel strings. In 1892, S. S. Stewart documented an experiment in which he measured the different tensions put on the instrument by gut and steel strings, concluding that "the strain of the wire strings is far in excess of that of the silk wrapped strings." Ever the musical businessman, he further surmised that for this reason "guitar manufacturers will not warrant their instruments to stand the strain forced on them in stringing with steel strings." In a later issue he noted that the popular instrument produced by the respected C. F. Martin Guitar Company "is a light built Guitar and will not stand being knocked about, or strung with steel wire strings." In fact, according to Stewart, many professional guitarists of the day, including the acclaimed Luis T. Romero, would not even tune their gut-strung instruments up to concert pitch, for fear of the strain on the guitar.[28]

Among the early BMG publisher/businessmen, only John Henning appears to have confronted the steel string issue head-on. A full-page spread for the "Henning Solo and Club Guitars" in *The Chicago Trio* features a large line drawing of the instrument, statements touting its playability and sound, and a catalog of its components, including a steel-reinforced neck. A feature of all Henning instruments, this reinforced neck allowed Henning to atypically claim that his instruments could safely carry wire strings.[29]

Convenience and frugality led many players to choose wire strings, but others may have chosen steel strings to get more sound from their guitars. Articles, letters, and even poems in the magazines often recognized the gut-strung guitar's "small voice" as one of its most charming characteristics, praising it as a subtle and intimate instrument of romance. But as this country's popular music styles developed, the guitar's restricted dynamic came to be seen as a liability. As later chapters document, the guitar underwent internal modifications (like Henning's steel-reinforced neck) as well as more significant design changes in the early years of the new century, nearly all inspired by the quest for more sound.

The early leaders of the BMG movement were banjoists and they most vigorously promoted changes to the guitar that drew the instrument closer to the banjo. Early on, the apparent goal of such hybrids was to induce guitarists to play a newer, progressive instrument that more closely resembled the banjo in timbre. The earliest guitar hybrid promoted in the BMG magazines emanated from S. S. Stewart's factory in Philadelphia, and its endorsers all had links to Stewart and his enterprise. Stewart's "Guitar Neck Banjo" had a banjo body with a resonating skin head and a fretted guitar neck carrying six strings. This promotion echoed attempts from the 1850s and 1860s by earlier banjo advocates to convert guitarists to the more progressive banjo by creating a new instrument. In an 1884 advertisement Stewart touted his "Six String Banjo," assuring guitarists that "these Banjos can be fingered at once by any Guitar Player, as the finger-board is the same as that of a medium size guitar."[30]

In a later article, Stewart advised ladies to abandon the unseemly guitar for the banjo, intimating that they could retain proper decorum by purchasing Stewart's own "Guitar Neck Banjo," playing guitar studies on it with no fingering changes.[31] While the guitar often appeared in illustrations of and in recital

NOTICE.

PROF. A. LOPES'
PATENT
Banjo-Guitar

One
Lesson for
Two Instruments,

TWO INSTRUMENTS
IN ONE.

The
Easiest
Banjo to learn is

Guitar & Banjo-Guitar.

The Banjo-Guitar.

Front View.

Back View.

The public may obtain from this New, Correct and Practical Method a fair Musical Education; and proficiency both as Soloist

and Accompanist will be quickly acquired, as it is written in a very easy and progressive manner.

The merit of this work is already testified to by a great number of competent people, as being a Book that contains the instructions and explanations from the beginning to the end, which simplifies the difficulties of beginners in studying music. This advantage is not usually found in other methods, as they generally give in the front of the book only the first rudiments of music, leaving the student completely in the dark when proceeding to the most important studies.

This Book also contains Modulation : the Building, Inversion of the Chords and Bass, and a limited number of Vocal exercises with Guitar accompaniments, very instructive to beginners wishing to Sing and accompany themselves.

Sheet Music.—For the order of Vocal and Instrumental pieces in sheet music published as a *Progressive Series of Lessons* in connection with the instructions given in this Book, see Regulations on next page.

All the pieces in this Method and the Sheet Music are arranged for One or Two Guitars ; and there is also published the Piano part for the same, so that every piece can be played either by One Guitar (Solo), Two Guitars, or Guitar and Piano (Duetto), or Two Guitars and Piano (Trio).

BANJO-GUITAR.

Great Improvement in Banjos.—This instrument is Stringed, Tuned and Played precisely like the ordinary Guitar, so that this Method and the Sheet Music are both applicable to the New Instrument; and a still further advantage is, that the Guitarist has nothing new to learn, and the beginner learns Two instruments at the same time, as Lessons on the Guitar are also applicable to the Banjo-Guitar.

For further information of the Banjo, see enclosed circular.

N.B.—Learning the Guitar (or any other Instrument) by ear or figures, is loss of time and money, for what is learned to-day may be forgotten to-morrow. In learning by NOTE you have the advantage of constant Progress.

A. LOPES, Brooklyn, N. Y.

Numerous manufacturers, including S. S. Stewart, produced hybrid banjo-guitars. This advertisement promotes an instrument marketed by Brooklyn guitar teacher Antonio Lopes at the beginning of his *Instruction for the Guitar* (New York, 1894). (courtesy of Eli Kauffman)

programs for Banjo Orchestras, experts who wrote articles about these ensembles for *Stewart's Journal* sometimes called for the hybrid Guitar Neck Banjo rather than a guitar to provide a harmonic underpinning. Dominga Lynch, the young European-trained guitarist, even composed a waltz specifically for Stewart's new instrument. Despite Stewart's claim that the piece had been "Especially written for the Guitar Neck Banjo," Lynch's "Enterprise Waltz" actually differed in no way from guitar pieces of the same nature.[32]

While a certain musical aesthetic might have been at work here, Stewart's desire to displace the guitar with the banjo, as well as his drive to create and dominate the national market for the banjo, provided the more likely impetus behind his Guitar Neck Banjo. Nonetheless, hybrid instruments, including versions of guitar-neck banjos, remained a significant presence in the BMG movement well into the 1930s. Such experimentation was fueled by the demand for more sound, an interest in "progressive" innovation, and manufacturers' drive to create new and competitive products for an expanding market. Later chapters will describe how these three points—coupled with the BMG community's insistent privileging of the banjo and mandolin over the guitar—contributed to a new American interpretation of the guitar.[33]

Not all editors imitated S. S. Stewart by maintaining a stranglehold on opinions expressed in their journals; despite his enthusiastic promotions for the banjo, Clarence Partee welcomed other voices to the pages of his journal. From the beginning of *Cadenza's* run, his treatment of the guitar remained generally evenhanded, reflecting his interest in appealing to the broadest range of advertisers and readers. As a result, *Cadenza* offered a variety of articles about the guitar that document a range of opinions as well as a gradual shift in attitudes toward the instrument over the magazine's thirty-year run. And although the banjo's advocates regularly challenged Europe's hegemonic hold on musical culture, serious guitarists saw the Old World as a musical touchstone. Early articles about guitar in *Cadenza* by R. S. Chase, Alfred Chenet, and Richard Tyrrell, among others, took a conservative, Eurocentric, and occasionally highly romanticized attitude toward the guitar.

The first issue of *Cadenza* offered a brief introduction to the instrument, "The Guitar and Its Teaching," which outlined a broad history of the guitar as well as an estimation of its status in 1894. The article's author, R. S. Chase, identified the usual early- and mid-nineteenth-century composer/players—Sor, Giuliani, Legnani, and Regondi—as well as several listed less frequently—Conradin Kreutzer and Leonard Schulz, for example. Chase recognized a decline in the guitar's popularity outside of Spain and Italy, crediting "the introduction of the pianoforte into all houses where the least taste for music exists." He noted a revitalization of guitar studies since the mid-1880s, but observed that "comparatively few of our modern instructors realize the possibilities of the instrument," blaming the abandonment of expressive playing for tasteless bombast on the use of steel strings. Chase complained that the guitar in 1894 appeared most often as an accompanying instrument and that teachers were most interested in volume and rapid execution of incomprehensible scales.[34] Chase's report emphatically confirms the attitudes of banjo advocates like Stewart, Gatcomb, and others who relegated the guitar to a secondary role in support of the banjo.

The next issue of *Cadenza* offered a decidedly more positive outlook on the guitar in the 1890s with an article titled "The Guitar and Its Progress in America." Alfred Chenet—an experienced guitarist, composer, and teacher—seemed to be answering Chase when he asserted "in the past eight or ten years the guitar has made wonderful progress in this country." Chenet agreed that the guitar was a superior accompanying instrument, but claimed its glory was as a solo instrument. He placed it in the same category as the harp, organ, and piano, recognizing that "it carries its own accompaniment, with its rich sonorous bass and wealth of pretty chords and harmony." He cited the compositions of American-born guitarists such as W. L. Hayden and Justin Holland as well as American-based guitarists including Manuel Lopez, Luis T. Romero, and Charles de Janon. Chenet recognized progress for the guitar, as well, in the proliferation of well-constructed American guitars from manufacturers like Martin, Bruno, Vega, and Washburn, among others. He claimed that most guitar students in the United States at that time were adults "determined to succeed," rather than unmotivated children. He also acknowledged American guitar teachers for their "new and improved systems of teaching, better adapted to ... our American guitar school." Chenet ended his article by encouraging guitarists to participate in ensembles, suggesting an idiosyncratic group of three guitars, two mandolins, and a banjo.[35]

Most other contributors who wrote about the guitar for *Cadenza* in the late 1890s touted its European roots. These include Irish-born Richard Tyrrell (b. 1850) who played clarinet, flute, double-bass, and violin as well as guitar and whose credits include a stint with the Marine Band in Washington, D.C. Tyrrell's many articles confirm a well-rounded musical mind, significantly more familiar with standard classical repertoire, music theory, and composition than most BMG writers. He wrote extensively for *Cadenza* beginning in 1896, and later for the *American Music Journal*. He wrote primarily about the guitar, but offered articles on popular and classical music and compositional techniques in *Cadenza* and on the clarinet and band music in *American Music Journal*. A conservative musician, Tyrrell preached respect and deference for the traditional, skeptically questioning the latest fads. In an article about how to study the guitar, he drew on his experience as a professional band musician, comparing the standardized teaching of orchestral and band instruments to the looser standards for the "parlor class of instruments." He chided BMG teachers whose insufficient musical training contributed to a disdain for the tried and proven, holding up Matteo Carcassi's *Method* and Johann Kaspar Mertz's technical advice as exemplars of systematic and rationalized methodologies, even sixty years after Carcassi's method first appeared.[36]

Other contributors to *Cadenza* in the 1890s offered histories of the guitar that ranged from the breathlessly romantic to levelheaded attempts to document the instrument's past. Unsurprisingly, the guitar's Old World connections were highlighted in these histories. Madame Giulia Pelzer, sister of the celebrated Victorian guitarist Madame Sidney Pratten (1821–1895), traced the guitar back into antiquity, tying it to Apollo's lyre as well as the Arabs, Italians, Spanish, and Germans. Her hyperbolic history not only linked the guitar to Europe's fine art tradition but also put the instrument in the hands of "Bach, Mozart, Haydn,—even the mighty Beethoven himself—[who] played the guitar, because it was an instrument of easy conveyance, and capable of expressing every variety of harmony and modulation." William J. Kitchener's more sedate three-part history also reached back into the ancient world but effusively highlighted the earlier nineteenth century, citing the careers of Carulli, Carcassi,

Aguado, Sor, and Giuliani. He also recorded Berlioz's and Paganini's attraction to the instrument, but the most recent guitarist Kitchener documented was J. K. Mertz, "the last of the old school."[37]

The status of the guitar in America from the 1890s to the early years of the twentieth century probably lay somewhere between Chase's pessimistic view and Chenet's considerably rosier picture. Significantly, despite their championing of the guitar as a solo instrument, both men clearly recognized that the fortunes of the guitar in America had become tied to those of the banjo and mandolin, primarily as an accompanying instrument in the developing plectral ensembles. This dual role remained a point of debate for the remainder of the BMG era, with non-guitarists calling for minimal technical standards suited to playing simple accompaniments for banjo and mandolin, while guitarists championed a sophisticated technique appropriate to a more demanding solo repertoire.

The BMG magazines also published music; guitar solos appeared in the early BMG magazines, reflecting much of the published literature available to guitarists. Most pieces were simple dances, composed to appeal to a student's taste and technique—tuneful, rhythmically square, in easy keys of two sharps or less, and utilizing open strings and the first position. Slightly more advanced solos might be theme and variations, usually on a popular or folk song. Clarence Partee's charming variations on "Believe Me If All Those Endearing Young Charms" stands as a particularly good example of these works aimed at the advanced amateur player.[38]

But several of the early magazines promoted and sometimes published works for solo guitar that appear to have been aimed at the advanced or even professional performer. In the 1880s and 1890s, the most demanding pieces of this solo repertoire were arrangements of standard, non-guitar fare by Europe's recognized masters. These included moderately challenging transcriptions by C. H. Stickles of two of Felix Mendelssohn's "Songs without Words," as well as C. F. E. Fiset's arrangements of works by Bach, Chopin, Grieg, and Schubert. Unlike song arrangements aimed at amateur performers, these guitar settings did not serve as thematic material for variations or fantasy divisions, but offered accurate reproduction of the original, suggesting a more high-minded conception of instrumental music, much along the lines preached by John Sullivan Dwight. Many apologists and arrangers within the BMG community concurred with Dwight, and such solo arrangements of works by Europe's master composers reflected an attempt by guitarists to reinforce the connections between the American BMG movement and Europe's cultivated tradition.[39]

But leaders of the BMG community were not solo guitarists, and they strove to elevate the plectral instruments by other means. When chronicling

The Boston Ideals responded to growing interest in the mandolin by incorporating it into their performances. (*Gatcomb's Musical Gazette*)

the early days of their movement, many early-twentieth-century BMG commentators recognized S. S. Stewart's invention of the soprano banjo or banjeaurine as a seminal moment, principally because it had prompted the development of multi-part plucked-string ensembles that mirrored the elite string quartet or symphonic orchestra. Stewart and other manufacturers followed the banjeaurine with a variety of instruments, creating a family of hybrid banjos (and eventually mandolins) that covered a pitch range comparable to that of the traditional string quartet. In short order, professional players established banjo ensembles comprised of several banjos supported by one or more guitars. The Boston Ideals, perhaps the most famous of the early ensembles, was a quintet that had strong connections to L. B. Gatcomb's operations. The Ideals started as a banjo quartet in 1883 but within four years had expanded to include mandolins. Significantly, although the Ideals were a mixed ensemble, they apparently did not blend mandolins and banjos in their performances, but worked in ensembles of sized banjos (a banjeaurine and two banjos) or mandolins (first and second mandolin and mandola) supported by one or two guitars. Although the Ideals played light classics, their most famous

A multi-talented ensemble—the Vanderbilt University Glee, Banjo, Mandolin and Guitar Club. Note the sized banjos, including the banjeaurine being held in the first row. (*Gatcomb's Musical Gazette*)

piece, "The Darkey's Dream," surely played on the banjo's minstrel-show connections.[40]

Semiprofessional and amateur bands of banjoists and guitarists sprang up across the nation, imitating the early professionals. While many of the ensembles were purely amateur, others were founded and/or led by professional players or teachers. Through the 1890s most of these ensembles identified themselves as "clubs" and appeared in high schools and on college campuses, often in association with a glee club or chorus. And while the preponderance of the music for these ensembles remained popular dances, some of these new BMG ensembles imitated cultivated European ensembles, performing a more refined repertoire of classical and light-classical works.

Almost without exception, the guitar remained an essential part of these ensembles through the 1890s, supporting the melodic activities of the banjos or mandolins in everything from duos to large-scale plucked orchestras. And although the guitar appeared prominently on the mastheads of BMG magazines, it remained firmly in the background of the BMG ensembles. As the century drew to a close, developments in the BMG movement contributed to a slow intensification of the debates and conflicts highlighted in this chapter.

These developments included the evolution of the BMG clubs into mandolin orchestras, the creation of more hybrid instruments for this ensemble, the ongoing distrust of the traditional guitar and guitarists as foreign, and the emergence of a new generation of American guitar soloists. The following chapters continue the story of the guitar in America by examining these developments.

Chapter Four

INTERLUDE

A New Generation of Guitarists

The history of the guitar in America remains largely a history of players. Before the late twentieth century no important American composer wrote for the guitar and no American guitarist achieved any lasting reputation as a composer. Although the guitar had enjoyed some popularity in this country before 1850, only after the 1870s did American-born guitarists begin to garner attention as teachers, performers, and composers. Some of them achieved sufficient technical polish and sophistication, in fact, to warrant inclusion in Philip Bone's influential, international, and encyclopedic *Guitar and Mandolin: Biographies of Celebrated Players and Composers*, first published in 1914. Despite their accomplishments, however, most of these musicians remain virtually unknown, even among guitar aficionados. A later chapter will evaluate the careers and contributions of the two most important American guitarists of the early twentieth century, William Foden and Vahdah Olcott-Bickford; but the following pages resurrect some of the lesser-known guitarists active through the BMG era.

Four figures appeared regularly in late-century BMG literature and programs, recognized as important teachers, performers, and composers. Ironically, although America's BMG movement claimed them as its own, all four—an African American, a Spaniard, a Colombian, and an American born of Spanish parents—stood outside the racial boundaries promoted by the BMG community. The oldest, Justin Holland (1819–1887), was known principally as a pedagogue. Born a free African American in Virginia, he spent his teens around Boston, where his early guitar mentors included Spaniard Mariano Perez and William Schubert. In 1841, Holland enrolled in Oberlin College, one of only a handful of colleges available to blacks. He supplemented his musical studies with intense language study so that he might read the great guitar pedagogues in their original languages. He set up shop in Cleveland in the mid-1840s, teaching

Justin Holland. (James Trotter, *Music and Some Highly Musical People* [Boston and New York, 1885], courtesy of Gaylord Music Library, Washington University in St. Louis)

music there for the rest of his life. Although Holland turned out hundreds of arrangements for solo and duo guitars as well as songs for voice and guitar, his reputation as one of America's most influential guitar pedagogues rested on his method books. Holland received recognition beyond the guitar community, too, and was included in James Trotter's 1878 compendium of African American musicians, *Music and Some Highly Musical People*. The popularity of his methods, especially his *Comprehensive Method for the Guitar*, rested on Holland's systematic approach to musical and technical skills. But more importantly, his adherence to the traditional techniques of Europe's early guitar masters supported the conservative approach to the guitar to which America's BMG community generally subscribed.[1]

Although born in Madrid, Luis T. Romero (1854–1893) was very often claimed for America in the BMG literature. He landed in California from Spain in his teens, where he studied guitar with another Spaniard, Miguel Arrevalo. Romero established himself as a performer and teacher in San Jose, California, but eventually moved to Boston, where he enjoyed considerable success. When Romero appeared in a concert in Philadelphia in April 1891 on the same bill with a pianist, a vocalist, and several banjoists, a pre-concert article (probably a paid promotion) in *Stewart's* identified Romero as "The Greatest Living Guitarist." He must have lived up to these hyperbolic promotions, for a series of short blurbs and stories in *Stewart's Journal* continued to promote him enthusiastically until his premature death from tuberculosis in 1893. As reported by Stewart and his contributors, Romero's repertoire consisted primarily of his own arrangements of or variations on such well-known classics as Beethoven's "Le Desir,"

Luis T. Romero. (Philip J. Bone, *The Guitar and Mandolin* [1914])

"The Prayer" from Handel's *Moses in Egypt*, Verdi's *Rigoletto*, and Stephen Foster's "Swanee River." After his death, most of Romero's works disappeared from the pages of BMG magazines, but his "Fantasie Americaine," a set of variations on American tunes, remained popular for another twenty-five years.[2]

Romero was a virtuoso player and his compositions were significantly better than most American works of the period. Yet Romero's major contribution to the BMG movement rested in some ways in the role assigned him by Stewart. Prior to Romero's East Coast appearances, Stewart had taken a dim view of the guitar, using it in his *Journal* primarily as a negative foil for the banjo. When Romero's playing forced Stewart to admit that the guitar had potential in the hands of a virtuoso, the banjo manufacturer attributed it to his Spanish heritage, mistakenly reporting the guitarist's work with the Spanish Students on their famous American tour in the early 1880s. Stewart used Romero's Spanish heritage as a way to set the guitar, its music, and its players apart from the all-American banjo. The Spanish-American War brought out a real xenophobia in *Stewart's Journal*, and as we shall see, the guitar's connection to Latin musicians remained a negative marker for the instrument, contributing to the BMG community's drive to create not just an American repertoire, but also an American instrument on which to play that repertoire.

Manuel Y. Ferrer (1828–1904) was cast in a similar role in the BMG movement. Born to Spanish parents just north of the Mexican border, he spent his entire career in California. Settling in the San Francisco area around 1850, Ferrer created a lasting reputation as a respected performer and teacher. He was best known in the BMG community as a composer, in part because of his distance from the competition on the northeastern seaboard, the seat of the BMG movement. His most famous student, Vahdah Olcott-Bickford, who studied with him in his final year, regularly promoted his music, identifying Ferrer (alongside Luis T. Romero) as a signature representative of America's guitar composers, comparable to Spain's Francisco Tárrega. In 1914, Philip Bone identified Ferrer as an "American guitarist . . . of pure Spanish parentage," implying that that heritage gave him a natural affinity for the instrument and its expressive voice. Like Romero, Ferrer's reputation among America's guitar players stood in part on an essentialist reading of his ethnic roots, a reading grounded in an American jingoism coupled with a suspicion of the musical foreigner.[3]

Charles de Janon (1834–1911) also joined the ranks of American guitarists of Latin extraction. Born in Colombia, he came to New York with his family in 1840. As a self-taught guitarist, de Janon satisfied the BMG community's expectations of the Latin guitarist whose skill owed as much to innate racial characteristics as to disciplined study. Although the BMG magazines continued to lionize de Janon as a masterful performer, concert announcements, program listings, and reviews disappear from their pages before the 1890s. Nonetheless, the BMG journals' leading guitar advocates regularly cited him as an important guitarist/composer whose many compositions and arrangements were considered on a par with those of Romero, Ferrer, and some of the earlier European guitar masters. In fact, when the American Guild of Banjoists, Mandolinists and Guitarists created their "Standards of Attainment" in the mid-teens, the repertoire list for professional guitarists included several works each by de Janon, Ferrer, and Romero, as well as Johann Kaspar Mertz and Luigi Legnani.[4]

Given that women were also seen to share an innate sensibility and sensuality with these Latins, we should not be surprised that they, too, seemed inherently linked to the guitar. Despite his early antipathy for the guitar, S. S. Stewart found it in his interests to promote two female guitarists. Having unequivocally asserted in 1885 that "the guitar, as a ladies' instrument, when compared with the banjo, is decidedly vulgar," the following year Stewart reported a well-received recital featuring Meta Bischoff (b. 1867), a young Chicagoan, assisted by John Henning, a banjoist whom she subsequently married. Her inclusion of Legnani's challenging solo "Theme and Variations, op. 237," indicates that as a guitarist she stood out from the crowd. Of course, Stewart's enthusiasm for Bischoff probably had less to do with her playing than her association with Henning, who played and sold Stewart banjos—or the full-page advertisements the Chicago couple bought in the magazine. The only child of immigrant guitarist Wilhelm Bischoff, Meta Bischoff was born in New York City, but the next year the family moved to Chicago, her father's first American home. Bischoff studied guitar with her father and began performing publicly at age eight and teaching at eleven. She married at nineteen; their honeymoon became a concert tour, and the Hennings appeared in private recitals on the East Coast before returning to Chicago to resume performing and teaching. Bischoff-Henning's

Meta Bischoff-Henning. (*Chicago Trio*)

guitar solos eclipsed her husband's more modest banjo solos and garnered very favorable reviews. News reports hyperbolically named her "the most wonderful lady guitarist and banjoist in America," indeed, "the most beautiful and accomplished banjo and guitar artist in the world." In addition to works by her father, she played her own compositions as well as pieces by Legnani, Sor, and de Janon. It seems likely that Bischoff-Henning also participated actively in her husband's musical business, though she left no mark in either of her husband's magazines beyond advertisements for her compositions and recital notices for her student ensembles. The Hennings remained active in Chicago after the demise of his second magazine, *The Chicago Trio*, in 1898, operating Henning's Banjo, Guitar and Mandolin Conservatory at Steinway Hall until at least 1899.[5]

Dominga I. Lynch, the second female object of Stewart's attention, began her guitar studies around 1890 in Paris, but they were cut short by her unplanned return to Philadelphia only a year later. By late 1894 she had found a position there as an instructor of guitar, piano, and theory in a local music academy. She appears to have been the first teacher in the BMG magazines to advertise solely as a teacher of guitar. In addition to contributing several arrangements and original solos to *Stewart's*, Lynch published two thoughtful and articulate articles offering technical and performance advice to guitarists. Lynch's classified advertisements vanished from the *Stewart's* near the end of 1897.[6]

Each of these women played a pioneering role in America's late-century guitar community. Bischoff-Henning appears to be one of the first native-born guitarists to display an accomplished technique in public performances; Lynch's articles represent some of the earliest serious discussions of applied guitar technique in the BMG periodicals. Nonetheless, the BMG community reflected the values of America's late Victorian society and neither woman could transcend conventional expectations and roles. Regardless of her apparently superior skills as a soloist, Bischoff-Henning played a supporting role to her husband in his musical and business activities, promoted principally as her father's protégé or her husband's discovery. Although Lynch wrote articulately and persuasively about guitar technique, once male guitar teachers followed her articles with similar technical commentary, she disappeared from the pages of *Stewart's*. Numerous married couples worked together in BMG ensembles or in teaching studios, and in nearly all cases, articles and promotional materials depicted the female partner in a supporting role. Such examples derived from expectations and presuppositions about the role of women in American society as well as the role of the guitar in BMG musical activities.[7]

Despite the continued publication of images and reports that reinforced such conventional attitudes, beginning in 1897 and through the first decade of the next century, *Cadenza* promoted a number of young women guitarists whose work as performers and teachers certainly rivaled that of their male peers within the BMG industry. *Cadenza's* promotion of these competent and professional women alongside male musicians documented a change not just in attitudes toward women but in their role and place within the BMG community.

Two female guitarists to achieve significant recognition on their own merits first appeared in the same issue of *Cadenza* in 1897. Elsie Tooker (1879–c. 1934) of San Jose, California, and Jennie M. Durkee (b. 1877) of Chicago received glowing praise for their solo turns in separate concert notices.[8] Unlike many BMG soloists cited in the magazines, Tooker and Durkee did not promptly disappear but continued to garner positive notices in the periodicals. The following year, *Cadenza* featured a photographic portrait and biographical sketch of the up-and-coming nineteen-year-old Tooker. Born in Utah, Tooker began her study of the guitar when she was seven years old, learning the instrument from her mother. At the same time, the family moved from Utah to California and most of Elsie's professional activity centered on the San Francisco area. She favored the works of the Italian prodigy Giulio Regondi as well as solos by Luis Romero, William Foden, and Manuel Ferrer. Both Tooker women appeared in *Stewart's Journal* and Elsie wrote the "Ladies of the Banjo, Mandolin and Guitar Realm" column briefly in 1901. Tooker toured professionally in the Romany Trio (guitar, cello, and soprano) in 1902–3 and appeared in BMG magazines into the early teens. One of the few BMG guitarists to have recorded, she left a guitar solo and two violin-guitar duets on a 78, probably from the early 1930s. Tooker remained an active performer through the 1920s and into the 1930s, appearing regularly as a guitarist on several San Francisco radio stations as well as leading a female ensemble of guitars and mandolins.[9]

Elsie Tooker at age nineteen.
(*Cadenza*)

Jennie Durkee, the subject of several biographical magazine articles, remained in the public eye as a BMG celebrity for more than twenty-five years. Daughter of George B. Durkee, a Chicago instrument builder and designer, at fourteen she moved to St. Louis to study with virtuoso William Foden. In 1903 she began a long career as an active performer and well-respected teacher in Denver, and notices of her recitals and concerts, as well as those of her students, appeared regularly in *Cadenza* and *Crescendo*. When a craze for Hawaiian music erupted in the mid-teens, Durkee not only took up the ukulele but also wrote a method book for this faddish instrument, identifying her approach to the ukulele as an "American Way." She played ukulele in promotional concerts for Lyon & Healy and appeared in 1922 as a featured performer at the convention of the American Guild of Banjoists, Mandolinists and Guitarists. An attendee observed that Durkee "played 'Il Trovatore' on her ukulele in such a manner that all of us were looking around to see if she had not put one over on us and concealed the New York Symphony Orchestra behind the palms somewhere." By the mid-1920s, Durkee had links to Vahdah Olcott-Bickford and her American Guitar Society on the West Coast. Her final notice in the BMG magazines documented a performance at a fellow guitarist's funeral in Los Angeles in 1925.[10]

Gertrude Miller (b. 1879), another young guitarist active through the first decade of the new century, also appeared in *Cadenza* in 1899. A native of Vinton, Iowa, she began guitar studies with her father at ten, performing first in public at thirteen. The Miller family appears to have had a connection to

Elsie Tooker Howard (seated at center with a mandolin) and a "gypsy" BMG ensemble. (courtesy of the Tooker-Howard family).

Josephine Mertz, the widow of the guitar virtuoso Johann Kaspar Mertz, as well as to the family of Italian guitarist Zani de Ferranti; her repertoire included works by these virtuosi as well as Fernando Sor, Luigi Legnani, Giulio Regondi, and William Foden. In 1905–6 Miller created an early American Guitar Society, which included such notable members as Jennie Durkee in Denver and Carl W. F. Jansen, a prominent Chicago guitarist. In 1915 Vahdah Olcott-Bickford identified Miller as among "the best known American guitarists," and even forty years later she, her sister, and father were recognized as "excellent guitarist-performers."[11]

Despite the admiration given Latin guitarists and the success of women as players and teachers, the preponderance of active BMG members remained Anglo men. And although their dominant position in society and the BMG movement gave them a leg up on female and Latin players, white men also had to build careers and reputations around social and cultural expectations. While the emotional and sensual nature of women and Latins predisposed them to performance, Anglo men, with their (supposed) superior intellectual skills and less temperamental nature, had to prove themselves as composers, conductors, pedagogues, and businessmen. Even when these men demonstrated sophisticated performance skills, promotions and biographies highlighted their more intellectual talents. The study of harmony or even passing acquaintance with orchestral or band repertoire signaled a musician's advanced musical skills and the BMG literature regularly touted such training or experience when found in a plectral player. And even when a male ensemble director had only children under his direction, magazine promotions or reviews highlighted his "conducting."

Alfred Chenet (b. 1854), a native of Ottawa, Canada, received his first guitar instruction in Montreal but his principal musical studies focused on brass band music, a point highlighted in his earliest biography. By 1882 Chenet had relocated to Boston, where he directed the French-Canadian Institute as well as a band he founded there. He began teaching guitar in Rochester, New York, in 1884 and continued that work in St. Louis the following year. By 1886 Chenet had returned to Boston, and secured a teaching position at the Boston Conservatory around 1896. The magazines recognized him as an active composer, too, and his studies and pieces were published and promoted in the BMG magazines through the 1920s. His one extended article, "The Guitar and Its Progress in America," offered Chenet credibility, too, as an enthusiastic authority on the guitar familiar with the repertoire and techniques of the Old World masters.[12]

Another Boston-based guitarist, Walter Francis Vreeland (1868–1927) became one of the most active proponents of the guitar in America; the BMG magazines highlighted his wide range of activities that included writing articles, directing ensembles, performing as a soloist, and publishing numerous works for guitar. A native of Newark, New Jersey, Vreeland studied music in New York with members of one of the many professional mandolin and guitar ensembles that sprang up after the popular success of the Spanish Students in the 1880s. Like many of these ensembles, The Venetian Troubadours was comprised principally of Italian immigrants. Vreeland joined the group when he was fifteen, apparently performing with them until he moved to Boston in 1889. Although Vreeland continued to perform, touring the Lyceum circuit with Boston's Imperial Banjo, Mandolin and Guitar Quartet, he followed the BMG career model, concentrating on teaching and directing ensembles in the Boston area. He established himself as an authority with several serial articles in *Cadenza,* including a three-part discussion of the guitar as an accompaniment instrument. Widely respected in the BMG community as a solo guitarist, Vreeland performed at the 1915 Guild convention. A biographical sketch promoting Vreeland's performance noted that he favored Legnani's music, but was expected to play Tárrega's "Capricho Arabe" as well as solos by Pettoletti and Mertz. Two years later, Vreeland was the subject of another long biographical essay that touted his quick and skillful adaptation to the latest fads of Hawaiian steel guitar and ukulele. Vreeland certainly embodied the ideals of the BMG community: American-born but trained in the tradition of expressive Latin musicians; a respected performer who played the works of the European masters; an enthusiastic and articulate spokesman for the community who wrote with authority and experience about the plectral instruments; a multi-instrumentalist equally adept with any traditional or new plectral instrument; a composer whose works remained popular for many years following their publication; a pedagogue who understood and passed on not only the traditional techniques of Europe's old masters but the skills necessary to play the latest musical fads; and a savvy entrepreneur who translated these musical skills and experience into a successful business.[13]

In 1897 *Stewart's Journal* introduced a young Canadian guitar soloist and his new approach to guitar technique and repertoire to its readers. In offering something other than the predictable dances and variation sets regularly published for guitarists, C. F. E. Fiset (1874–1966) claimed to be breaking new ground with transcriptions that retained "the original harmonic construction" of pieces written for piano, orchestra, or cello. As importantly, Fiset's articles and transcriptions claimed a role for him in the community as a scholar, pedagogue, and skilled harmonist. Born to a musical family from Quebec, Fiset was raised in North Dakota, where he taught himself guitar. A college graduate, he began his teaching and performing career in Montreal before he turned twenty. He returned to the United States to teach in upstate New York and eventually settled in Minneapolis where he performed and taught. Unlike most American guitar and banjo soloists, Fiset did not perform his own original compositions, but performed virtuoso works by European guitarists of previous generations as well as his own transcriptions of works by Bach, Mendelssohn, and other European masters. He remained a regular contributor to *Stewart's* until its demise at the turn of the century, and his sophisticated contributions—technical articles and arrangements of non-guitar pieces—stand in marked contrast to much of the guitar-related materials in the BMG magazines.[14]

Fiset's promotional materials highlighted his abilities as a player but, true to form, emphasized his training and technical innovations. *Stewart's* followed suit with typically hyperbolic support: "C.F. Elzear Fiset to day [*sic*] ranks at the head of all living guitarists. Having discovered and perfected a new system of fingering, he is enabled to play many of the most intricate works for the violin and for the piano, retaining the original harmonic construction." These three themes—attention to correct harmony, an innovative fingering system, and intellectual access to a sophisticated non-guitar repertoire—pointed up Fiset's skills as harmonist, pedagogue, and musical authority. Additionally, his claims stood on a rhetorical dismissal of the work of previous generations of guitarist/composers. Fiset called for new music for the guitar, since "very little classical music was published for the guitar at this date [the late 1890s], and that little was incorrectly harmonized." In addition, Fiset found it necessary to devise a new right-hand fingering system, "as that [fingering system] taught in guitar methods was totally inadequate for the rendition of rapid scale and chord passages." In support of these goals, Fiset first offered *Journal* readers accurate transcriptions for solo guitar of works by some of the Old World's most revered composers, surely selected in part to highlight the guitar's connection to Europe's elite music. A comparison of Fiset's editions and arrangements with the typical guitar solo appearing in the BMG magazines clearly illustrates his significantly higher standards and more highly developed musical sophistication. Bach's music offered him the opportunity to display his skills as a harmonist and performer capable of comprehending and negotiating the challenges of baroque counterpoint much like a pianist, cellist, or violinist. Likewise, Fiset's arrangements of works of the previous generation (Schubert and Chopin) or of conservative and tuneful works by contemporaries (Grieg and Mascagni) showcased his understanding of the strictures of academic musical training. And as one review noted, Fiset's recital performance of these transcriptions "was a revelation of the possibilities of the instrument."[15]

Stewart's promoted Fiset especially as an authoritative pedagogue/performer whose ideas about guitar technique transcended the work of earlier generations. Beginning in 1899, Fiset produced a series of columns for *Stewart's* titled "A System of Technique for the Guitar." The series featured one article that focused on his system of left-hand fingering, supplemented by extensive musical examples (including excerpts from Ferranti and Regondi, as well as Mendelssohn's violin concerto), but Fiset's most interesting technical ideas involved the right hand. He reviewed the right-hand techniques of his most significant predecessors, offering examples from Carcassi, Sor, and Ferranti and identifying their advantages and disadvantages. He eventually offered six rules governing right-hand articulations, suggesting the use of the thumb on all strings for slow scale passages and, more significantly, the consistent alternation of thumb/middle/index (*pmi*) on fast, unaccompanied scales. Fiset's *pmi* pattern appears to have been adopted by few players or pedagogues (it never appeared again in any of the BMG periodicals), but it indicates that some *fin de siècle* American guitarists were looking beyond the tried and true for a new way to play the instrument.[16]

Fiset remains little more than a footnote in the history of the guitar in America, but a brief technical aside may lead to a greater appreciation of his work. The significance of Fiset's *pmi* rotation derives from its equalizing each digit. In the older, most commonly used *pipi* alternation, the stronger, heavier thumb generally sounded the strings with an accent, giving scalar passages a strong/weak/strong/weak pulse (**pipi**). In much the same way that bowed string players plan down and up bow strokes to accommodate accents and phrasing, early guitarists arranged the strict thumb/index pattern insuring that the thumb struck on metrically strong beats—down beats, strong beginnings or endings of phrases, etc. Traditionally, a three-finger pattern like Fiset's (*pim* or *pmi*) would naturally emphasize the thumb, creating a triplet pulse—strong/weak/ weak (***pim*** or ***pmi***), but he makes no metrical accommodations for the stronger stroke of the thumb, treating it as an equal to the other fingers. Although Fiset's system never took hold, its implied basis—evenness of attack and sound across the strings from each finger—has become a keystone of modern classical guitar technique. Building on the ideas of Francisco Tárrega, twentieth-century pedagogues and performers like Emilio Pujol and Andres Segovia developed right-hand alternation patterns that demanded evenness and balance throughout. In the same way that pianists through the nineteenth century abandoned harpsichord fingerings that implied specific accents, phrasing, or articulations, guitarists in the early years of the twentieth century gradually abandoned "accented fingerings" whose roots were in the sixteenth, seventeenth, and eighteenth centuries.

It is worth noting that the focus of Fiset's innovations—a more modern right-hand technique and a more sophisticated guitar repertoire—were being promoted at the same time by European guitarists, especially Francisco Tárrega (1852–1909) and his disciples. Tárrega, too, produced numerous transcriptions of standard non-guitar pieces, pointing out a new repertoire for guitarists. Likewise, Tárrega's new approaches to the right hand revolutionized the classical guitar, contributing not just new techniques but helping create a new generation of players with new technical and musical skills and standards. Fiset's work indicates that although the community of guitarists in the United States remained conservatively parochial, some American players were in tune with the significant developments taking place in Europe.

Cornelius Daniel Schettler (1874–1931), one of America's better-known guitar soloists active in the final years of the century, may well have known about the important developments taking place in Europe. A native of Salt Lake City, Utah, he first attracted attention in 1898 because of his three years of guitar studies in Munich, Vienna, and Berlin. While his European training clearly put Schettler in an elite minority among America's BMG musicians, he remained an American BMG guitarist, subject to conventional expectations, at one point backpedaling from his overseas experience: "Although recognizing the value of foreign training, Mr. Schettler considers America as having taken the lead of late years, both in the manufacture of high grade instruments and in music, ensemble work for the guitar and mandolin having become very popular and having engaged the attention of many talented artists."

Like his peers, Schettler had to establish himself as something other than a good performer. He offered several articles to *Cadenza*'s readers over the next few years, one assessing the status of the guitar while others dealt with specific techniques. Despite his European training, Schettler followed the party line, decrying incompetent and unethical teachers while announcing that the world's best guitarists were American. In the area of technique, Schettler attempted to reconcile American and European approaches to the guitar. He endorsed an unsupported right hand, contradicting nearly all American pedagogues but wholly in line with the new thinking in Europe. At the same time, he appears to have endorsed holding the guitar as banjoists held their instruments, resting it on the right thigh at a severe angle, a technique used only by American players.[17]

In 1904 C. L. Partee sponsored Schettler's appearance at the annual Guild Convention Concert at New York's Carnegie Hall. Schettler shared the bill for this high-visibility concert not only with banjoists, mandolinists, and various ensembles, but also with William Foden, a guitar virtuoso from St. Louis. Partee made much of the distances these two guitarists had to travel to appear in this concert, even promising to alert *Cadenza's* readers when each had begun his long journey to New York. Peter Danner has identified this concert as the high point of Schettler's career, after which he "returned to Utah and was little heard from thereafter." Danner's estimation is essentially correct. Schettler appears to have performed well; Richard M. Tyrrell critiqued Schettler's phrasing, but allowed that "on the whole he showed a great mastery of the instrument, some of his bass movements being noticeable for their clearness and power." But Foden, whose performance followed Schettler's, dazzled the audience with his virtuosity, drawing ecstatic applause the night of the concert and detailed rave reviews in following weeks. More importantly, while Schettler appears to have continued to base his promotions on his playing (modeling himself on Europeans?), Foden slowly transformed himself from a midwestern player to an East Coast authority—composer, author, teacher, and historian. Although both Schettler and Foden parlayed their initial performance success into business deals, including publications with C. L. Partee, Schettler never achieved the kind of fame enjoyed by Foden. Schettler continued to perform but was overshadowed by Foden from the first, and never again found a place in the BMG spotlight.[18]

Two other guitarists active in the early years of the twentieth century deserve notice, in part because each promoted his performing career at least as aggressively as he promoted his composing or teaching. Carl W. F. Jansen (b. 1868) maintained an active career as a teacher and performer in the Chicago area into the 1930s. Born in Norway to Swedish parents, he spent most of his teens in Sweden. In 1886, Jansen both took up the guitar and emigrated to the United States, working the transatlantic passage as a seaman. None of his biographical entries in the BMG magazines documents a teacher and Jansen may well have been self-taught, like so many of these early guitarists. Jansen's first notices in the BMG journals occurred in 1903, when he appeared as a guitar soloist at a Guild Convention Concert in Philadelphia. He retired to a Michigan

C. W. F. Jansen with his harp-guitar.
(*Crescendo*)

farm in 1933, but for thirty years before that he pursued a lively performing career in the upper Midwest. Like so many of the period's more accomplished guitarists, Jansen gravitated to the compositions of Mertz and Ferranti, but had a special interest in chamber music, regularly performing violin and guitar duos by Paganini and a quintet by Mauro Giuliani for strings and terz guitar. Unsurprisingly, when Jansen performed this work at a Guild Convention Concert in Chicago, the bowed string quartet was replaced by mandolins, a mandola, and a mando-cello. Besides playing terz guitar, Jansen appears to have been one of the few players regularly to use the harp guitar as a solo instrument. He contributed several articles to the BMG magazines, highlighting his interest in chamber music and the harp guitar. In addition, Jansen published a number of solo guitar works in this country and Europe, one of which won second place in an Italian composition competition in 1920. While he never received the kind of overwrought praise offered to players like Schettler, Fiset, or Foden, Jansen maintained a consistent professional presence in the BMG world for nearly thirty years.[19]

Another persistent presence in the BMG community, Johnson Bane (b. 1861) spent the bulk of his career touring as a solo performer. At one point, the editor of a magazine asked readers to alert him to Bane's most recent performances, since mail for the guitarist, forwarded to the magazine's offices, had begun to collect. Bane's recital programs appeared frequently in the magazines and confirm that he seldom played any of the standard guitar literature, preferring instead a nearly unchanging repertoire of arranged light classics by

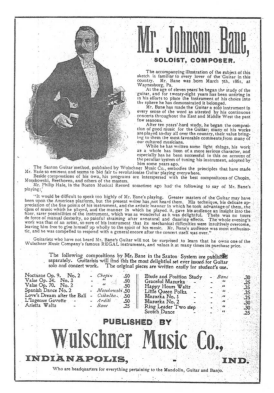

A promotion for Johnson Bane and his "Saxton System." (*Crescendo*)

Ethelbert Nevin and Moritz Moszkowski as well as his own compositions. This unique repertoire grew out of Bane's almost exclusive use of an open-string tuning system that he promoted as the "Saxton System." Full-page advertisements promoted Bane's concert performances as well as his instruction books and anthologies (in both "Spanish" and "American" tunings). Although recognized by guitar proponents in the BMG movement as one of the most important and visible advocates for the solo guitar in America, Bane's idiosyncratic tuning and restricted repertoire kept him on the periphery as a performer or composer, and he remains today little more than a curious footnote in the guitar's story in America.[20]

Hundreds of other guitarists figured in America's BMG movement, many typically promoted as composers, teachers, ensemble directors, and arrangers. An extended list might include the hyperprolific Winslow L. Hayden (d. 1886), who published over one thousand works for the guitar; Marguerite Lichti, guitar soloist featured at the 1923 Guild Convention; and William J. Kitchener (b. 1861), an English organist turned plectral player who appeared regularly as a guitar soloist in New York but was even more highly regarded as a pedagogue, ensemble director, author of historical articles to the BMG journals, and composer of a number of popular solos. The magazines highlighted P. W. Newton's (b. 1868) work as a pedagogue, harmonist, and composer, while A. J. Weidt received regular notices as the composer of dozens of guitar solos, duets, and arrangements. But a line must be drawn somewhere and this seems an appropriate spot to do so.

Further biographical sketches of guitarists active in the BMG movement would hew to the themes outlined above. Performance served to confirm an individual player's skill, yet it ranked behind composition and pedagogy as a measure of the individual's value to the musical community. Even the most talented player strove for respect in the BMG community as a businessperson engaged in teaching or composition and publishing. Despite their calls for innovation and creativity, America's guitarists remained tradition-bound, adhering to conventional roles, techniques, and repertoires. The compositions of Europe's mid-nineteenth-century guitarist/composers—Mertz, Regondi, and Legnani—remained the standard by which a player established his bona fides and to which a guitar composer aspired. Women and Latin players made important contributions to the BMG guitar community and were admired for their natural affinity for the instrument, yet the BMG leadership regarded the talented Latins as suspiciously foreign and generally patronized women as merely supporting figures.

These attitudes reflected the conservative elements of the BMG community but their erosion through the 1920s and 1930s played a part in changing the guitar's role in America's musical culture—as guitar players superseded guitar composers, improvised popular tunes displaced published classical standards, and the guitar became more closely associated with sex and sensuality in the hands of racial and social outsiders. But these changes were gradual and the next chapter considers how the guitar's fortunes remained tied in the first decades of the new century to the conventional attitudes and to the creation of new ensembles featuring America's newest favorite instrument: the mandolin.

Chapter five

TRANSITIONS

From the Parlor to the Concert Hall

Following S. S. Stewart's unexpected death in 1898, his heirs and business partners succeeded in keeping the business, including his *Journal*,
afloat for several years into the new century. But conflicts arose among
the different parties (at one point leading to the publication of both a New
York and a Philadelphia *Stewart's Journal*), and the business and periodical
eventually expired. In some ways, *Stewart's* had outlived its original purpose,
for beginning in the early 1890s the BMG community underwent a dramatic
change in its musical and commercial focus.

By the turn of the new century, the mandolin had replaced the banjo as
the primary instrument in the BMG ensembles. Not merely a replacement of
one instrument for another, this shift from the banjo to the mandolin affected
the constitution and repertoire of America's plectral ensembles through the
first quarter of the new century. This shift to the mandolin was accomplished
in part by the invention of new instruments, a development that had a direct
impact not just on the guitar's role in the ensembles but on the instrument's
physical design, too. Coupled with the appearance of a coterie of players,
teachers, and advocates in the BMG community who asserted the guitar's role
as a refined solo instrument, these changes redefined the guitar's place in the
BMG movement and pointed the way to a redefinition of the instrument, its
repertoire, and its role in America's musical culture.

At the same time that Stewart was laying the foundation for his manufacturing and publishing business in Philadelphia, New York's theater audiences witnessed the beginnings of the new musical fad that was to dominate the BMG
movement. In 1880, an ensemble of Spanish musicians disembarked from the
S. S. *France* in New York harbor. The *New York Times* identified them as a
"Spanish student troupe" that had garnered significant attention two years earlier at the international Paris Exposition. Numbering somewhere between fifteen

and twenty-five players, the Figaro Spanish Students created a sensation in a nearly four-month run at Booth's Theater. This ensemble, playing strictly from memory, featured nine *bandurrias* and five guitars in a repertoire ranging from traditional Spanish folk songs and dances to Beethoven sonatas. From all accounts, the Spanish Students were an immediate hit.

The ensemble was built around the *bandurria,* a wire-strung plucked instrument that carried the melody and countermelodies while the guitars provided harmonic and rhythmic accompaniment. To nonmusicians, the *bandurria* resembles the round-backed mandolin, with a teardrop-shaped body, courses rather than individual strings, and an aggressively bright sound. Reports differ as to what happened to the troupe after their run in New York, but it hardly matters. Their initial success inspired imitators, and new Spanish student ensembles immediately sprang up in their wake. Playing on the racial stereotypes of the day and assuming (correctly) that no one knew the difference, Italian musicians called themselves Spaniards, pretended to be students, and substituted the round-backed "potato bug" or Neapolitan mandolin for the *bandurria.*[1]

Many of these early mandolin ensembles were professional or semiprofessional and because the mandolin and violin share the same tuning, many of the Italian pretenders were musically literate violinists. The "new" Spanish student ensembles followed the lead of the "Original Spanish Students" (as the real Spaniards came to be known), playing arranged folk and popular songs, but the musical literacy of the new ensembles allowed them to tackle more sophisticated light classical works, as well. Banjos were not, of course, used by the Spaniards, but banjo ensembles like the Boston Ideals felt the pressure and added mandolins to their performances, though early on the instruments were not played together. Ethnic costumes and music remained popular through the 1890s, but after the turn of the century most BMG ensembles eventually reserved such musical posing only for special concerts.[2]

As had happened with the banjo ensembles, amateur mandolin clubs grew up in the wake of the professionals. And although mandolin playing and mandolin ensembles eventually became a craze, it was a craze that had to percolate for nearly twenty years before boiling over. Through the 1880s and much of the 1890s, banjos and mandolins participated as equals in these clubs (always with the harmonic support of the guitar, of course), but by the turn of the century, the mandolin had overtaken the banjo.

And once the craze took hold, mandolins could be found everywhere, from vaudeville to western mining towns. Professional vaudevillians like the Five Musical Nosses continued the tradition of ethnic costumes, while educational institutions incorporated mandolin ensembles into their curricula. Professional and semiprofessional adult bands emphasized their elite, classical aspirations while social service organizations like the Salvation Army offered cultural uplift

The Musical Nosses, as Spanish dandies. Other promotional photographs depicted the Nosses as a contemporary saxophone quintet. (*Crescendo*)

to their charges through mandolin and guitar clubs. And plectral teachers built their studios around youth and adult ensembles.

These new mandolin ensembles quickly became the catalyst for a number of significant changes in the BMG movement. Mirroring the invention of Stewart's sized banjos, instrument manufacturers created sized mandolins, matching the ranges of the traditional bowed-string instruments. And as mandolinists, mandola players, and mando-cellists came to see themselves as plectral versions of violinists, violists, and cellists, their clubs became "orchestras," mirroring the traditional string ensemble. Mandolins and banjos had their own sections, and in some cases, these plucked orchestras were augmented with percussion and woodwinds. Guitars, grouped together in a section and occasionally reinforced by a piano or harp, continued to play an integral, but supporting, role in these new BMG orchestras.[3] Many of these "orchestras" were merely re-named clubs with only four to ten players, but others had up to fifty players and festival ensembles regularly numbered one hundred or more players. In many cases, BMG advocates saw these plucked-string orchestras as partners or extensions of more traditional ensembles. One observed that the mandolin orchestra "is coming gradually into prominence and will some day take its proper place side by side with the military band, the choral club and even the proud symphony orchestra."[4] Most mandolin orchestras continued to play a popular dance-based repertoire but some emulated their bowed-string counterparts by taking on Mozart, Grieg, Beethoven, and even Wagner.

Mandolin ensembles were not just popular in high schools and on college campuses, but were considered part of America's music education system. (*American Music Journal*)

As the mandolin's fortunes rose through the 1890s, articles and advertisements in the BMG magazines reflect its increased popularity. In trying to appeal to the more up-to-date teachers and players of the mandolin while not alienating those dedicated to the banjo, *Cadenza* presented the three instruments as co-equals, encouraging cooperation and mutual support within the BMG community. As early as 1895, Clarence Partee issued a call for a national organization to represent the BMG community, suggesting the elevation not just of the music for the plectral instruments but also of their teaching. While such appeals seem entirely logical a hundred years later, they actually highlight the independence of the three instruments for most of the nineteenth century, confirming that players of the various instruments generally viewed their interests as disparate. These calls for cooperation confirm again that the union of the banjo and mandolin with the guitar in America's BMG movement was an artificial construct, and such self-conscious consolidating activities were necessary to legitimize the idea of a family of plectral instruments.[5]

The guitar continued to play an important role in the BMG community; *Cadenza* especially reflected its importance, with numerous articles as well as a long-running column devoted to the instrument. Its editors had the good fortune to attract some of the most important American guitarists or guitar pedagogues as regular contributors or columnists. The body of articles and

The Salvation Army String Band of Silverton, Colorado (Denver Public Library, Western History Collection, X-1757)

columns presented in *Cadenza* by Partee himself, Richard M. Tyrrell, Myron A. Bickford (1876–1961), William Foden, Vahdah Olcott-Bickford, and others comprise a fairly complete picture of guitar pedagogy, technique, and repertoire from the mid-1890s into the 1920s.

More significantly, the columns and articles written by these contributors document a gradual shift in attitudes toward the guitar in America over the magazine's thirty-year publication history. The earliest approach, discussed in chapter 3, was manifested in the Eurocentric writings of R. S. Chase, Alfred Chenet, and Richard Tyrrell, among others. A second stage, promoted primarily by Partee and supported by the contributions of the virtuoso William Foden, championed a new American guitar school, built on progressive ideals and pyrotechnic values. Proponents of this view recognized some contributions by earlier European players, but as often aggressively attacked these traditions of early and mid-century Europe, in favor of an American repertoire and American players. The final stage represented in *Cadenza*, characterized perhaps as a "mature conservatism," sought to unite the technical virtuosity of the American school with the traditions of repertoire and expressive playing

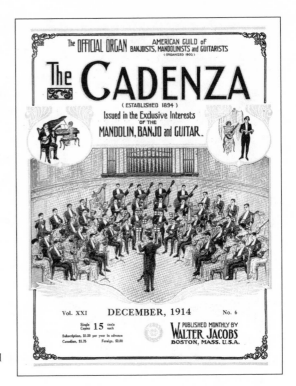

An idealized BMG
Orchestra includes banjos,
guitars, and sized mandolins
as well as standard orchestral
instruments. (*Cadenza*)

associated with European, especially Spanish, players. Leading proponents
of this approach to the guitar and its literature were Myron A. Bickford and,
especially, Ethel Lucretia Olcott, Bickford's musical and marital partner from
1915 on.

Clarence Partee himself contributed to the debate, offering a series of articles titled "Practical Hints for Guitarists" in 1897–98. Partee took his cues from
his earlier contributors, especially Chenet and Tyrrell, recognizing the guitar's
popularity as an accompanying instrument but encouraging its use by soloists.
Like most BMG writers who dealt with the guitar but did not play it seriously,
Partee considered it a difficult instrument to play well and blamed inadequate
teachers, poor fingering systems, and an overabundance of unnecessary scorda-
tura tunings for many of the challenges to the guitar student. Partee addressed
each of these impediments over the course of his series; other articles discussed
ornaments, special effects, accompanying techniques, and the use of the transposing capo d'astro. The penultimate article in the series contains Partee's
recommendations to insure good teaching. He offered students (and inexpe-
rienced teachers) a step-by-step outline of musical and technical topics to be
covered as well as a recommended practice routine. Partee concluded with a
promotion for his new method book, noting that it included "suitable extracts

from the methods of the best classic writers for the guitar, Carcassi, J. K. Mertz, Ferdinand Sor, M. Giuliani, Kuffner, Carulli, and others."[6]

Despite this appeal to the historical witness of earlier players, Partee abruptly changed his tune, challenging the hegemony of these nineteenth-century European guitarists. Partee's attack on Europe's past masters might easily be dismissed as aggressively negative marketing—belittling competitors (even those long dead) to boost his products—had he not continued this theme and expanded his critique of the European tradition with even more aggressive language in 1901. While some other BMG apologists might have only given lip service to the earlier generations, none was so bold as to charge them with technical and compositional ineptitude, as Partee did.

> [I]t is very certain that not one of [the earlier players], even at his best, ever equaled the technical accomplishments of the best American guitarists of the present time. . . . [O]ur best performers have attained artistic heights previously unknown. . . . While the greatest of the compositions for the instrument ever produced, so far as known, were written by men like Legnani, Regondi, Sor, Giuliani, Mertz, Carulli, Carcassi and a few others, it is also true that a vast amount of studies, music, and exercises written by these composers are practically valueless for modern purposes. While these men wrote some of the very best of guitar music, . . . they also wrote some of the very worst that it has ever been our lot to encounter.

Partee did not restrict his critiques to guitarists of the past but included contemporary European guitarists and composers, too. Amazingly, in the midst of this harangue, Partee admitted that foreign musicians held an edge in "instrumentation, orchestration and harmonization" because they have "always been closer students of harmony, theory and instrumentation than the Americans." He conceded that foreign plucked-string ensembles were "more artistic, finished, and musically perfect" than Americans.[7]

Later readers incredulously wonder how Partee could justify ranking American guitarists before Europeans who surpassed them with more skillful and harmonically correct arrangements, as well as more polished performances. Partee did not limit his criteria to the purely musical, however, and in a twist of logic that reaffirms the commercial connections of America's musical culture, he identified manufacturers and publishers alongside performers and composers as major contributors to American superiority. "It has remained for American manufacturers, publishers, performers and composers of modern times to develop the guitar and mandolin to a point previously unknown, not only as regards the construction of the instruments, but in technical accomplishments and in composition as well."[8] Partee conceded the superiority of the Old World's musical culture, but to his mind, the New World's musical industries trumped the foreigners with numbers—more instruments, more music, and more magazines; with technology and technique—newer designs, louder instruments, and faster players; and with innovation—new sorts of instruments, new (albeit crude) compositional techniques, and new special effects. The new American guitar school was built on these precepts: greater numbers, more power, increased speed, and leapfrogging innovation.

Partee served as the principal apologist for this new "American guitar school," but its most famous figure was the virtuoso guitarist William Foden (1860–1947). Of all the publishers, composers, performers, and personalities of the American BMG movement, Foden undoubtedly remains the best known. The subject of a monograph as well as numerous journal articles, Foden is the only nineteenth-century American guitarist/composer whose works still appear with any regularity on recital programs or recordings.[9]

Foden's career and contributions will be examined in detail in a later chapter, but several general observations about his approach to the guitar can be considered here. He offered a decidedly less romanticized view of the guitar than many of his contemporaries, focusing almost exclusively on technical control of the instrument. Foden's own compositions, though often charming, derive for the most part from technical rather than musical ideas. Performance reviews lionized his prodigious pyrotechnic feats, especially his playing of arpeggios and tremolo. And while he clearly respected the contributions of earlier generations of European guitarists, Foden cited works by Sor, Legnani, and Ferranti more often as examples of specific techniques or special effects than as great works of music.[10] Foden never advanced beyond technical considerations in any of his columns, giving the impression that physical control of the instrument paired with intellectual control of the rules of harmony made the guitarist a musician.

Unlike Partee, who readily disparaged the first generation of guitarists, Foden respected aspects of their music. Nonetheless, his purely technical approach to their music, his limited performing of it, and an apparent disinclination to encourage its use by others can hardly stand as an endorsement of these composers. Foden's approach to the guitar—coupled with his awe-inspiring technique, challenging compositions, and concert programming—reinforced Partee's identification of an American school of guitarist/composers based on technique, design and technical innovation, and commerce.

At nearly the same time that *Cadenza* introduced William Foden as its guitar columnist, its most active competitor, H. F. Odell's Boston-based *Crescendo*, presented Vahdah Olcott-Bickford (née Ethel Lucretia Olcott) (1885–1980) in a similar role. The most significant American guitarist of the generation following Foden, she offered a marked contrast to Foden both as a columnist and as a performer and personality. Beginning in 1904, her first notices in the magazines focused on her performing activities, but she contributed articles to the periodicals as early as 1906.[11] She ran "Guitarists' Round Table" for *Crescendo* from 1912 to 1916, at which time she and Foden switched allegiances. She became the guitar columnist for *Cadenza* (1916–22), while Foden took over *Crescendo*'s "Guitarists' Round Table" (1916–27).

In her articles and columns, Olcott-Bickford established an approach to the guitar that redefined the American guitarist, subverting Partee's commercial leanings and challenging Foden's focus on technique. Her earliest articles for the *American Music Journal* and *Crescendo* offered insights into the repertoire of an early-twentieth-century guitarist, but an article from June 1911 proved to be more significant. While her title hinted at a discussion of the business opportunities for the BMG teacher, Olcott-Bickford suggested instead that the commercial focus of the BMG community, which for many members offered an aura of professionalism, actually detracted from both the professional and public image of teachers and performers of the trio instruments. In the process, she vigorously attacked the image of the BMG professional as a multi-instrumentalist, a dearly held tenet of the community.

> I **do** think that **as a class** [teachers of guitar, banjo, and mandolin] are inclined to lean more to the commercial side of things than are teachers of piano, voice, violin, etc. Just why this is the case, I can find no other reason, than that the violinist, pianist, vocalist, or cellist is more apt to **specialize on** his instrument, to devote himself to it alone, giving none of his attention to even attempting to teach or master any other instrument. . . . On the other hand, take a teacher of banjo, mandolin or guitar, and we know that we usually find that the teacher who teaches one of the three, teaches **all three** . . . giving the pupils the idea that **their** fumbling and strumming on the guitar is guitar playing. [emphasis original]

This early article touched on a number of themes that would dominate Olcott-Bickford's contributions to *Crescendo*, *Cadenza*, and the *Serenader*: single-minded dedication to mastery of the guitar; its regular appearance as a solo instrument in formal concert settings; and, most importantly, expressive and artistic performances supported by masterful technique. She held out the hope that America might soon see a resurgence of sophisticated guitar playing comparable to that of violinists, cellists, and pianists on their instruments.[12]

Through the teens, Olcott-Bickford presented to *Cadenza* readers a new understanding of the requirements for virtuosity on the guitar. She assumed in the professional guitarist a formidable technique based on the foundational work of the earliest generations of players and teachers. Additionally, she required that this player put his or her technique at the service of the art of music, expressively interpreting music from a range of periods and styles as the composers indicated. Olcott-Bickford was calling, in fact, for a new breed of guitarists/musicians. As will be seen in a later chapter, Olcott-Bickford's call was eventually met, but not by American guitarists.

Foden never recommended specific repertoire for performance, but one of Olcott-Bickford's earliest articles pointed American guitarists to many of Europe's old masters for appropriate guitar solos, mentioning Sor, Giuliani, Legnani, and Mertz in two articles. At the same time, she encouraged guitarists to consider solo works by such American composers as Charles de Janon and her teacher, Manuel Ferrer. She even identified several solos by Foden, recognizing one as "pretty" and noting that one of his widely known theme and variation sets utilized all the technical facets of the guitar.[13] In a later column, she asserted that guitarists desiring the "commendation of musical critics and music-lovers . . . will have to play a grade of music that is worthy of the instrument at its best, and such as their contemporaries on the violin or piano would be glad to play. They will also have to bring to these numbers the richness and beauty of tonal quality of which the instrument is capable, and charming and expressive interpretation."[14]

In 1914 *Cadenza* published several feature articles devoted to the "Standards of Attainment" promoted by the American Guild of Banjoists, Mandolinists and Guitarists, including a list of sixteen pieces for the "Artist" level. This list featured several works by Luis T. Romero, J. K. Mertz, Luigi Legnani, Charles de Janon, and Manuel Y. Ferrer, as well as one each by Fernando Sor, William Foden, Pietro Pettoletti, and Francisco Tárrega. By and large, these pieces present greater technical challenges to the player than interpretive, suggesting that Olcott-Bickford's call for more artistic playing had made little headway against Foden's technique-driven aesthetic. Most of the works on this list disappeared from recital and concert programs well before the middle of the twentieth century; of the sixteen pieces, only Tárrega's "Capricho Arabe" remains a staple of contemporary players.[15]

It is difficult to determine how stringently or how broadly the BMG leadership enforced these professional "Standards" or how many players achieved this level of play. Fortunately, the BMG magazines offer evidence of a professional repertoire in articles, reviews, concert programs, and advertisements that document a recurring repertoire divided between works from previous generations of nineteenth-century guitarist-composers and newly composed pieces or arrangements, often by the performers themselves.[16] Among approximately three hundred pieces several works stand out, having been performed by a variety of players on numerous occasions. The most popular pieces, virtuosic variation sets, confirm that Foden's approach to solo playing dominated the tastes of the BMG community.

The titles of about two dozen works by Foden and Mertz appeared consistently in the BMG magazines in recital and concert promotions, programs, and reviews as well as in biographical sketches of performers. While American guitarists performed dances and song arrangements by both men, their large-scale fantasies and variation sets attracted the most attention from performers, commentators, and audiences. These included Mertz's settings of operatic selections from *The Barber of Seville*, *La Traviata*, *Rigoletto*, and *The Merry Wives of Windsor* and Foden's arrangements of selections from *Faust*, *Der Freischutz*, and *Lucia di Lammermoor*, as well as his variation sets on popular songs like "Old Black Joe" and "Annie Laurie." But two works—one by each composer/guitarist—appear to have held the attention of America's guitarists and fans for much of the BMG era.

Between 1904 and 1933 Mertz's "Fantasie Hongroise," Op. 65 no.1 appeared on the programs of no fewer than seven performers, including C. W. F. Jansen, George C. Krick, the German guitarist Louise Walker, and William Foden. An article devoted to Mertz in *Cadenza* in 1911 attempted to explain the work's popularity.

> [Mertz's] Three Morceau Op. 65 are stellar examples of his best work. . . . They are very complicated and one needs a command of the entire fingerboard to master their intricacies. Fantasia Hongroise, the first of the group, is the most beautiful and the oftenest played. It is divided into three parts, a Maestoso, an Adagio and an Allegro. The Maestoso is bold and forceful with sections of rare charm. The Adagio is plaintive and appealing while the Allegro, brilliant and vivacious, has some delightful modulation. As a whole the work is unique, grand, having fire, passion and romanticism of Hungarian music.[17]

The "Fantasie Hongroise" stands at the head of the set that also includes a "Fantasie Originale" and "Le Gondolier." The three works are concise examples of the art of the mid-nineteenth-century guitar virtuoso: alternating lyrical melodies with furious scales, tremolos, and arpeggios built on a stable (and predictable) harmonic foundation, all held together with a (sometimes bombastic) virtuosity designed to showcase the player/composer's technique.

Foden, more than any other American and perhaps even more than any European guitarist/composer, assumed the mantle of Mertz's aesthetic and compositional approach, especially in his large-scale works. While the most extensive investigation of Foden's career and music attempts to link him almost directly to the late eighteenth century, Mertz's compositional technique offers a more relevant touchstone for understanding Foden's approach to the guitar. Foden, like Mertz, created variation fantasy sets on operatic or traditional themes based on two principles: the use of lyrical and expressive themes and the decoration of these same themes with pyrotechnic scales, arpeggios, and tremolos. A recent evaluation of Mertz's "concert fantasies" emphasizes his use of lyrical expository materials that both attract a listener's attention and camouflage virtuosic passage work. Foden's most popular variation sets adhere closely to Mertz's process, especially in his savvy choice of lyrical melodies as thematic material.[18]

Although he aggressively promoted his variations on "Sextette from Lucia di Lammermoor," Foden's setting of "Alice, Where Art Thou?" appears a more likely candidate for his most popular work with American players. Between 1899 and 1921 this piece appeared in repertoire lists or recital programs for six guitarists including (besides Foden himself) his student George C. Krick, BMG activist J. J. Derwin, and a young Ethel Lucretia Olcott. Audiences and critics, too, appear to have preferred this work to his others. Foden included this piece and his "Lucia" variations in his first significant performance outside the Midwest, and a reviewer cataloged not only the minutiae of his awe-inspiring technique but also the audience's preferences.

> One is at a loss to find words to adequately describe Mr. Foden's playing upon the guitar, for he is more than a virtuoso, he is a thorough master of the instrument in every phase and detail. He has invented and mastered effects unknown to many guitarists and he executes trills, runs, tremolo passages with three fingers, tremolo with the second finger (across the strings) intricate chord combinations, melodies with intricate accompaniment and sustained passages with a clearness of technic and fullness of tone usually only associated with the harp or piano. His playing was a delight to all present for the reason that he brought out every phrase and every effect with the greatest clearness and facility, without the least apparent effort. The 'Sextet from Lucia' and the 'Favorita Fantasie,' as played by Mr. Foden, well displayed the capacity of both the artist and the instrument, but probably his rendition of his own transcription of 'Alice, Where Art Thou?' most quickly won the hearts of the audience. This, Mr. Foden's first appearance in the East, will long be remembered by those who heard him.[19]

The success and popularity of Foden's piece—indeed, the value and popularity of his variation set within the BMG community—rested on the transformation of a sentimental, familiar vocal number into an extended, complex instrumental work. While the surface display of truly virtuosic technique impressed the listener, the actual execution of these pyrotechnics frequently remained incomprehensible to even most good amateur players. More important than pyrotechnics, however, were familiar melodies in familiar settings that reinforced what a listener already knew—specifically about a particular piece, but more generally about how a piece of music proceeds. Foden chose thematic material—especially in his settings of popular songs—whose musical features reinforced a listener's sense of the familiar with lyrical melodies, simple and clear phrases supported by basic diatonic harmonies, and slow, expressive tempos.

As importantly, Foden's variations supported the goal of BMG apologists to elevate the plucked instruments and their music by overlaying the familiar with a façade of scales, arpeggios, and tremolos that referred to the European fine art tradition. As a result, the significance of these pieces for listeners was not merely the pyrotechnics, but Foden's ability to transform the familiar into an elevated masterpiece. Foden, more than any other player in the American BMG movement, realized the movement's dream of creating a cultivated American voice. Foden modeled his arrangements of popular American songs on Mertz's treatments of elevated operatic themes, creating variation sets mimicking Mertz's revered models. In this way Foden established that American themes were also worthy of such treatment and, therefore, as valuable (cultivated) as Mertz's refined operatic models. Foden's variation sets balanced the accessible and the authoritative, offering the former in accurate settings of familiar themes and the latter in highly complex, notated variations supported with detailed dynamic and expression markings. BMG critics and audiences of the era looked on Foden's works as progressive masterpieces at the pinnacle of solo guitar literature, realizing the dream of many of America's cultivated musicians: to create a distinctly American elevated music.[20]

Of course, while nearly all members of the BMG movement appreciated Foden's work, few could play it. For most BMG enthusiasts, including many guitarists, the mandolin orchestra served as the focal point of their musical and cultural refinement. And, as was always the case, cultural progress in the BMG movement went hand-in-hand with musical business. Promoters of the plectral instruments not only acknowledged the commercial significance of these large ensembles for the BMG community, but also actively discouraged solo and chamber music in favor of the mandolin orchestra.

> The mandolin orchestra is the foundation stone of the entire small instrument industry. If it were not for the mandolin orchestra, the manufacturers would have no incentive in making the fine instruments they are putting out today; the publishers would have no encouragement whatever in issuing mandolin orchestra music. . . . It is the real mandolin orchestra with the instrumentation mentioned above [mandolin, banjo, and guitar] that is making our industry so successful. . . . Solo playing is alright; quartette playing is a little more interesting than solo playing; but on account of the social side of the mandolin orchestra, where a lot of players meet together weekly for rehearsals, that is the organization to which more attention should be given because in that lies the future success of the entire industry.[21]

America's elite cultural organizations—including orchestras, choral societies, and opera companies—most often developed over years, usually created and supported by a group of interested patrons. Mandolin orchestras, on the other hand, more often sprang up as part of a BMG teacher's commercial package of musical instruction and promotions. These teachers not only provided rehearsal space in their studios, scheduled and promoted recitals, arranged repertoire, and conducted the ensemble, but also sold music, instruments, and lessons to its members. As many editorials in the BMG magazines pointed out, the successful BMG teacher/director handled his or her activities—including creating, directing, and sustaining ensembles—not as an artistic vocation but as a business.[22]

The business plans, cultural predilections, and aesthetic tastes of the powers behind the BMG ensembles—teachers, manufacturers, and publishers—clearly determined the nature of the music played and heard in the BMG community. The clearest cases of business-driven musical creation involved instrument manufacturers who not only promoted new (often hybrid) instruments, offering BMG professionals workshops in salesmanship, teaching techniques, and ensemble formation, but also published ensemble music which called specifically for their new instruments in performing configurations promoted in their workshops.[23]

From the beginnings of the BMG movement, its leaders committed themselves to the creation and promotion of "good music," music that not only entertained its players and listeners but also enlightened and uplifted them.[24] BMG promoters, like so many Americans, recognized masterworks by Mozart, Haydn, Beethoven, Mendelssohn, Verdi, and others as elevating and inspiring classics. Many also readily condemned the salacious songs and dances of bars and brothels—including, for the most part, jazz—as musical trash. Most BMG enthusiasts walked a line between the two extremes, embracing cultivated classics because of their status but programming popular and novelty numbers to appeal to the less developed tastes of beginning students and a broader audience. As a result, the repertoires of America's BMG amateurs and professionals ranged from transcriptions and arrangements of Beethoven, Mozart, Schubert, and Dvořák symphonies to hundreds of cookie-cutter cakewalks, waltzes, schottisches, and one-steps. Minstrel song and dance numbers continued to appear on both amateur and professional programs, as did such musical fads as ethnic dialect songs (principally German, Chinese, and Japanese novelties), Hawaiian numbers, and syncopated dance tunes. Articles about concert programming regularly suggested a blend of heavy classics (early in the concert) and lighter popular numbers (at its end), but always included an admonition to program only "good" music.[25]

As Americans worked to identify their musical culture in the early years of the twentieth century, a significant distinction between "good" popular music and its less savory counterpart resided in the fact that the "good" music was notated and performed by trained, literate musicians. Despite the predominance of memorized arrangements and spontaneous improvisations in earliest jazz, proponents of "good" jazz depended on notated arrangements. For the advocates promoting "good" music in the BMG community as well, a critical characteristic of worthwhile music resided in its being notated, allowing for faithful realizations of the piece from the printed score in the venerable western classical tradition. By the early 1920s, even popular syncopated music—if rendered by note-reading ensembles—might be considered "high-class": "Today syncopated music is used considerably, but it is of a decidedly better class, and many of the prominent orchestras playing dance work are using especially arranged music of a very high class, and are not striving for noise and gymnastics, but rendering their music with the taste and finish in music expression of a symphony orchestra."[26] The formal and harmonic structures of the vast majority of BMG pieces—solos and ensemble music—remained formulaic dances or predictable songs, the stuff of improvising dance ensembles or later jazz bands. But BMG advocates calculated the worth of a piece of music on its existence as a formally notated piece and evaluated its performance as an accurate realization of this notation.

Music publishers' desire to tap the wallets of a music-buying public undoubtedly exerted considerable influence, too, since notated music stood as but one part of a controlled commercial system of recurring creation, replication, and consumption. Attempting to retain control of their musical products, early-twentieth-century publishers, including those in the BMG movement, denigrated ill-trained teachers and musical illiterates (often including jazz players) as inept musical bottom-feeders, taking advantage of the hard-working professional teachers and dedicated, musically literate students.[27]

The BMG magazines reinforced the dedication to musical literacy by publishing nearly eight hundred ensemble pieces featuring banjo or mandolin with guitar accompaniment. But these pieces were just the tip of a publishing iceberg.[28] Many of these pieces appeared in the magazines as duets, with a solo melodic instrument part on one page and the accompanying guitar part on another. Magazines also published duo or trio reductions of large-scale pieces as a sales ploy, introducing music to ensemble directors and players, enticing them to order a complete set of parts. Several magazines published complete ensemble pieces; most importantly, *Cadenza* presented some two hundred pieces with complete or nearly complete sets of parts for banjos, mandolins, guitars, hybrid plucked instruments, and standard orchestral instruments. *Crescendo* also offered some works in complete parts for mandolin orchestra.

This ensemble repertoire remained consistently and conservatively dominated by popular (and often out-of-date) dances. Of almost eight hundred ensemble pieces using guitar from the magazines, fewer than fifty—including arrangements of several minuets by Beethoven as well as a polonaise and a mazurka by Chopin—might be characterized as something other than a popular dance. Earlier waltzes, mazurkas, and schottisches subsequently gave way to one-steps, two-steps, and fox-trots in the later journals, although the more contemporary dances never completely replaced the older forms. This published repertoire of dances probably served the dual function of light concert repertoire as well as actual dance music. The vast majority of the BMG dance numbers were characterized by a steady pulse, regular phrases, predictably repeated sections, and standard "guitar keys" of C, G, D, A, and E major and their relative minors.[29] The style of ensemble guitar parts published in the late 1920s remained virtually identical to those published over thirty years earlier in *Stewart's Journal*, utilizing only the guitar's chordal capabilities, with unchanging bass/chord alternations. Guitarists generally played root position chords in the security of the guitar's first position while barre chords, the bane of the beginning guitarist, appeared infrequently. Following the guidelines of BMG theorists such as Richard Tyrrell and P. W. Newton, BMG composers and arrangers seldom ventured beyond I, IV, and V harmonies. Reading such a repetitious guitar part could hardly have presented much of a problem even for beginning players.[30] These simple guitar parts reinforced the attitude of the BMG leadership toward the guitar: while difficult to play well, the guitar could be made accessible to beginners with dumbed-down music and watered-down techniques. While some of these simple guitar parts reflected ineptitude on the part of the composer or arranger, in many cases they reinforced both the pedagogical and functional approach to the guitar of most nineteenth-century guitar tutors, including Matteo Carcassi's very popular and widely used *Method*.

Guitar solos for the amateur generally reflected the same technical limitations as the ensemble works but sometimes emulated the models offered by Foden and Mertz's virtuosic variation sets. As in the ensemble repertoire, popular dances comprised a significant portion of the solo works, but the solo literature included more arrangements of popular and traditional songs as well as theme and variation sets on both preexisting and original tunes. Many BMG composers, handcuffed by their own limited training and talent, seldom rose above cliché when attempting to create guitar solos, a testament to compositional ineptitude and minimal training. On the other hand, the naiveté and simple mindedness of many other solo works reflected a desire to appeal to the beginning student. Like most ensemble works appearing in the BMG magazines, these solos conformed to the standards of the day for popular music: dance forms with regular and predictable structures, square rhythms, basic harmonic schemes built on the tonic-dominant relationship, and simplistic melodies derived from these harmonies. The simplest pieces featured open-string chords, unfretted bass notes, and standard chord shapes in formulaic harmonic patterns. Despite their compositional limitations, these pieces apparently filled a need, many proving quite popular with student players and teachers. Compositions by the Boston-based teacher and composer Winslow L. Hayden stand as particularly obvious examples of this sort of piece, principally because his works continued to appear in the BMG journals nearly forty years after his death in 1886.[31]

Many other players' works, while neither innovative nor particularly memorable, were nevertheless simple and charming. J. C. Folwell's 1906 composition "Mistletoe Waltz" represents such works.[32] Folwell's choice of a waltz reflects the overwhelming preponderance of solo waltzes in the BMG magazines, which account for over 25 percent of all guitar solos from the magazines and occur more than twice as often as the next most popular dance, the march or one-step.[33] The waltz enjoyed a renewed popularity in late-nineteenth- and early-twentieth-century America, a popularity often attributed to Charles K. Harris's 1892 waltz song "After the Ball." Instrumental waltzes shared this wave of popularity with vocal settings, their success derived from the physical proximity of the dancers and their breathless whirling about the dance floor. Titles of numerous instrumental waltzes in the BMG magazines probably conjured up some of the "sexual undercurrent surrounding the dance." Folwell's "Mistletoe Waltz," Frank Bone's "Fascination Waltz," A. J. Weidt's "Girlie Waltz," and William Foden's "Sweet Whispers Waltz" may have been as attractive to amateur guitarists for the imagined subtexts of their titles as for their music.[34]

Correspondence in the guitar advice columns in *Cadenza* and *Crescendo* also reflected a significant interest in solo arrangements, with numerous requests for information about solo guitar settings of piano, operatic, and orchestral music as well as popular songs and Sousa marches.[35] Creative interpretations of pre-existing pieces—reharmonizations, introduction of new countermelodies, complex rearrangements of rhythmic figuration, for example—were not a part of the process for these guitar arrangers, whose goal remained accurate replication of a preexisting model. The challenge to the arranger remained almost entirely technical: the reduction of a piano, vocal, or orchestral piece to the six strings of the guitar by choosing an appropriate key and artfully negotiating octave transpositions to accommodate the range of the guitar. The easiest solo arrangements followed the "bass solo" format, setting a melody on lower strings with basic, first position chords above. Other pieces appear to be reductions of solo piano arrangements, built with thick block chords. In their attempts to stay true to their models, some arrangers created moderately demanding works from a technical perspective, forced by the range of a melody to traverse the full fingerboard of the instrument. Complex rhythms as well as awkward shifts and barre chord shapes in upper positions placed these pieces beyond the capabilities of the beginning player. Nearly all such pieces featured lyrical portamento and expressive vibrato, reflecting the prevailing attitudes about the guitar's intimate and vocal character. Many advocates for the instrument touted its use by serenading lovers as well as its connection to Iberian or Italian folk musicians. Lyrical love songs and folk songs (or popular songs assuming a folk aura) appear most often as appropriate subjects for solo guitar arranging.

The theme and variation sets published in the BMG magazines reflected the works of Foden and Mertz discussed earlier. Nonetheless, their target consumer remained the accomplished amateur, not the professional performer. This is not music for the beginning guitarist, nor does it address the professional virtuoso, although a beginner could aspire to play it and a semiprofessional player might find it an agreeable diversion. It makes technical demands—including an ability to traverse the fingerboard with facility and developed right-hand arpeggio and scale techniques—commensurate with those of an intermediate player. Six variation sets appeared in the BMG periodicals, all conforming to the BMG community's standards for good, but not elitist, solo music. Several offer technically demanding variations, but all appealed to the accomplished amateur guitarist. The themes were familiar, having long been appropriate fare for refined parlor and music room performances. Harmonies and phrase structures remained uniformly simple in both themes and the variations derived from them.[36]

These theme and variation sets, more than any other guitar music in the magazines, confirm the values of the BMG community. Like their more demanding models by Foden and Mertz, they offered the illusion of elite, authoritative music, detailing dynamics, articulations, and tempi. At the same time, thematic familiarity, static structures and harmonies, and changing surface patterns insured a vernacular accessibility. These works, neither purely popular nor strictly elite, reflected the status of America's BMG community, which strove to be broadly egalitarian while promoting elitist pretensions.

As the twentieth century opened, the BMG leadership remained remarkably consistent in pursing the movement's original goals: parity with America's elite musical communities and market share within the country's developing mass-market consumer culture. To satisfy the first goal, the American BMG community adopted standards of technical and musical attainment for its three principal instruments and self-consciously imitated European musical institutions and musical forms, especially in its creation of the mandolin orchestra. To satisfy the second, the BMG manufacturers created instruments and published music intended to satisfy the tastes and techniques of musically unsophisticated amateurs. For the most part, the businessmen, teachers, and players who contributed to the BMG periodicals had neither the training nor the talent to create music that could successfully address both concerns. The results—idiosyncratic arrangements of European standards (elevated art music in the vernacular) or formulaic and ephemeral dance tunes scored and promoted like symphonic literature (the vernacular promoted as elevated art)—betray the limits of their creators as well as the constraints of such commercially driven composition.

As we have seen, the BMG leadership employed the guitar and its music to support these musical and commercial ambitions. But during the second decade of the new century, a rift slowly opened between America's serious guitarists and this leadership. While guitarists called for higher technical and performance standards, the BMG industry focused on creating and promoting not just more accessible music, but instruments that might be learned and played more quickly and easily. While guitarists searching for more sophisticated music found themselves drawn more and more to their European musical roots, BMG publishers aimed for the lowest common denominator in players and listeners, even more vigorously promoting America's popular songs and dances. And as the BMG leadership touted the new American mandolin orchestra as the answer to its calls for an elite status for the banjo and mandolin, guitarists found themselves not only inaudible in these ensembles but eventually pushed out of them altogether. The stage was set for a redefinition of the guitar and its role in America's musical culture.

Chapter Six

INTERLUDE

The Guitar as Icon

In recent years cultural historians have expended considerable energy "read-ing" the guitar, especially the electric guitar, for its symbolic value. By exam-ining not just the instrument's sounds, but its appearance, its uses, and what is said or written about it, observers have interpreted the guitar as an icon capa-ble of conveying important cultural information. As a result, scholars and social critics have identified the guitar in the second half of the twentieth century as a conveyor of authenticity and sincerity (through the acoustic steel-string guitar of the rural bluesman or urban folkie), youthful rebellion (in the solid-body elec-tric played by rockers from Buddy Holly to late-century punks), and male sexual prowess (in R&B, electric blues, and heavy metal), among others.[1]

Although it had not yet achieved such an iconic status, a century earlier the guitar also represented ideas and values reflecting aspects of American culture. Among the various themes connected to the guitar several stand out, in part because on the surface they seem to mirror some associations that became linked to the guitar in the late twentieth century, including gender or sexual identity and racial difference. But as the following pages demonstrate, the ico-nography of the guitar in the BMG era offers a different understanding and interpretation of the instrument based on the mainstream musical and cultural values of the BMG movement.

One of the most popular images involving the guitar in the late nineteenth and early twentieth centuries linked it directly to the ancient lute, often conflat-ing the histories of the two instruments. In much the same way that the steel-strung acoustic guitar represented musical/cultural authenticity and emotional sincerity in the popular music of the late twentieth century, the troubadour's lute offered the late Victorian guitarist historical and cultural validity. Many maga-zine articles held up the medieval troubadour, serenading his lady with his lute, as an ancient predecessor of the BMG enthusiast, and some BMG advertisers

Washburn advertisement featuring a
troubadour theme. (*Chicago Trio*)

utilized this same theme. For example, a late-nineteenth-century advertisement
from *The Chicago Trio* used the image of a serenading "lutenist" to promote
Lyon & Healy's Washburn brand instruments. While the sentiment of the text
was decidedly contemporary ("A Summer Night, /A Pretty Girl . . .—make life
worth living."), the advertisement's image placed the protagonist/musician and
the object of his attention in an earlier time and another place. Stylized visual
clues—the serenader's cape, knee socks, and buckled shoes as well as the girl's
"peasant maid" outfit, including an apron and bowed shoes—place them in the
ancient past, a stylized troubadour courting a maiden. But the straight headstock
and six tuning pegs of his instrument identify it as a guitar.[2]

Other illustrations featuring a medieval theme invariably depicted a male
figure serenading a female. In a cover illustration from *Crescendo* a group of
men, one a lutenist, perform for a carriage full of women. The foreground of
this cover, a silhouette of a modern BMG orchestra under its conductor, links
this lute serenade to the contemporary plectral ensemble and instruments. In
the most overt adoption of the medieval theme, a number of BMG clubs that
sprang up across the country in the second decade of the new century called
themselves "Serenaders." A column devoted to news of local chapters featured
the name, complete with "illuminated" letters, imbedded in a picture of a pair
of medieval musicians singing and playing at a castle's wall.

A *Crescendo* cover
featuring a lute serenade
with a BMG ensemble in
the foreground silhouette.

Poems and stories, too, played on the twin themes of the guitar's roots in
the lute and the lute-playing troubadour serenading his love. In a poem from
Cadenza, its author considered the rewards of musical talent on the piano, violin, and guitar. By the poem's final stanza, he had rejected the rewards of the
piano (fame) and the violin (art) for that of the guitar (love), with which he
might serenade his love, "like a merry troubadour."

> *If I could play the soft guitar*
> *As Foden does (unrivalled star),*
> > *I'd neither make the grand, grand tour,*
> > > *Nor take to solitude, I'm sure,*
> > > *But like a merry troubadour,*
> > > > *To Laura's home I'd steal away,*
> > > > *And 'neath her vine-draped window play.*
> *I'd want no one but her to hear;*
> *No audience would listen with kinder ear.*
> > *And on the strings of my guitar*

I'd music bring forth, sweeter far
(to her),
    Than grandest strains of Rubenstein,
    Or Ole Bull, Paganin.

Despite attempts by the BMG leadership to have their instruments recognized in formal concert halls by sophisticated audiences, poems and stories like this one regularly rejected the more cultivated piano and violin—instruments requiring years of training and practice—for the more familiar and more easily mastered guitar. The BMG leadership wished to depict their instruments as cultivated, but poems and stories in their magazines more often celebrated the immediate emotional and romantic rewards of the guitar.[3]

Such depictions of the guitar as an instrument of medieval troubadours, ostensibly based on historical realities, actually appealed to a broadly popular mythology of the Middle Ages derived from earlier Victorian fiction and poetry represented by Sir Walter Scott's *The Lay of the Last Minstrel* (1805), *The Lady of the Lake* (1810), and *Ivanhoe* (1820). In this mythological world, the troubadour, a model of chivalric duty, participated in noble wars, religious mysteries and searing romance, serenading deserving damsels, brave knights, and noble kings with his lute. Jackson Lears has identified this Victorian medieval mythology as a reaction to the overly rational and emotionally constricted society of that era: "Peasants, saints and seers haunted American imaginations around the turn of the century. Journalism, fiction and verse celebrated the simple faith of the charcoal burner and the ecstasy of the mystic. . . . To feel drawn toward medieval mentalities was to participate in the recovery of primal irrationality, to share the primitivist impulse of the late nineteenth century." The medieval troubadour could easily join this cast of irrational medieval characters. According to the BMG magazines, the troubadour inhabited an easy world of love and luxury and his music served but one purpose, to enhance the activities in the "courts of love." One BMG contributor noted that "the assembly of the Troubadours and story tellers [at medieval castles] was the picture of a mirthful, soft and luxurious life." Their songs—supported by the lute—conveyed an irrational and probably dangerous language of love. Such medieval characters peopled not just BMG advertisements, but also stories and illustrations in general interest magazines, invariably carrying the same message. "The medieval world of the magazines was populated by jolly friars, winning jongleurs, passionate lords and ladies. . . . The legendary lovers embodied the emotional vigor pervading the new imagery of the Middle Ages. . . . Their twentieth-century personifications of medieval children . . . signified not just intense piety but a range of imagination and emotional life which seemed impoverished in modern society."

While the BMG apologists probably intended to imbue their instruments with the noble traits of the medieval court, their stories and depictions invariably focused on the pursuit of a desirable woman by the musician/lover. By associating the guitar with serenading lutenists attending available women, the BMG magazines encouraged readers to picture themselves in exotic and (potentially) erotic roles and situations. These depictions allowed readers to dally with the "primitivist impulse" of the late Victorian era and to experience vicariously the more intense emotional life of the medieval lovers and musicians.[4]

Such a mythical association of the guitar with the lute and medieval Casanovas seems innocent on its face—a case of bad history, perhaps or, at worst, a cynical advertising ploy. In fact, this picture of the lute/guitar as a tool in the hands of overly sensual and irrational figures had real-world correlations in America's late Victorian culture. Lears notes that part of the Victorian interest in the Middle Ages stemmed from the reaction of a native-born, educated, middle-class, and Protestant mainstream to an immigrant, illiterate, and (usually) Roman Catholic underclass. He suggests that the mainstream looked on this underclass as direct heirs of the medieval musicians and lovers— emotional, hot-tempered, artistic, and a bit dangerous.[5] These same biases appeared regularly in the BMG magazines, whose publishers and contributors both admired and distrusted Latin musicians, especially guitarists. One BMG writer not only linked medieval troubadours to Latin musicians, but also noted that the guitar's transformative powers might even touch an Englishman.

> No doubt owing to its peculiar adaptability as accompaniment to the human voice, the guitar was very popular with the minstrels of past ages and it will ever be associated with the pictures of the love-sick troubadours pouring out their hearts' burdens to the queens of their fancy. That the more ardent natures of the Spaniards and Italians should be stirred by the persuasive and sensuous strains of their favorite instrument is not surprising, but how great the influence of the guitar must have been, is shown by the fact that even the less sentimental English were incited to romantic furor by it. . . . If the performer on the guitar consider his instrument not simply as what it is in itself, but as connected with all the outpouring of sentimental passion with which it has been associated, it would seem a necessary consequence that his touch should become more sympathetic, and that the greatest charm of all musical interpretation, "feeling," should permeate his every endeavor.[6]

In the second half of the twentieth century, the guitar's association with America's black underclass and the blues made it a cultural and racial marker, associating the instrument negatively with irrationality and sensual behavior, including dance and illicit sexual activity. While banjo proponents of the BMG era sometimes linked the guitar to black players to bolster their image of the banjo as a Caucasian instrument, at this time the guitar was more often tied negatively to Latin characters, whose artistic and amorous accomplishments linked them to the medieval troubadours. In much the same way that they promoted medieval links for the guitar, editors and contributors to BMG magazines regularly highlighted the guitar's traditional associations with the Latin cultures of Spain and Italy in poems, articles, news blurbs, and gossip.

By the late nineteenth century, American musicians and critics alike assumed the superior qualities of northern (German) music built on the intellectual and spiritual precepts of scientific harmonies. Seductive rhythms and sensuous melody, on the other hand, dominated southern (Italian and Spanish) music. Earlier in the century, John Sullivan Dwight had articulated the contrasts in his praise of Nordic Jenny Lind's chaste and chilly music, which overcame that of the sensuous south. "The Northern Muse must sing her lesson to the world. Her fresher, chaster, more intellectual, and . . . colder strains come in due season to recover our souls from the delicious languor of a music which . . . has degenerated into mere sensibility, and a very cheap kind of superficial, skin-deep excitability."[7] In another article involving Lind, Dwight asserted: "'Italian *song* and German *music*'—there is the whole story in a nutshell. . . . [I]n this century at all events, Germany is the 'land of real music,' and [musicians should] seek to become baptized into the spirit of the great composers, the immortal HANDELS, MOZARTS and BEETHOVENS . . ."[8]

The guitar—an instrument often used in simple, rhythmic performance to accompany light, sensuous love songs—appeared incapable of the complex, scientific art of music as created by the German masters of counterpoint and harmony. In an early column devoted to the guitar, S. S. Stewart archly reported a sexual reading of the instrument: "One of our correspondents, in a wandering eulogy on the guitar, declares that instrument to be the 'exponent of sexual love.'" Stewart primly chose not to print his correspondent's "wandering eulogy," which in all likelihood promoted the guitar's cheap and superficial sensuality.[9]

Associations of the guitar with southern Europe, warm weather, and even hotter blood often supported jingoistic affirmations of the banjo's superiority as a homegrown American instrument.

> When'er I hear the mandolin trilling its tuneful lay,
> To me brings thoughts of Italy o'er seas, far, far away.
> 'Tis the home of instruments tho' it strayed beyond its call,
> There are many fine players there, but the U.S. leads all.
>
> And when I hear the sweet guitar, my thoughts are all on Spain,
> On the Cuban war so recent, the wrecking of the Maine.
> In the homes of high or lowly, in palace or in hall,
> Are heard artists without number, but the U.S. leads all.

To the banjo last I gladly turn, down south before the war,
'Twas there the banjo came to light, its flames reached the world o'er.
Everywhere it went with success, in countries great and small,
They have players they take pride in, but the U.S. leads all.

While the poet appears to be praising the trilling mandolin and the sweet guitar here, his lines, in fact, attack both instruments. The mandolin—perhaps like the Italian immigrants flooding America in the late 1890s—"has strayed beyond its call." When the guitar turns the poet's thoughts to Spain, they stand in stark contrast to the "sweet guitar," for he recalls the carnage of the *Maine*, purportedly sabotaged and sunk by Spanish agents, and the ensuing Spanish-American War. The poem attempted to turn the reader against both foreigners and their instruments, while promoting the banjo with allusions to the United States' recent military successes and growing international influence. In the midst of the Spanish-American War, Stewart attacked Spain's music as clearly inferior to America's intellectual and progressive music (especially that for the banjo).

> Spain's history is one of the most romantic among nations, and in all arts, save the greatest, she has given treasures to the world. Had her unreasonable pride been tempered by a drinking at the fountain from which music springs, toleration might have arisen; . . . Spain has not produced a single composer of note . . . Of virtuosi she can make a display at the present time; they however are exceptionals [*sic*] and do not reside in their native land. If the continual playing of frivolously sensuous airs on the mandolin and guitar could make a nation musical, Spain ought to be the most musical country in the world. Indolence, perhaps a natural languor, which has dulled perception and intellectual ambition, prevents the people of the Peninsula from regarding these instruments and the music to be obtained, in the light we view them in this country.[10]

Like the cowardly and scheming Spanish military, the guitar and its Latin players were more commonly seen as unpredictable, if not dangerous. In one entry of his serialized musical memoirs, banjoist Albert Baur noted that earlier in the century, "it was almost impossible to procure a reliable guitar teacher" in New York City. He recounted the story of a guitar instructor, "a hot-headed, black-eyed Spaniard, and one of the best performers I had ever heard." Hired to teach guitar lessons at a private girls' academy, this Spaniard quickly fell in love with a student. The guitarist's obsession drove his student to flee to Europe and led to his dismissal. Baur concluded his cautionary tale:

> I felt positive that the fellow was out of his mind, but he talked so rationally that I could hardly believe it. He stayed with me nearly four hours that day, long enough

to thoroughly disgust me with him and all his kind. I met him quite a number of times afterwards; each time he seemed to have sunk lower than the time I had seen him before. He had taken to drink, and every time I met him he spoke of his great trouble. . . . I heard that he went from bad to worse and died in filth and rags, a victim of intemperance. I can not say as to the correctness of my information. . . . Were I to mention his name, many guitarists of to-day would remember him. He traveled with the Spanish Students for some time as a solo guitarist.[11]

While condemning neither all Spaniards nor all guitarists, Baur certainly implied links between this individual's irrational behavior, nationality, and guitar playing. In formal discussions of the guitar and its capabilities, most writers pointed approvingly to its strength as a subtle accompaniment to the voice. Yet even this positive characteristic, especially when coupled with Latin performers, invariably insinuated the guitar as a tool of wooing (in the American parlor) or of seduction (under Spanish balconies on warm summer nights). Even when used in its most appropriate role of accompanying the voice, the guitar projected a sensuality and sexuality that threatened the decorum of late Victorian America.

Although many characterizations of Latin musicians from the BMG magazines displayed distrust and hostility, at times they also reflected a grudging respect for the musical and expressive skills of these dangerous foreigners. No less a caricature than the negative depictions, positive images credited Spanish, Italian, Mexican, and South American musicians with a natural affinity for the guitar and an inherently expressive and artistic nature. Articles and reviews in the magazines recognized the artistry of such guitarists as Luis Romero or Manuel Ferrer as natural components of their Spanish heritage. American and English writers who described the place of the guitar in Spanish life often sounded a condescending tone, but could not hide their admiration of graceful, free, and emotionally expressive performances by Spanish men, women, and children.

The guitar, song, and dance form the joy of all, and the repose of sunburnt labor in sunny Spain. . . . In every venta [sic] and courtyard, in spite of a long day's work and scanty fare, at the sound of the guitar a new life is breathed into their veins. . . . [S]upper is no sooner over than some dark-eyed performer tunes his instrument and commences his song with which the audience are in raptures, expressing themselves by beating with their feet, clapping their hands and joining in the chorus. . . . The performers, however, are seldom scientific musicians, their musical powers are inborn. . . . In order to feel their full power the performer should be a sprightly maiden of Andalusia; whether taught or untaught, she wields her instrument with the same grace as her fan or mantilla. It becomes part of her very self. . . . About her performances there is an indescribable abandon, a fire, and grace, which could not be possible with the ladies of more northern climates and more tightly laced zones. . . . As the Spaniard is warlike without being military, salutary without being graceful, so he is musical without being correctly harmonious; he is just a prima materia [sic] fashioned by nature, and he treats himself as he does the raw products of his native soil, leaving art, learning and industrial development to the stranger.[12]

Fictional accounts in the magazines especially reinforced both the negative and positive caricatures of Latin musicians. Beginning in the late 1890s, *Cadenza* offered readers several serialized stories by C. E. Pomeroy, a banjo enthusiast. Each story featured a Latin protagonist whose playing of one of the three plectral instruments brought him or her good fortune in love and life. "Evangeline and Her Mandolin" was set in Spain while the hero of "Sancho and His Banjo," besides being an Mexican aristocrat, was an expert shot, skilled knife-thrower, and consummate performer who played perfectly by ear. In the course of the story Sancho learned to sight-read and simultaneously memorize the most difficult music.[13]

The middle story of the three, "Carrara and His Guitarra," presented a plot of usurped and mistaken identity in which the hero and villain respectively embodied the positive and negative traits of the Latin personality. The two men, who had grown up together in Italy, were nearly identical twins physically, but were opposites morally and artistically. Nicolai Bruno, the smooth-talking schemer, was "a handsome man, of dominating presence, debonair, faultlessly dressed, brushed and booted." Bruno posed as a guitar virtuoso (an appropriate role for a foreigner), acquiring fame and wealth while his shy friend, Angelo Carrara, anonymously played Bruno's music and even taught Bruno's wealthy students. In a nod to the troubadour, the author links Cararra to ancient nobility, contrasting him to the scheming Bruno as "absolutely an artist . . . , generous, learned, affable and loveable at first sight."[14]

Illustrations of the two men contrasted Bruno's dark and oily suavity with Carrara's doleful sensitivity. Unsurprisingly, by the end of the story Carrara's artistry and nobility, inspired by love for a woman mistreated by Bruno, triumphed. Carrara's (fictional) artistic pedigree surely elicited admiration from BMG readers, for he had studied guitar with Dionisio Aguado, an early-nineteenth-century Spanish virtuoso and pedagogue, and had acquired his amazing technical skills from "a close study" of Paganini, whom he knew personally. Carrara's skills allowed him "to attack, without hesitation, many of the concertos hitherto deemed possible only to the violin." This story links many of the basic tenets of the BMG world: the guitar's pedagogical pedigree (Aguado), its links to Europe's finest musicians (Paganini) and music (violin concerti), its ability to communicate directly the innermost feelings of the human heart, and an admiration and suspicion of foreign musicians whose cultural predilections and racial tendencies encouraged effortless and emotional musical expression.[15]

The end of his story relates that once music had led him to his true love, Carrara put his guitar aside to become a successful businessman. Despite his exceptional skills, Carrara, like other protagonists in BMG fiction, did not make his living as a professional musician, only occasionally taking up his guitar to accompany himself or his wife in their favorite love song. Turn-of-the-century America had an ambiguous attitude toward professional performers, and stories like Carrara's confirm it. Professional musicians remained suspect in America, in part because of the long-standing association of the theater (where most public music was heard) with unsavory activities and in part because so many musicians were, in fact, foreigners. Although not all professionals were unscrupulous and shifty figures like Carrara's evil twin, the distrust of easy emotional expression (manifested in artistic performance by expressive foreigners) resonated in the BMG movement. The movement's emphasis on music as a business of teaching and selling, on amateur ensembles, and on musical performance as technical accomplishment stand in part on the distrust of artistic, foreign professionals. Such suspicions resonated with long-held negative views of professional musicians (from Aristotle on) and corresponding positive appreciations of the devoted amateur performer. For many in the BMG community, the true artist aspired to anonymous amateurism, sharing his or her music only with close friends and family, while responsibly and productively pursuing a career in business or industry.

The conclusion of Carrara's saga reinforced another image of the guitar in its description of his instrument as a link to his romantic past, reminding him how music had brought him and his love together. In the 1890s and early years of the twentieth century, stories and poems in *Cadenza* distilled the BMG community's appraisal of the guitar—an ancient, expressive instrument, associated with amorous serenading—in sentimental and nostalgic narratives and poems. These stories and poems invariably valorized the guitar as a receptacle for memories of amorous emotions. In one particularly overt case, the magazine cited a purportedly true newspaper story about a man and woman separated by a lover's spat. When, nearly fifteen years later, he wistfully took up his guitar to strum a few chords, a note from his lost love, written and hidden in the guitar on the night of their quarrel, fell out of the instrument. He rushed over to her house, played the guitar for her once again, and all was forgiven. "He says that, with the first touch of the guitar, the bitterness of fourteen years was forgotten, and that the music he had so long neglected came as a balm to his feelings."[16] If such restorative powers could be attributed to the guitar in a fact-based news item, little wonder that fictional narratives in the BMG magazines regularly touted the guitar's ability to transport a listener or player to another time, place, or emotional state. Its emotive powers were so strong that only a glance at or an idle strum across the strings of a guitar could bring a flood of memories and emotion.

> *Neglected now is the old guitar*
> *And moldering in decay;*
> *Fretted with many a rift and scar*
> *That the dull dust hides away,*
> *While the spider spins a silver star*
> *In its silent lips to-day.*
>
> *The keys hold only nerveless strings—*
> *The sinews of brave old airs*
> *Are pulseless now; and the scarf that clings*
> *So closely here declares*
> *A sad regret in its ravelings*
> *And the faded hue it wears*
>
> *But the old guitar, with a lenient grace,*
> *Has cherished a smile for me;*
> *And its features hint of a fairer face*
> *That comes with memory*
> *Of a flower-and-perfume haunted place*
> *And a moonlit balcony.*
>
> *Music sweeter than words confess,*
> *Or the minstrel's power invent,*
> *Thrilled here once at the light caress*
> *Of the fairy hands that lent*
> *This excuse for the kiss I press*
> *On the dear old instrument.*[17]

Other poems recount the actual playing of the instrument with substantially the same effect—evocation of strong memories and emotions across time.[18]

As significantly, however, such poems put the guitar in the hands of women. In the late twentieth century, the guitar's phallic imagery overrode its feminine shape, in part because the modern electric guitar had lost its female curves and resembled a modernist tool rather than a Rubenesque body. But a century earlier, the guitar had been an instrument of and about women, with the poems, stories, and images of the BMG movement reinforcing the association. The BMG community's conceptions of the female mirrored those of late Victorian society, in which women were conventionally relegated to the role of helpmate, muse, and mother. At the same time, the movement, focused as it was on music, rearticulated ancient mythologies and deep-seated prejudices about women and music. These ranged from an appreciation of feminine intuition and sensuality as positive and direct links to musical expression, to suspicion and fear of the same sensuality coupled with female sexuality as dark and dangerous snares for good Christian men. In many ways, the BMG community offered the female musician, especially the guitarist, the same condescending respect and inquisitive fear it directed to the talented and charismatic Latin musician. The woman guitarist was a significant figure in the BMG community, a figure revered and displayed, but also distrusted as part of the confused and confusing mix of Victorian social conventions, artistic representations, commercial manipulations, and sexual mores.

Linda Phyllis Austern has described early modern literary and visual depictions of women and their relationships to music as fantasies.[19] BMG literature and images depicting women guitarists stood firmly on such fantastical relationships. The narrator or the point-of-view in many poems and stories about the guitar in the BMG journals was male, but often the depicted guitarist was a woman, whose mere touch of the instrument elicited rapturous love from a male listener. These pieces recounted the power of the guitar (and its female player) to elicit fond memories of romantic love. Even authoritative "historical" articles by such experts as Madame Giulia Pelzer promoted the romantic and expressive nature of the guitar. She began an article in 1899: "The guitar is the instrument of romance; for the expression of sentiment, love, chivalry, and deep poetic feeling, it is decidedly superior to any other. . . . Everywhere through the annals of the past we find that, with the march of the humanities, the guitar is brought forth to aid and heighten the charm and attraction of romantic truth and fiction."[20] The evocative and emotional powers of the instrument were regarded as mysterious and magical; women, like medieval troubadours and Latin musicians, were thought to possess an intuitive, childlike ability to draw these powers from the guitar.

Most women guitarists who appeared in the magazines did so principally in supporting or accompanying roles, documented in photographs and recital notices of BMG ensembles. In the late 1890s and early years of the twentieth century, a number of BMG ensembles consisted of only women and girl players. And, while women occasionally served as music directors for such groups, in most cases men directed them. In one of the more overt representations of male control within the BMG community, formal portraits of some ensembles superimposed a male director's image floating just above the assembled women.

The women of The Manzanita Club presided over by its hovering director. (*American Music Journal*)

These halftones graphically confirmed prose descriptions of the ensembles, which seldom identified players but enthused about their leaders. A photographic portrait titled "P.W. Newton" depicts the BMG authority contentedly sitting with his mandolin as an anonymous female guitarist (his long-suffering wife, perhaps?) stands attentively before him. This particular picture epitomizes widely held attitudes toward women and the guitar, both waiting patiently to serve their masters. Such images offered a late-Victorian interpretation of centuries-old attitudes toward women, men, and music in which "music and feminine nature were widely perceived as similarly sensual, affective, and in need of strict rational control to benefit men and their narrow perception of women."[21]

In some BMG fiction, women exerted their power over men through the guitar; as in earlier literature, these female guitarists were depicted as enchantresses, casting spells over and inspiring love from male auditors.[22] One of the more fantastic guitar fictions in the BMG magazines opened with an account of a young Russian woman capturing the heart of a young nobleman by singing a patriotic air to quell a riot in Moscow. When the couple journeyed to meet his father, a rural lord with Neanderthal tendencies, the old nobleman welcomed the young lovers to his country castle by filling it with dead cats and dogs, and gathering a murderous crowd of peasants to greet the pair. Prince Feodor led his love to a desolate music room, hoping that his father's violence might be mitigated by the artistic setting. Unruffled, young Olga

> selected a rare old guitar and also a quaint lute. She then sat down upon a divan, placed the lute by her side, took up the guitar and began to play. She chose an old French madrigal . . ., and she played it with bewitching effect. . . . [D]usk was creeping in and filling all the place with shadows. Still Olga played on, the wailing notes of the guitar pulsating through the air and filling the whole room with

BMG pedagogue P. W. Newton and his mandolin supported by an anonymous woman and her guitar. (*Griffith's*)

entrancing melody. The dusky shadows shut in closer and closer until the room was in a mist of darkness—magical, enchanting darkness that rang with the murmuring music.

The magic of the intoxicating music was so great that Feodor [the son] still held his first position, while Alexis [his wild father], though still immovable, had gripped his hands so tightly that the nails had sunk into the flesh.[23]

In the end, the misanthropic Alexis and his mob of feral peasants succumbed completely to Olga's guitar and lute. They cleared the castle of filth and rot, happily preparing a magnificent wedding feast, as the young couple were joyously reconciled to a miraculously civilized Alexis, who doted on Olga, spending hours at a time listening to her play and sing.

Olga with her guitar personifies the healing and enchanting powers of music as the author repeatedly reinforces the mysterious forces of music and women with his choice of adjectives: ear-haunting, bewitching, entrancing, enchanting, intoxicating. Here, too, the ancient lute and the modern guitar are united in the person of Olga, a magical woman whose musical powers held sway over not only a civilized and rational man (Feodor), but also an unruly urban mob, a group of marauding peasants, and a homicidal nobleman. Despite the exotic setting and her amazing skills, however, the story concluded with a depiction of Olga as a middle-class Victorian woman, waiting to be elevated and completed by a civilized and loving man. Olga (like the dutiful Victorian wife) not only offered her mate inspiration but also acted as a buffer against and interpreter of the unruly world of dark and dangerous emotions. In playing this role, she embodied the ancient image of the nurturing, maternal Musica, linked to the "Archetypal Feminine[,] . . . the mysteriously creative vessel which brings forth the male in itself and from out of itself, which nourishes and protects within all bodies."[24] With her inexplicable powers, Olga created a haven of love and tranquility for her man, reconciling him with his emotional family and nurturing him for his important work in the world. Undoubtedly, she would also be a devoted and loving mother to Feodor's children, a role foreshadowed in part by her association with the full-bellied lute.[25] Olga's tale emphatically rearticulated the conventional wisdom that unmarried girls be trained musically, providing them skills that would aid them in finding a civilized mate and in creating a proper family and household. Clearly, music served Olga in this manner, for her musical skills literally ennobled her, lifting her (through her husband) from a faceless, urban working class to a well-deserved aristocracy.

Of course, the early twentieth century witnessed a gradual change in attitudes toward women and the roles they played in the American family and society, a change fostered in part by the suffrage movement, greater educational and employment opportunities, and a gradual relaxation of social and sexual mores. And while most depictions of women and the guitar in the BMG literature reflected conventional attitudes toward both (the BMG community was, of course, as much a conservative industry as an artistic movement), a series of magazine covers for *Cadenza* in the early years of the new century offered more up-to-date images.

Late-nineteenth-century magazine images of women slowly progressed from "The American Woman" (a mature and refined Victorian housewife) to the "New Woman" (a younger woman in transitional settings between home and society at large), and finally to the "American Girl" (young, single, athletic, and adventuresome), identified by various names (Gibson Girls, Christy Girls, and Fisher Girls, most famously).[26] *Cadenza* featured its own cast of girls on the magazine's covers for four years, from late 1901 to September 1905, coinciding with the very popular and ubiquitous artwork of Charles Dana Gibson, Howard Chandler Christy, and others.[27] *Cadenza* was clearly imitating other magazines (and the developing advertising industry) in its use of the female face and figure to attract readers and subscribers. This same promotional attitude also encouraged the magazine's depictions of real women players, often highlighting their attractive good looks and charming personalities.

Before *Cadenza*'s series of magazine covers, images of such young women had appeared in BMG advertisements only irregularly. One of the earliest appearances of these girls, an atypical advertisement from 1897, featured a halftone of two fashionable young women, one playing a guitar and the other holding a guitar-shaped mandolin. Although the guitarist directed her gaze at her playing hand, her partner engaged the reader with a frank and direct stare. Several years later, a series of advertisements featured the recurring image of a young woman lounging in the back of a punt, playing an instrument that appears to be a cross between a mandolin and a guitar. This young woman bears a remarkable resemblance to the Gibson Girls, wearing fashionable clothes, apparently enjoying outdoor activities, and looking directly at the viewer with an open and inviting gaze. Her relaxed posture and crossed legs (which reveal a bit of stockinged ankle), made her stare all the more inviting. Stories and illustrations described how water, especially flowing water, "softened the Gibson Girl," confirming for male viewers that her steely resolve could eventually be broken down. The location of this fashionable musician on water clearly pointed up her potential availability.[28]

These two advertisements reflected the general use of young women in turn-of-the-century magazine illustration, but they were only two isolated examples in the BMG literature. In the spring of 1901, however, *Cadenza* began its four-year campaign of covers featuring women instrumentalists. These depictions, clearly modeled on the popular Gibson Girl, were all produced by W. L. Hudson, an all-but-unknown magazine illustrator. *Cadenza's* letterpress offered no introduction or explanations for these new cover illustrations, but they first appeared as the magazine's publisher prepared to move his operation from Kansas City to New York City. Such a dramatic move from the far west to the urban east coast marked a radical change for *Cadenza* and its publisher. As noted earlier, changes in the magazine's content—such as articles about the violin and the piano and more notices of East Coast BMG personalities—reflected Clarence Partee's intention to raise the standards and content of his "western" magazine. The addition of new and changing images on the cover of the magazine may have been a similar move, calculated to reflect an up-to-date urban publication capable of attracting a cultivated city readership. At the same time, the use of the female figure also reflected separate appeals to female and male readerships. Women might identify with and imitate these fashionable female musicians (and perhaps join the BMG movement) while men would be drawn to the covers (and into the BMG community, too) by the opportunity to associate with (or at least watch) these pretty and available girls.[29]

Like those of general interest magazines, Hudson's *Cadenza* covers featured young and attractive female figures. Hudson, however, conflated the modern images of these women (young, fashionable, direct, and beautiful) with some of the standard associations about the history and character of the guitar (ancient, refined, exotic, and sensual). Many of his earliest covers placed these women musicians in a stylized "classical" world featuring pastoral settings, temple columns, flowing robes, and garlands of flowers. The instruments in the hands of these young musicians were stylized as well, sometimes

One of W. L. Hudson's "classic" guitarists, in a setting that reinforces the classic, exotic, and sensual nature of the instrument. (*Cadenza*; courtesy of James Bollman)

resembling a cross between the ancient lute, mandolin, or guitar, at other times looking like a hybrid cello-guitar. In most cases, these women appeared unaware of the viewer, focusing on their music or on tuning. When a player occasionally appears to have noticed the reader's attention, she raised her eyes, staring back unblinkingly, much like the unabashed Christy girls.

These magazine covers reinforced a number of the BMG community's attitudes toward the guitar discussed earlier. The "classical" settings recalled the guitar's ancient history, while its physical conflation with the lute echoed a number of the guitar histories from the magazines as well as ancient associations of the lute with the maternal female. Additionally, the odd hybrid instruments reinforced their exotic and foreign roots. Children sometimes appeared in this mythical world, and their presence highlighted not just the maternal but also the irrational and emotional character of music and women.

Despite the exoticism of the instruments and the costumes, Hudson eventually brought his women into the modern world. Beginning in September 1901, Hudson's covers featured a more contemporary look. Hudson's young women, following the same trajectory of the Gibson and Christy Girls, came to reflect

Vol. 9   September, 1902   No. 1

A Hudson Girl in transition,
perhaps returning to school
with her guitar, golf clubs,
and steamer trunk. (*Cadenza*;
courtesy of James Bollman)

the modernization of the American girl, a "more self-assured modern woman,
equally adept at sports, high society, or her studies."[30] The September 1902
cover returned firmly to the early twentieth century, depicting a young woman
waiting for a train. A late summer sun hovers on the horizon, rising on her future
or setting on her past, but certainly implying that this young guitarist faced
change. She may be leaving the countryside, perhaps for college. The college
girl, "an entirely new type of woman for society to assimilate,"[31] appeared often
in illustrations by Christy, who "imagined college as a place where girls formed
friendships and took up sports that would make them better mothers and
wives."[32] Like the Christy College Girls, this modern Hudson Girl was athletic
as well as artistic, evidenced by her golf clubs resting against her steamer trunk.
Another September cover featured two refined female musicians on an elegant
terrace, while two men play lawn tennis in the distant background. In both
cases, Hudson visually linked the guitar—in the hands of cultivated women—to
leisure-time athletic activities of the educated, fashionable, and moneyed class.

    Hudson's female banjo and mandolin players, reflecting the BMG drive
to improve the instruments' standing in refined society, often maintained

Vol. 10   December, 1903   No. 4

THE CADENZA

Established 1894   Whole Number 76

*An Educational Monthly Magazine Devoted to
the Literature and Music of the Violin,
Mandolin, Guitar, Banjo, Zither, Harp and Piano*

The C. L. PARTEE CO., Publishers, 5 East 14th Street, near Fifth Avenue, New York,
Subscription, $1.00 per year in advance. Single Copies, 10 Cents.
Foreign subscription, 5 shillings.

Copyright 1903, by Mr. and Mrs. C. L. PARTEE

St. Nick with a new guitar
prowling behind a demure
(and wide-awake) Hudson Girl.
(*Cadenza*; courtesy of James
Bollman)

a restrained decorum and propriety. Hudson's guitarists, on the other hand, sometimes displayed a more relaxed fashion sense. While other musicians wore proper long-sleeved, high-collared dresses and maintained tightly wound, nononsense hair, his guitarists might appear in a sleeveless, low-cut summer dress or with stylishly mussed hair. In December 1902, Hudson depicted a lovely mandolinist demurely receiving her new instrument on Christmas morning; a year later a guitarist, waiting up for a late-night visit from Santa, offered the viewer a sidelong stare. A furtive St. Nick, standing in for the male magazine reader, stalks this second Hudson girl, her new guitar in hand. While Hudson may not have consciously depicted his female guitarists as more relaxed or more sensual than his other players, the iconic guitar undoubtedly reinforced the perception of such women as emotional and sensual. Even after Hudson's girls disappeared from *Cadenza*, the magazine featured covers that continued to play on Hudson's themes. The female figure continued to predominate and drawings and paintings reiterated the BMG links to ancient classicism, female sensuality, medieval lutes, and troubadours.

Have you read the "Gibson Romance Series?" We will send them on request

"WHEN THE LIGHTS ARE LOW"

A Gibson advertisement that plays on female expectations ("intimately personal instruments") and male hopes ("they break down conventional reserve"). (*Crescendo*)

By the 1920s ensemble photographs conveyed the growing divide within the BMG community: more traditional performers appeared in gowns and tuxes in a concert hall setting, while younger players with their tenor banjos, Hawaiian guitars, and ukuleles were more often depicted less formally, sometimes in relaxed shirtsleeves or matching sweaters, on a dancehall stage. And as the musical styles became more rhythmic, more jazz-influenced, the new hybrid instruments— including the arch-top guitar—figured more prominently and assertively in depictions of instruments.

A Gibson advertisement from 1920 points to some of the changes that were to come as the guitar became less feminine and more a (female) instrument upon which a man demonstrates his technique, control, and passion. References to love, courting, emotion, and sensuality persisted, but they were enhanced with a veiled sexuality. This Gibson advertisement, featuring a fashionable young musical couple before a fire, attempted to touch as many themes as possible. The sketch shows a mandolin-playing girl demurely looking down and away from her guitarist partner, who boldly leans toward her with an assertive stare. The advertisement's text plays on the (female) themes of emotional expression and intimacy, observing that "[m]usic itself is a medium for expression of our innermost emotions, and the Mandolin and Guitar seem to be the most *intimately personal* instruments." But in a play on the traditional association of musical expression with the release of dangerous passions, the text also euphemistically notes (for the hopeful male reader?) that such music-making can also "break down conventional reserve." The advertisement additionally observes that readers can learn to make music (as well as achieve intimacy and break down reserve) with these instruments quickly and nearly effortlessly. As if readers needed more convincing, a small boxed caption above the picture offers "Gibson Romances," fictionalized stories whose plots hinge on Gibson instruments, for the asking.

Nearly a hundred years later, a twenty-first-century reader might regard such romantic promotion as quaint or needlessly subtle. But while such advertisements appear backward, they actually pointed to the future of the instrument and the industry, demonstrating that America not only had created a new instrument for its new musics but was in the process of creating a new musical culture in which sound, image, function, business, and art each played a role. These images further demonstrate that the guitar—an instrument whose traditional shape and uses tie it so closely to the human body and the human heart—will continue to play an iconic role based on both ancient themes and new definitions assigned to it by new generations of players and listeners.

◄← *Chapter Seven* →►

A NEW INSTRUMENT

T he nineteenth century witnessed important changes in the construction of musical instruments as growing audiences for public concerts in
Europe and America filled larger and larger venues. These larger halls
created a need for more powerful instruments, leading to the development of
reconfigured bowed instruments capable of carrying higher-tension strings, more
powerful winds and brass, as well as larger pianos built around larger, heavier,
and stiffer steel frames. The guitar, too, underwent alterations in this period,
but proved more difficult to update than most other instruments. As a result, for
most of the century, the guitar remained an intimate instrument more suited to
the salon or the parlor than the concert hall. In the last two decades of the nineteenth century, however, European and American luthiers strove to create guitars that met the demand for more sound. While European builders, especially
in Spain, focused on modifying the guitar's traditional design, in America several
trends—technical, organological, commercial, and musical—coalesced, leading
to a new kind of guitar suitable for a new kind of music-making.

Numerous book-length studies document the guitar's various configurations as well as experiments in guitar design by nineteenth-century builders.
Among the European builders active through that century, Antonio Torres
(1817–1892) remains the most significant, credited with the creation of the
modern classical guitar. Recent evaluations recognize Torres less as a pioneer
responsible for innovative design and construction techniques and more as a
synthesizer who refined earlier experiments. Sophisticated fan-bracing, larger
bodies, and domed or arched soundboards—significant features of the Torres
guitar—had all appeared earlier in the century in guitars by other Spanish
builders, but Torres was the first to unite them in his instruments. His designs
were emulated by many Spanish luthiers, most famously the Ramirez family
workshop, which produced several instruments for Andres Segovia, including
the guitar he played in many of his most important debut concerts in Europe
and North and South America.[1]

American guitar builders and manufacturers followed different paths in their quest for more powerful instruments, paths partially documented in articles, serial columns, and advertisements in the American BMG magazines. The most important American organological experiments were the use of wire rather than gut or silk strings, the development of hybrid guitars, and the production and promotion of larger instruments with more strings, culminating in massive harp-guitars with twenty or more strings. Chapter 3 dealt with steel strings in the BMG movement and touched on the development of the banjo-guitar, an early hybrid. The following pages focus on other hybrid instruments that influenced the history of the guitar in America.

By the late nineteenth century, the American guitar's most obvious change was its increased size. It had developed a larger lower bout, with a more pronounced waist. In general, even these larger instruments were designed for gut strings. The increasing use of steel strings eventually led to a different kind of American guitar, more strongly braced to withstand the greater tensions of steel, but such instruments became widespread only in the 1920s. In his overview of the careers and instruments of Carl and August Larson of Chicago, Robert Carl Hartman cites George Gruhn, crediting the brothers with construction developments leading to a flat-top steel-string guitar. Hartman notes that while August Larson patented a number of design changes as early as 1904, neither of the most prominent guitar manufacturers, the Gibson Company and the C. F. Martin Company, manufactured flat-top guitars designed specifically for steel strings until well into the 1920s.[2]

The most important change for America's guitars occurred almost inadvertently, as instrument manufacturers and the BMG leadership focused more and more of their energies on the mandolin and mandolin-based ensembles. This increased attention to the mandolin grew in large part from the desire of the BMG manufacturers to expand their markets and see greater profits with new products. But as importantly, they continued to work just as hard to elevate the plectral instruments into the concert hall, to their mind a logical destination for the evolving BMG ensembles. Leaders of the BMG movement considered both their commercial and cultural activities to be in the service of "progress" and regularly described instruments, techniques, ensembles, teachers, and performers as "progressive." BMG apologists brandished the terms in promotions to confirm up-to-the-minute fashion, but more significantly, they were used to communicate a scientific and philosophical point of view standing on a middle-class appreciation of the values of industrial capitalism. For these musical businessmen and manufacturers, as for many Americans of the time, progress was a universal phenomenon, validated by the evolutionary science of Charles Darwin and explicated by the philosophical writings of Herbert Spenser. "For Americans, evolution provided scientific proof, taken from the evidence of a physical universe, of the purpose, mission, and meaning of America. Evolution was proof of progress—unceasing, inevitable progress. And America was and is, as all Americans believe, the living, national embodiment of progress."[3]

Nineteenth-century America's fascination with technical progress, manifested in an avalanche of inventions and patent applications in all areas of life, also led manufacturers and tinkerers alike to create new, progressive instruments. Almost inevitably, promoters who regularly touted the banjo as "America's instrument" came to see nineteenth-century developments in banjo design and its elevation into higher American society as evidence of a musical manifest destiny. Such progressive/evolutionary rhetoric became the philosophical underpinning of the BMG community, as manufacturers experimented with a variety of hybrid blends and sized families of banjos, mandolins, and guitars.

While developments in banjo design began in the 1880s, only in the final years of the nineteenth century did American instrument builders begin to seriously experiment with the design of the traditional Neapolitan mandolin. This instrument exuded an old-world charm with its bowl body and was regularly confused (often intentionally) with the medieval or renaissance lute. Such associations, as well as its use by Italian immigrants, relegated the mandolin to the realm of mythological lovers or the folk, a tool for wooing minstrels or dancing immigrants—clearly not an instrument of the progressive age. It was perceived as fit for love songs or rustic dances but not serious art music. As a result, when progressive BMG manufacturers created a new physical design for the instrument, they also tried to create new cultural and class associations for it.

The most successful innovator to tackle the mandolin, Orville Gibson (1856–1918), abandoned the flat top and bowl body of the traditional instrument for a mandolin with a carved and arched top and back, inspired by the violin. In time, Gibson "Florentine" mandolins sported the violin's f-holes, too. Gibson's mandolins proved significantly more powerful than the "potato bug" Italian instruments and eventually dominated the American market. Orville Gibson gave up his interests in the company early in its history, but his successors at the Gibson Mandolin-Guitar Company promoted their new instrument as a plectral version of the violin, spotlighting it as an instrument suitable for the performance of high-class music. Like earlier banjo soloists, mandolin virtuosi took on standard works from the violinist's repertoire, like Mendelssohn's Concerto or Beethoven sonatas. When manufacturers offered sized mandolins corresponding to the instruments of the violin family, the string quartet repertoire opened to mandolinists, too. In addition, directors of plectral ensembles strove more and more to create large ensembles modeled on traditional string orchestras.[4]

The guitar was an essential element of the early mandolin ensembles described in chapter 5, but *Crescendo* documented growing dissatisfaction

An illustration from a 1908 Gibson advertisement in which the new Gibson mandolin sweeps the potato bug mandolin into the "Dead Sea." Note that the bugs are being pushed off the "Eternal Progress Platform." The advertisement plays on a xenophobic suspicion of Latin immigrants, as the foreigners are gleefully thrown back into the sea by the all-American Gibson. (*Cadenza*)

with the traditional guitar and its role in the progressive mandolin ensembles, which grew in size, popularity, and (sometimes) musical sophistication. Although numerous solo guitarists operated successfully in the BMG community, the BMG leadership continued to regard the guitar as too difficult for most players to master and too quiet to have much of a role in large ensembles. Additionally, as mandolin ensembles expanded their repertoires to include serious works for string quartet or chamber orchestra, the guitar's role in these ensembles diminished. As a result, the instrumentation and repertoire of these mandolin ensembles had a direct impact not only on the guitar's role in the BMG movement but also on its design and construction.

Both of *Crescendo*'s editors penned long columns and fervent editorials for their magazine about developments in mandolin ensembles, promoting new hybrid instruments and innovative approaches to orchestration for these ensembles. While neither man attacked the guitar or its composers as some of their predecessors had, their approach rested on minimal expectations for the instrument within the mandolin orchestra. Of the two, H. F. Odell, *Crescendo*'s founder and first editor, was more negative about the guitar even as an accompaniment instrument in small mandolin ensembles. In 1909 he observed, "The purpose of the guitar in the mandolin orchestra being for accompaniment work only, the simpler the part, the better. . . . [I]n fact the guitar may with good effect be omitted entirely in certain strains. . . . The six string guitar cannot do all that a harp or piano can and guitar parts in which an attempt is made to play both melody and accompaniment are to be avoided." In a continuation of this column several months later, Odell noted that while the guitar might function as "an excellent instrument for accompaniment . . ., a piano carefully played is

The Polish Plectral Symphony—an ensemble modeled on the bowed string ensembles of the European tradition with sized mandolins. Gibson's promotional claim declared the company's goal of making all BMG players "Gibson-ites." (Gibson Catalog, 1921)

probably the most satisfactory instrument for accompaniment work in a mandolin orchestra." By way of example, Odell explained that his quintet of two mandolins, mandola, and two guitars had recently eliminated both accompanying guitars in favor of a harp. He reported that the resulting ensemble (two mandolins, tenor mandolin, mando-cello, and harp) "was fairly successful but it was impossible to get a harpist to play the grade of music we wished to, so we dropped the harp and used a piano." The lineup of pitched mandolins in his new ensemble mirrored that of the traditional string quartet. This correspondence, coupled with the choice of harp or piano to support the mandolin quartet, not only reflected musical tastes or convenience, but also documents the activities of the BMG leadership as they associated the new, progressive mandolin with the elite performing ensembles, the concert hall, and the cultivated repertoire of the European classical tradition. Promotions from the Gibson Mandolin-Guitar Company in the early 1920s emphasized that the ensembles of the 1880s and 1890s were merely "clubs," quite different from the "modern Mandolin Orchestra as made possible by the creation of the Gibson Tenor-mandola, the Gibson Mando-cello and the Gibson Mando-bass."[5]

While Odell seems only to have tolerated the guitar in his ensembles, his editorial successor, Walter K. Bauer, found a place of sorts for the guitar in his

A mandolin quintet covering the full string gamut with mandolins, mandola, mando-cello, and bass mandolin. (Gibson Catalog, 1921)

"plectrophonic orchestra." Bauer's ensemble included oboes, flutes, and percussion as well as choirs of banjos and mandolins that corresponded to a symphonic ensemble's brass and string sections. A third "accompaniment choir" included guitars and piano. While this inclusion seems positive, Bauer appears to have doubted the guitar's real contributions to his model ensemble, and in a later article titled "The New Era of Instrumentation Part Three—The Tenor Guitar," he welcomed this newly invented instrument as a replacement for the Spanish guitar. Bauer's enthusiasm for this hybrid probably derived from its similarities to the popular (and loud) tenor banjo. The tenor guitar retained only the guitar's body shape, taking on the tenor banjo's steel strings, tuning in fifths, and right-hand plectrum technique.[6]

Although Odell and Bauer hedged on the complete banishment of the guitar from the mandolin ensembles, others were not so circumspect and eliminated the instrument from their orchestrations. Despite her dedication to the guitar as a solo instrument, guitarist Ethel Lucretia Olcott was drawn into this debate by such attacks on the guitar, devoting one of her early "Guitarists Round Table" columns in *Crescendo* to a defense of the guitar in mandolin orchestras. While little of her argument in favor of guitarists remaining in these ensembles rests on musical considerations (she focuses primarily on the futility of mandolin ensembles attempting to imitate bowed string ensembles), the fact that one of America's foremost authorities had to argue for the guitar's

NEW 7-PART MANDO ORCHESTRA

COMPRISES
1—Piccolo Mando
2—First Mando
3—Second Mando

4—Tenor Mando
5—Mando-Cello
6—Harp
7—Bass Mando

WHY NOT START ONE NOW?

PRICES
OF MANDOS
RANGE FROM
$18.00
to
$75.00

Competent critics everywhere have been so gratified with the results achieved by the Chicago Seven Part Mando Club that we wish to place before the public particulars of this new orchestration. It is rich in harmony and sound from a musician's standpoint, as all the parts of the regular string quintet are represented and all the instruments yield the same quality of tone. The playing of the most simple number becomes a source of delight to the cultured listener. An Orchestra formed upon these lines is able to produce not only the popular music of the day, but can also give a correct reading of the lighter classical numbers.

WORLD'S LARGEST MUSIC HOUSE

Lyon & Healy

WRITE
FOR
BOOKLET

FREE

Wabash Avenue and Adams Street

CHICAGO

Gibson was not the only company pushing the new mandolin ensemble. In this advertisement Lyon & Healy promote their ideal mandolin orchestra—without a guitar. (*Crescendo*)

continued inclusion indicates how serious the problem had become within the BMG movement. Unsurprisingly, part of Olcott's argument rests on commercial considerations, as she implies dire consequences for players (who would lose access to good music) and for publishers and instrument manufacturers (who would lose business).

> With all due respect to the progressiveness of the modern director, I [put] to you the question, *Is it for the ultimate progress and betterment of the mandolin orchestra of the future, to eliminate the guitar?* Personally, I can not but feel that it is a big step backward, instead of a step forward; a step backward not only in the beauty, originality, and effect, and purpose of the future mandolin orchestra, but in my opinion, it will lessen the general interest in both the mandolin and guitar. Not only this, but as a result, the publishers will, through lack of demand, necessarily cease publishing good things for the combination of mandolin and guitar. . . . People will lose interest in the instruments. Publishers will cease to put out the good and distinctive mandolin orchestra parts they now are publishing. Even people who now play the mandolin and guitar, will give it up for the violin and other orchestral instruments, where they can receive more remuneration . . . then is the dawn of the day for mandolinists and guitarists to relegate their instruments to the chamber of antiquities.[7]

Such an active defense of the ensemble guitar, coupled with comments like those cited above by Odell, Bauer, and others, reflected a new attitude toward the guitar from the BMG leadership. In the early years of the BMG movement, its apologists had consciously courted the guitar, linking it to the banjo and eventually the mandolin to improve the image of these two instruments. But by the second decade of the twentieth century, mandolin advocates asserted that the mandolin club had evolved into a plucked-string orchestra without need of guitar support. This gradual shuffling of the guitar to the periphery of the American mandolin orchestra, coupled with a growing specialization among BMG players, eventually encouraged American guitarists to more actively pursue a solo repertoire, and (as will be seen in later chapters) prepared them to enthusiastically embrace the instrument's European heritage, as presented by Miguel Llobet, Andres Segovia, and other European virtuosi.[8]

But before these Spaniards had a significant influence on American guitar-playing, American manufacturers, inspired by the progressive ideals of evolutionary capitalism and evolutionary art, continued their experiments with hybrid instruments. As earlier manufacturers had blended the very popular banjo with the guitar to create the guitar-neck or six-string banjo, later manufacturers, especially the Gibson Mandolin-Guitar Company, experimented with ways to unite the extremely popular mandolin with the guitar. The result, the arch-top guitar, proved unsuitable for traditional guitar literature and of little interest to mandolin ensembles, but eventually became an independent and important instrument on its own, separate from both the mandolin and the traditional guitar. This new instrument engendered a new technique as well, as it established itself in America's burgeoning popular music, ranging from jazzy dance orchestras to hillbilly string bands.

Like its smaller cousin, the early arch-top guitar mimicked the violin with a carved top and back. Most significantly, this instrument appears to have been designed from the start to carry steel strings. While the earliest designs utilized a typical pin bridge, Gibson's early models sometimes incorporated a metal stay secured to the base of the guitar. This stay reinforced the bridge, allowing it to be strung like the mandolin with steel strings. By the teens, however, Gibson guitars became even more like the brand's mandolins, featuring a metal tailpiece to secure steel strings, a violin-inspired floating bridge, and a more sharply angled neck. Early versions of the new Gibson mandolins and guitars featured round or oval sound holes but by the mid-1920s Gibson designers, led by mandolinist Lloyd Loar, made the violin connection even stronger by converting the traditional sound hole to paired f-holes.

The arch-top guitar, a hybrid blend of the mandolin and guitar, called for a hybrid technique, too. Mandolinists in BMG ensembles emulated violinists, playing only single-line melodies. While some virtuosi utilized "duo playing" (double-stops) in the occasional solo work, this technique was regarded as far too difficult for most mandolinists. Guitarists, on the other hand, were generally

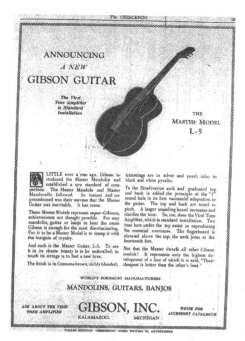

The CRESCENDO 19

ANNOUNCING
A NEW
GIBSON GUITAR

*The Virzi
Tone Amplifier
is Standard
Installation*

THE
MASTER· MODEL
L-5

LITTLE over a year ago, Gibson introduced the Master Mandolin and
established a new standard of comparison. The Master Mandola and Master
Mandocello followed. So instant and un-
precedented was their success that the Master
Guitar was inevitable. It has come.

These Master Models represent *super-Gibsons,*
achievements not thought possible. For any
mandolin, guitar or banjo to bear the name
Gibson is enough for the most discriminating.
For it to be a Master Model is to stamp it with
the insignia of royalty.

And such is the Master Guitar, L-5. To see
it in its chaste beauty is to be enthralled; to
touch its strings is to find a new love.

The finish is in Cremona brown, richly blended;

trimmings are in silver and pearl; inlay in
black and white pyralin.

To the Stradivarius arch and graduated top
and back is added the principle of the "f"
sound hole in its first successful adaptation to
the guitar. The top and back are tuned to
pitch. A larger sounding board increases and
clarifies the tone. So, too, does the Virzi Tone
Amplifier, which is standard installation. Two
tone bars under the top assist in reproducing
the essential overtones. The fingerboard is
elevated above the top; the neck joins at the
fourteenth fret.

Not that the Master dwarfs all other Gibson
models! It represents only the highest development of a line of which it is said, "Their
cheapest is better than the other's best."

WORLD'S FOREMOST MANUFACTURERS
MANDOLINS, GUITARS, BANJOS

ASK ABOUT THE VIRZI
TONE AMPLIFIER **GIBSON, INC.** WRITE FOR
ACCESSORY CATALOGUE
KALAMAZOO, MICHIGAN

PLEASE MENTION "CRESCENDO" WHEN WRITING TO ADVERTISERS

A Gibson advertisement announcing the new L-5 arch-top guitar. The text emphasizes the connection to violin (through Gibson's innovative mandolins) describing a "Cremona" finish and "Stradivarius" arch and top. (*Crescendo*)

restricted to chordal playing in most ensemble work. When this new mando-
lin-inspired guitar appeared, it combined the tuning and left-hand chordal
technique of the guitar with the right-hand plectrum technique of the mandolin. This new guitar became a plectrum instrument and, as befitting the newer
popular American music, a true rhythm instrument played with a percussive
attack derived from the mandolin. At the same time, the mandolinists who
took up this new guitar brought their single-line solo technique to the guitar,
allowing it to speak in the ensemble like the other melodic instruments.

Singer/guitarist Nick Lucas (1897–1982) described his early training in the
teens, tracing his development from a mandolinist to tenor banjoist to singing
guitarist. In the early teens, his older brother introduced him to the mandolin,
"the dominant instrument with Italians and the general public." Lucas notes
that his early performing experience contributed to his technique, "especially
with getting the right-hand tremolo technique," a skill promoted in many of
the BMG magazine columns devoted to the mandolin. In one of his earliest
professional gigs, Lucas performed primarily on a hybrid banjo-mandolin (he
mistakenly identified it as banjeaurine) with a banjo head and mandolin stringing. While he played the guitar for more sedate waltzes (as did most plectral
players in jazz dance bands), he played tenor banjo more often because of
its rhythmic drive and greater volume. The tenor banjo's greater popularity
derived in part, too, from its direct connection to the mandolin family. Tuned

Special Grand Concert Guitar, Style "O"
Artist's Model

Carefully selected, straight grain, graduated spruce top (sounding-board), finished in an exquisite blend from dark mahogany to sunburst; select, thoroughly air-seasoned maple rim and back, dark mahogany finish; highly polished throughout; select straight grain British Honduras mahogany neck reinforced and non-warpable, neck richly blended in shading of mahogany; veneered head-piece, front and back, front bound with ivoroid and handsomely inlaid with "The Gibson" in pearl and mother-of-pearl Fleur-de-lis; ivoroid bound convex solid ebony extension finger-board, with twenty-two ovaled, narrow frets; pearl position dots inlaid on finger-board and position dots on upper side of neck; ivoroid bound oblong sound-hole, inlaid with three rings of fancy colored woods; perpendicular compensating bridge, securing divided vertical string pressure and preventing sharping of tones in upper positions; elevated finger-rest with white copper clamp (Patented July 4, 1911). Top and back bound with ivoroid on outer edge of rim; improved extension string-holder; pearl nut; best quality nickeled machine-head. Body joins neck at fifteenth fret instead of twelfth fret, making the highest positions easily accessible. Width of sounding-board at bridge, sixteen inches.

Gibson instruments may be purchased from Gibson Agents, or, in territory where we are not represented, direct from us. Responsible parties may arrange for monthly payments to suit their convenience. For prices and terms see price list attached to inside of front cover. Price list of strings, supplies and parts furnished on request. Prices quoted are Net and not subject to further discount.

Always state whether gut or wire strings are wanted.
Agents must maintain prices marked "Net."

61

An advertisement from Gibson's 1921 catalog. The side view highlights the violin's influence—a severely angled neck, a floating bridge, tailpiece, and arched top and back. The front view shows how the instrument mimics the Gibson mandolins with its "Florentine" curls. (Gibson Catalog, 1921)

in fifths and played with a plectrum like the mandolin, the tenor banjo could be easily played by mandolinists.

Lucas achieved stardom as a singing guitarist, endorsing the Gibson instruments. In the mid-1920s the Gibson Company created a "Nick Lucas guitar" based on his preferences. Lucas noted that "at that time the guitar was practically obsolete. It was going out, and they had to do something." Lucas also published a multivolume guitar method and numerous solos, all of which focused on a right-hand plectrum technique.[9]

Lucas himself noted the significance of the mandolin for Italians and, unsurprisingly, a number of early jazz guitarists who specialized in playing the new plectrum style on the new arch-top guitars were first- or second-generation Italian Americans. These included not only Lucas (christened Dominic

Nick Lucas endorses the Gibson L-5 archtop guitar. (*Crescendo*)

Nicholas Anthony Lucanese) but also Eddie Lang (1902–1933, born Salvatore Massaro), the player usually credited with the invention of jazz guitar playing. Like many other plectrum guitarists of the 1920s and 1930s, Lang's early professional work was on the banjo; he turned to the guitar full-time only in the mid-1920s. His influential recordings of guitar duets with Lonnie Johnson are often pointed to as a highlight of the early jazz guitar genre, but Lang's work as a sideman in a variety of ensembles especially demonstrates how the plectrum guitar differed from the accompanying guitar of the BMG ensembles. Guitar parts in the BMG ensembles focused on single bass notes and block chords, so that even in more up-tempo dances the accompaniment was solid and square. Lang's accompaniments, on the other hand, often featured melodic commentary punctuated with chords, freeing the guitar from its stodgy bass/chord tradition.[10] Lang's approach to the guitar transcended the sound and style of the BMG community, becoming the basis for the evolving jazz guitar. But Lang's contribution to the world of jazz derived from the innovations of the manufacturers and players of the BMG movement: the progressive arch-top guitar and the highly developed plectrum technique of the solo mandolinist.

Italian American guitarists certainly had no corner on the instrument, but most white jazz and popular guitarists of this era began their musical activities with the mandolin or tenor banjo. Some maintained their musical connection to these instruments by playing the tenor guitar, a hybrid with a guitar body but tuned in fifths like the tenor banjo. Others found their own novel ways of linking the new arch-top guitar to their previous instruments. For example, Carl Kress (1907–1965) worked with Paul Whiteman's Orchestra and recorded with Bix Beiderbecke among others, playing tenor banjo and tenor guitar. When he switched to the six-string guitar in the 1930s, Kress maintained the tenor banjo's tuning in fifths, expanding it to accommodate the guitar's six strings.[11]

Despite the incredible popularity of both Nick Lucas and Eddie Lang as performers and recording artists, their appearances in the BMG magazines were limited to an advertisement for a plectrum method book and only brief notices, one being an announcement of Lang's premature death. While the tenor banjo became a regular topic in the BMG magazines, columnists often ignored its use in jazz combos, promoting it as a member of the mandolin orchestra. Most contributors to these periodicals disdained jazz, considering it at best unrefined and at worst dangerous. In a column from 1922, Vahdah Olcott-Bickford observed that if nature "implants a love of jazz in a human soul, she does not implant a love for the bewitching guitar in the same soul." In one of the oddest moments in musical historiography, she credited jazz's inherent primitivism to its origins in the war music of sixteenth-century Peruvian natives.[12] Whatever their rationale, the guitarists who wrote for the BMG magazines not only ignored jazz and pop players, but for the most part also ignored Gibson's innovative arch-top guitar, seeing it less as a guitar and more as an extended mandolin. Its body design, steel strings, and, most significantly, its plectrum technique clearly point to stronger mandolin than guitar associations. While not mentioning this new instrument by name, Vahdah Olcott-Bickford probably had it in mind in 1919 when she decried the increasing use of hybrid instruments in mandolin orchestras. She noted that teachers and serious performers had a responsibility to differentiate between "the serious, artistic fretted instruments and those of the hybrid 'jazz' variety."

> There is no doubt that in the past few seasons, the wild fad for "jazz" and the Hawaiian instruments has hurt the popularity of the old standbys, the really artistic fretted instruments. . . . I believe that the sooner the tenor-banjos, banjo-mandolins and other hybrid "jazz" instruments are eliminated from the clubs and orchestras . . . the better it will be for our instruments. For a dance orchestra, or for distinct "jazz" effects and popular topical "hits" of the day, the preceding named instruments are all right (for those who like them), but as such music is the only kind for which they are fitted or even intended, let directors bar them from the legitimate ensembles which are supposed to be "Mandolin Orchestras" . . . The poor beautiful guitar also comes in for its share of the ignominy bestowed upon the mandolin by these same people, for the reason that it so often is used to accompany the fierce onslaughts of the young "jazz" artist.[13]

An elegant duo—mandolin and harp-guitar.
(*Chicago Trio*)

This call for a return to the standard instruments of the mandolin orchestra also highlights the incursions of the Hawaiian or steel guitar, a hybrid instrument held flat on the player's legs and whose steel strings were fretted with a metal bar or slide. It eventually came to play a significant role in American popular music, but when the Hawaiian guitar (in the company of its smaller partner, the ukulele) first appeared in the BMG magazines in the early teens, it appeared to be an insubstantial fad, popular for its exotic sounds and the island costumes with which it was associated. Both instruments were embraced by professionals and amateurs alike, and many players reconfigured their standard guitars with devices marketed in the magazines. Despite snubs of these hybrids by Olcott-Bickford and other guitarists, the BMG magazines offered readers not only advertisements and promotions of the Hawaiian guitar and ukulele but also historical and instructional articles.[14]

While Olcott-Bickford called for a ban on most hybrids, many other guitarists accepted and regularly used the magnificent harp-guitar, a late-century hybrid manufactured by Gibson and others. While numerous variations were produced, the most common harp-guitar was comprised of an oversized guitar body with a standard neck carrying six fretted strings, augmented by a bank of unfretted bass strings. These additional basses (sometimes as many as twelve tuned chromatically) ran between an expanded bridge and an extended secondary neck or headstock. Most collectors and historians of the harp-guitar describe it as an extended guitar rather than a hybrid; contemporaneous BMG

1907 MODEL

SYMPHONY

HARP GUITARS

USED AND ENDORSED BY THE WORLD'S BEST ARTISTS

EQUAL IN TONE TO THE HARP

Heretofore there has been objection to Harp Guitars because of their being so clumsy and awkward to handle. This is overcome in the **Symphony** by an entirely new principle of construction so that they can be played with just as much ease as the ordinary instruments and are equally as desirable for either ladies or gentlemen.

The rich, deep, sympathetic tone is a revelation to those who have never before heard them and the five extra contra bass strings, which are tuned one octave lower than regular pitch, enable the performer to produce most beautiful effects which are impossible on the six stringed guitar.

WRITE FOR CATALOG No. 358

W. J. DYER & BRO.

SOLE FACTORS

SAINT PAUL, MINN.

The Dyer company based their harp-guitar designs on those of Chris Knutsen, which featured a resonating extension. Their advertisements emphasized the elite aspirations of the instrument. (*Cadenza*)

manufacturers and apologists, on the other hand, promoted its orchestral associations, calling them "Symphony Harp-Guitars," for example. Advertisements, editorials, letters, and columns regularly touted it as an economical replacement for the refined harp, an instrument popular in mid-nineteenth-century parlors and mentioned regularly in the early BMG journals as an appropriate accompaniment to the banjo or mandolin: "The harp is a beautiful instrument, and adds much to the strength of a mandolin club, but harps are very expensive. Now, for a comparatively small outlay of funds you can buy a splendid Symphony Harp Guitar. The clubs that are using them are enthusiastic in praise of their tone."[15] Additionally, full-page advertisements for Gibson's harp-guitar echo promotions of their arch-top guitar, pointing to a break with the guitar's past by touting design innovations inspired by the violin.

Harp- and lyre-guitars had been played in the mid-nineteenth century by some of Europe's best-known guitar soloists but achieved popularity in the United States only in the early years of the twentieth century. Despite its European pedigree, Walter A. Boehm, a contributor to *The American Music Journal*, *Cadenza*, and *Crescendo*, all but claimed to have invented the harp-guitar in 1897 in a search for "the perfect solo instrument." Boehm was not the only American experimenting with extended guitars in America in the late 1890s, but he was an indefatigable proselytizer for the instrument, promoting it through his teaching and performing as well as in the pages of the BMG magazines. His assertions and pronouncements often read like P. T. Barnum's, but no one could doubt his enthusiastic appreciation of both the instrument and the manufacturers' role in bringing this progressive instrument to progressive musicians: "The splendid improvement made during recent years in Harp-Guitar construction is one of the strong evidences that **progress** is the watch-word that impels the player and manufacturer to work hand in hand toward establishing a higher order of things than has existed in the past. In other words, that which has been, does not satisfy the progressive teacher **Now**. He calls on the manufacturer for something better right along."[16]

While it flourished only briefly in the BMG arena, the harp-guitar was ubiquitous, appearing in a variety of forms in refined chamber ensembles, pop groups, and massed mandolin orchestras. In fact, it appeared much more often in advertisements, articles, and columns than did the hybrid arch-top guitar, indicating that the harp-guitar struck a more resonant chord with the BMG leadership, a concrete example of many of the values of the BMG community. It had an historical foundation and high-art European link in the earlier use of extended guitars by Johann Kaspar Mertz and others, as well as a connection to the orchestral harp through its name and function in BMG ensembles.[17] Like the evolving piano or the high-rise skyscraper, the harp-guitar demonstrated a tendency in American design and technology to solve problems by building bigger. The harp-guitar was an ideal "progressive" instrument, in its melding of an earlier, classic form (the basic guitar shape carrying six principal strings) with current technology and science (an enhanced and complex superstructure). Naysayers who preferred only six strings were shamed for an antiprogressive stance with the example of J. S. Bach, who had preferred the antique harpsichord to the new piano:

> Death alone saved Bach from the ridicule of the then rising generation, for time and the piano proved Bach's satisfaction, and joys were but cheats that held him within narrow limits and belittled his gratifications by hedging his musical aspiration and inspiration with an instrument of dwarfed compensation. *Then it was the harpsichord versus piano; now it is Guitar versus Harp-guitar.* Bach's antiquated instrument is today but a museum curiosity and would remain such even if the mighty Bach were here to play it. . . . Listen, oh Teacher or Guitarist. *To remain the same while years and instruments advance is not becoming.* It does not even excuse Bach . . . .[18]

Despite the progressive talk surrounding the instrument, however, the harp-guitar only reinforced the position of the guitar and its players within the

A mandolin-led ensemble that mirrors a baroque chamber group with a bowed bass and plucked continuo. (collection of the author)

BMG community. Like its six-string version, the harp-guitar was generally recognized as far too complex for the average enthusiast to play well, yet manufacturers and commentators claimed that the rudiments of both instruments were simple enough for almost anyone to play acceptable accompaniments. As a result, while some advanced performers attempted solo work on it, most harp-guitarists were encouraged to play elementary bass/chord accompaniments for mandolins or banjos and never utilized the potential of the instrument's extended range. Harp-guitar solos and accompaniments published in the BMG magazines differed in no way from works for the standard guitar, since the only "harp effects" were bass notes transposed down an octave. An anthology of solos for the harp-guitar appeared in 1918, but it could hardly have offered an innovative use of its additional bass strings, since all the solos fit on the six-string guitar as well.[19]

While promotions for harp-guitars appeared in the BMG magazines as early as 1897, it did not reach its peak of popularity until after 1910. Photographs of ensembles, advertisements, and articles featuring harp-guitars increased significantly in the journals through the second decade of the twentieth century. For many ensemble directors, the harp-guitar became the preferred accompaniment instrument for a plucked-string ensemble. *Cadenza*'s "ideal mandolin club instrumentation" mirrored the bowed string quintet (two violins,

This refined Chicago ensemble utilized the orchestral harp in addition to three harp-guitars. (*Chicago Trio*)

viola, cello, and piano): two mandolins, tenor mandola, mando-cello and harp-guitar.[20]

Advertisements for harp-guitars in the BMG magazines indicate that several manufacturers dominated the market. While the Gibson Mandolin-Guitar Company (Kalamazoo, Michigan) manufactured its own instruments, William Stahl (Milwaukee, Wisconsin), and W. J. Dyer & Brothers (St. Paul, Minnesota) marketed harp-guitars built by the Larson brothers of Chicago. Their instruments, modeled on designs by Chris J. Knutsen, a West Coast luthier, incorporated an additional resonating chamber into the extended neck. Unsurprisingly, the Gibson Company eventually incorporated aspects of its mandolin designs, including the Florentine swirls and a tailpiece, into their harp-guitars. Gibson's advertisements for their harp-guitar emphasized its violin-inspired body design, tying it directly to their innovative and progressive mandolin.[21]

BMG magazines promoted other guitaristic instruments—some legitimate, some incredible concoctions— besides harp-guitars. Among the former, the terz guitar appeared regularly in the hands of Jennie Durkee, C. W. F. Jansen, and Vahdah Olcott-Bickford. The terz guitar corresponds to the standard guitar in the same way the violin does to the viola; it is a smaller, higher-pitched instrument, but played exactly like the standard guitar. The Italian virtuoso, Mauro Giuliani, published a number of works for the terz guitar in the early

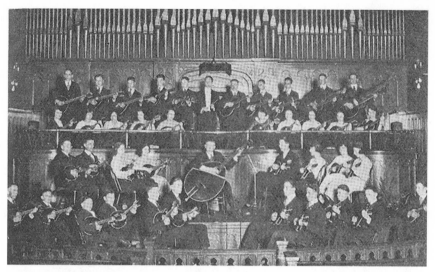

A true mandolin orchestra on a concert hall stage. Guitars and harp-guitars occupy the back row to the right of the conductor. (Gibson Catalog, 1921)

years of the nineteenth century, and contributors to the BMG journals consistently credited him with its invention. Durkee's father, George B. Durkee, an instrument designer and builder for Lyon & Healy in Chicago, constructed his daughter's terz guitar and promoted the instrument for use by soloists and ensemble players in the magazines. Besides performing solos and duets on the terz guitar, Olcott-Bickford wrote about it in her columns, encouraging its use in ensembles with standard guitars and harp-guitars. Jansen performed regularly on the terz guitar and featured it at the 1912 Chicago convention of the American Guild of Banjoists, Mandolinists and Guitarists, playing a quintet by Giuliani with a mandolin ensemble standing in for the bowed instruments.[22]

While harp-guitars built by the Gibson Company, Chris Knutsen, or the Larson brothers might on occasion have pushed the limits of design, structural integrity, and musical viability, few of them compare to the most bizarre instrument to grace the pages of the BMG magazines. De Main Wood, a guitarist and inventor from Rochester, New York, presented his "Orchestral Guitar" at a Guild Convention in 1906, performing the "Pilgrims' Chorus" from Wagner's *Tannhäuser*. Starting with a conventional six-string guitar, Wood added to it "six wonderful attachments invented and perfected . . . during the past twenty years." These attachments included a bank of bass strings plucked by the left thumb, a clockwork mechanism that plucked the instrument's first string in a mandolin tremolo, and another clockwork device that hammered bass strings to create a cello effect. Additionally, Wood added a moveable arm that not

De Main Wood and his Orchestral Guitar.
(*Cadenza*)

only fretted the highest string but also produced (according to a reviewer) a "good imitation of the voice" by means of a miniature bellows. This arm and bellows were connected to a mouthpiece manipulated by Wood's teeth and tongue. Amazingly, the steel/gut controversy spilled over to the evaluation of this extreme contraption and, according to *Cadenza*, the necessary use of steel strings compromised "the musical value" of this unique instrument. Nonetheless, the *Cadenza* reviewer enthused that "Mr. Wood's guitar is the only one of its kind, and it is not likely that another will be manufactured. . . . [I]ts invention and perfection by Mr. Wood is nothing short of marvelous. . . . The combined effects produced are really remarkable and probably nothing just the same will ever be produced on any other instrument." While Wood's instrument was not the last experiment with guitar design, it probably stands as the most extreme attempt at expanding the range, volume, and timbre of the conventional guitar. In carrying the progressive ideals of mechanization and hybridization very near the breaking point, Wood created a parody of the guitar rather than a practical instrument.[23]

By the close of the BMG era in the mid-1930s, the guitar family in America had divided according to function and corresponding design. Steel-strung instruments—arch-tops as well as stiffly braced flat-tops—and hybrids proliferated. While the faddish tenor guitar faded, the Hawaiian lap guitar found a place in American popular music, eventually becoming the pedal steel guitar, a ubiquitous presence in country and western music. The harp-guitar never transcended its musical and symbolic role in the more formal mandolin-based ensembles of the BMG movement, and as the movement stalled, so too did the harp-guitar's popularity. On the other hand, the hybrid arch-top guitar was taken up by urban jazz and pop musicians like Eddie Lang and Nick Lucas who desired more powerful instruments for live performance as well as for recording. Black and white rural players were drawn to this steel-strung guitar, too, probably for its durability and penetrating sound. In the mid-1930s, when joined with the new technology of electronic amplification, the arch-top guitar became the preferred instrument of America's jazz and pop guitarists, finally relegating the tenor banjo to an also-ran status.

Historians and fans of the guitar in America generally identify the birth of the modern guitar as the moment when the development of single-line jazz soloing (usually credited to Eddie Lang) was joined to the electric guitar (credited to a variety of individuals including George Beauchamp, Adolph Rickenbacker, Lloyd Loar, Leo Fender, and Les Paul). But in some ways the addition of electricity was merely icing on the cake. As outlined on the previous pages, the physical and technical roots of the new American guitar were planted firmly in the BMG movement's promotion of the mandolin family. America's new guitar first appeared when inventors and instrument manufacturers created the hybrid mandolin-guitar and mandolinists took up this new instrument with their plectrum technique.[24]

Despite this important development, American manufacturers continued to produce gut-strung guitars, and the leading guitarists of the BMG movement tried to ignore the impending schism within America's guitar community. While players including C. W. F. Jansen embraced new designs like the harp-guitar, most of the leading guitarists of the BMG movement focused on the traditional gut-strung guitar and the BMG repertoire of classically inspired saccharine dances and pyrotechnic variations. In 1918 William Foden offered *Crescendo* readers a two-article survey of odd guitar designs. He concentrated primarily on nineteenth-century oddities and did not address the steel-strung arch-top guitar at all. At the end of his second article Foden offered an evaluation of these eccentric guitars; it is difficult for a later reader not to hear in these lines a rejection of the changes in the guitar, its technique, and its music that roiled around Foden and his peers. "In all these inventions we can readily see a desire to improve the tone, power and detail of the guitar, and in general the inventors are to be commended for their efforts, but so far as my observation goes, no real and substantial improvement has been made in many years."[25]

Such a comment appears to have ignored the developments in American guitar design and construction of the previous two decades and points up the disconnection of the proponents of a traditional school of American guitar playing from their real-world situation. This disconnection certainly played a major role in the disintegration of this American school of guitar playing. And this disintegration was abetted by another musical force squeezing the BMG guitarists, as European players slowly made inroads into America's musical awareness, bringing a new instrument, a new technique, and new repertoire with them. This slow European invasion of America's guitar community culminated with

Andres Segovia's 1928 American debut, an event marking the beginning of the end for the gut-strung American guitar and the traditional school of American guitar playing. Following another brief interlude, the concluding chapters are devoted to Europe's reclamation of its guitar tradition and its role in the development of America's guitar culture.

Chapter Eight

INTERLUDE

The Wizard and The Grand Lady

S ince the 1960s popular guitar players have regularly become cultural
icons, with musicians such as Jimi Hendrix or Eric Clapton achieving
the status of pop music divinities. As seen in chapter 4, the BMG movement also had its share of acclaimed guitarists, some of whom achieved local
and regional distinction, while others including Johnson Bane, Jennie Durkee,
and C. W. F. Jansen became national figures. None, however, garnered the
notoriety heaped on Vahdah Olcott-Bickford and William Foden as performers, teachers, composer/arrangers, historians, and musical authorities. And
while their acclaim seems miniscule when compared to that given later pop
figures, these two players—The Grand Lady of the Guitar and The Wizard of
the Guitar—dominated America's guitar community from the end of the nineteenth century until they were squeezed out in the late 1920s by pop and jazz
guitarists on the one hand and European classical players on the other. Their
stories offer insights into the attitudes and values of America's guitar community in the important transitional period between the last decades of the nineteenth century and the late 1920s.

Born in St. Louis, William Foden (1860–1947) came to music as a young
child, playing first harmonica, then classical accordion, hurdy-gurdy, and drum.
At age seven, he began formal studies of the violin, turning to the guitar in his
teens under the tutelage of William O. Bateman (1825–1883), a local attorney
and skilled amateur player. Foden's earliest performing activities focused on
ensemble work; by his mid-teens he was directing a professional ensemble that
played parties and other entertainments in the St. Louis area. In columns for
Crescendo magazine thirty years later, he described some of his early work as
a mandolinist as well as the evolution of his Beethoven Mandolin and Guitar
Orchestra from an impromptu quartet of two mandolins, guitar, and harp organized in 1887. Reflecting his growing reputation, in the 1890s the ensemble

William Foden from his *Grand Method* of
1921. (courtesy of Gaylord Music Library,
Washington University in St. Louis)

became the Foden Mandolin and Guitar Orchestra. Foden remained actively
involved in the group until 1904 and it continued performing until August
1910. Anticipating the late-twentieth-century popularity of ensembles comprised of guitars only, Foden also created a short-lived guitar quintet whose
members included his student George C. Krick as well as Foden himself. Early
in his career as a guitarist (Foden offered no specific dates), he designed and
commissioned a six-string bass guitar, tuned a sixth below the standard instrument, which he used in ensemble performances.[1]

Like most BMG professionals of the day, Foden played banjo and mandolin as well as guitar, achieving considerable skill on all three. Also like other
music professionals, Foden made his living primarily as a teacher. He and his
brother followed the music business model so popular in the BMG movement,
opening a retail store in the late 1880s. Its demands on his time took Foden
from his teaching activities and the two brothers parted ways in 1890. Foden
opened his own store shortly thereafter, but once again abandoned the retail
business to concentrate on teaching and performing.

Foden's name first surfaced in BMG journals in the mid-1880s and
appeared regularly through the 1890s. Despite his focus on teaching (and later
on composing and publishing), Foden's reputation rested on his performance
skills. From the beginning he was revered with a mythic awe: in an early BMG
notice, several guitar enthusiasts described how they had traveled from Chicago
to St. Louis for a private audience, enthusing about his overwhelming

skills with the guitar. In a poem cited in chapter 6, Ole Bull, Paganini, and Rubenstein represent their instruments while Foden, described as an "unrivalled star," is the only guitarist mentioned. Although an aversion to travel limited his public appearances to the Midwest, through the 1890s he was consistently rumored to be America's premiere guitarist.[2]

Foden's first concert appearance outside the Midwest, a watershed event for the classical guitar in America, took place in 1904, when Clarence Partee brought him from St. Louis to New York's Carnegie Hall for the convention concert of the American Guild of Banjoists, Mandolinists and Guitarists. Partee, a former Missourian, certainly knew Foden's playing and his breathless reports in *Cadenza* contributed to the guitarist's revered status. The concert confirmed the rumors, and the East Coast BMG community responded to Foden's technical skills, special effects, and overall musicianship with amazement. Richard M. Tyrrell's astonished review of this performance reflected the consensus.

> And then the greatest guitarist of this, or we honestly believe any other country. We have seen the writings of the greatest masters, Sor, Legnani, Horetzky, Ferranti and Mertz, but nothing that this gifted artist could not encompass, as displayed by his remarkable rendition of, and brilliant execution in the Fantasie from Favorita and the variations on Ascher's "Alice." He seemed to bring out every conceivable possibility of the instrument. His right hand work in melody and simultaneous accompaniment being especially fine. The power and tone of his large concert instrument being vibrant and full. His manner of holding the instrument coinciding with our opinion, as against the stiff banjo born method, advocated by some. Mr. William Foden is not only a virtuoso on his instrument, but a most accomplished musician, as displayed by his transcription of the beautiful sextette from "Lucia." He is not sufficiently known in the east, but genius and ability like his cannot "hide its light under a bushel" very long.[3]

Foden took advantage of this enthusiastic reception, becoming a regular in Partee's magazine and publishing several works with Partee in the following year.

He appeared again at a Guild Convention Concert in 1911, in a program that also included mandolinist Giuseppe Pettine and banjoist Fred Bacon. The three men found themselves well-matched musically and by the end of that year not only were they touring as "The Big Trio," but Foden had also relocated to New York to facilitate their concertizing. Their tour took them throughout New England, across the upper Midwest, and into Canada, and audiences everywhere welcomed the trio as BMG royalty. Foden dedicated some of his later columns in *Crescendo* to the Big Trio tours, but focused principally on travel anecdotes, unfortunately offering little in the way of musical insights or commentary.

Foden remained in the New York area for nearly thirty years, and although he performed through these years, Foden devoted most of his professional energies to teaching, composing, and writing about the guitar. For nearly four years, beginning in late 1911 when he was most active as a performer with the Big Trio, Foden wrote twenty-nine columns for the *Cadenza* addressing a variety of musical and technical topics as well as answering queries from readers. While many contributors to BMG magazines wrote in an overwrought, expansive manner, Foden offered readers some of the driest, least adorned prose in these journals. Foden's columns reflect his skills as a player, focusing almost exclusively on very specific technical issues. Seventeen treated basic and advanced guitar technique, ranging from fingering systems to harmonics while the last eleven articles in the series, titled "Elementary Harmony as Applied to the Guitar," introduced guitarists to the basic tenets of musical theory. Foden never advanced beyond technical or theoretical topics in any of his *Cadenza* columns, giving the impression that physical control of the instrument and intellectual control of the rules of harmony made the guitarist a musician.

Unlike other columnists, Foden neither offered a suggested repertoire nor mapped out a regimen of particular studies for students. And although he clearly respected the work of earlier generations of guitarists, he never advocated the actual performance of their works in his articles. Foden's own programs resembled those of other American guitar soloists at this time, featuring primarily his own compositions and arrangements with only the occasional work by earlier composers. Aside from one or two pieces by his teacher William Bateman, Foden generally limited his performances of earlier works to a few pieces by Mertz and Ferranti. Only one program from the BMG magazines documented Foden publicly performing a work by a member of the earliest generation of classical guitarists, when he played a sonata movement by Fernando Sor.[4]

Foden's own compositions fall generally into two genres: simple and popular dance forms, especially waltzes, or virtuoso variation sets. As described in chapter 5, Foden's theme and variations owe much to the works of Johann Kaspar Mertz, and these two composer/guitarists remained paradigmatic figures for America's guitar community into the late teens. During his New York years, Foden published not only many of his guitar compositions, but also his two-volume *Grand Method for Guitar* (1921). In tracking the publication record of his works in the BMG magazines (principally through advertisements or promotional blurbs), one gets the impression that Foden's publishing ventures never fully satisfied him. While his method and many of his solos were issued by commercial music publishing houses, some of his most famous compositions were self-published, often promoted as available by subscription only. Among these was his set of variations on "Sextette from Lucia di Lammermoor," which the composer promoted as "the most wonderful Guitar Solo published," offering it by subscription only at the astronomical price of $10. Despite Foden's insistent advertisements, it appears that only the composer himself ever performed the piece in public. While Foden had little apparent success making his "Lucia" variations a popular piece with other players, his advertisement for it clearly identified what American guitarists and audiences looked for in a professional guitar solo: "The Great Sextette from Lucia is the most wonderful Guitar Solo published. Ten pages of instruction are contained in this beautiful arrangement. Passages in single and double notes. Tremolo for one, two and three fingers, arpeggios, cadenzas. All positions marked, fingerings for both hands fully indicated." This advertisement describes not only Foden's compositional style (discussed in chapter 5) but also the expectations American audiences and critics had for early-century professional guitarists. They expected a familiar tune (an arrangement), virtuoso technical fireworks (passage work, tremolos, arpeggios, and cadenzas), and a rational, explicable relation to current pedagogy ("ten pages of instruction," often little more than clear position and finger indications).[5]

For America's BMG community, the true musician was the player who could set and perform an elevated classical work (operatic or orchestral) on the guitar while honoring the composer's original harmonies and voice-leading. Such skills demonstrated a sophisticated understanding of the technical possibilities and limits of the guitar as well as an appreciation of some of the finer points of the rules of harmony and counterpoint. The BMG community, despite its hopes and pretensions, remained generally unsophisticated in musical matters, appreciating such arrangements for their mimicry of the original, but even more enthusiastically acclaiming the pyrotechnic skills demanded by the arranger/performers' variations. Foden remained this country's most acclaimed guitarist by fulfilling such expectations as a sophisticated performer and knowledgeable arranger.

Although his publishing ventures met with only moderate success, Foden worked hard to consolidate his role as America's most revered guitarist. As noted above, he wrote a column for *Cadenza* for several years in the mid-teens. In early 1917, however, Foden switched allegiance and became a monthly columnist for *Cadenza*'s crosstown rival *Crescendo*. Foden's stewardship of "The Guitarists Round Table" lasted until March 1927, an impressive run; as he noted in his farewell column, "for the past ten years, my monthly column has appeared in it without a single miss."[6] His subjects included not only technical matters and Big Trio tours but also arcane historical subjects. While the tone of his historical and theoretical articles ranged between dry and pedantic, the columns that show him at his best were responses to readers' technical questions. Foden became almost effusive when writing about right-hand "Touch and Tone," a subject he covered not only in *Crescendo* but also in earlier *Cadenza* columns and in his method. He devoted several columns to aspects of right-hand technique, especially the stroke or articulation of the strings, a technique he thought "still seems to be misunderstood, or, at least is vague, to most amateurs, and to some professionals."

Numerous columns dealt with subjects he chose ("Temperaments," "Hebraic Instruments," "Jongleurs, Minnesingers and Meistersingers") and reflect his serious, almost academic bent. Foden undoubtedly gleaned the content of such esoteric articles from dictionaries, encyclopedias, and contemporary musical treatises, and these articles offer little information about America's BMG community. One can only surmise the bemused response to such erudite topics by a magazine readership that still requested advice about steel or gut strings or the use of open "Spanish" tuning.

More importantly, however, these articles highlight a role Foden strove to play within the BMG community. Having been recognized since the first decade of the century as America's foremost guitar performer and composer, Foden attempted through his columns in *Cadenza* and especially *Crescendo* to consolidate his roles into one—America's foremost authority on the guitar. The byline of his earlier *Cadenza* columns had identified Foden simply as "Virtuoso." When he assumed *Crescendo*'s "Guitarists Round Table," however, his appellation expanded to "Virtuoso, Composer and Historian." Foden's method book, extensive theoretical articles in *Cadenza*, and wide-ranging historical articles in *Crescendo*, together with his acclaimed performances and significant compositional output, stand as an impressive oeuvre that united the creative, technical, and scholarly aspects of the early-twentieth-century guitar world in America. Foden, ever the technician, reflected contemporary ideology in his drive to rationalize the world of the guitar and to demonstrate his control of this world. Foden's predilection to consider music more a business than an art has been noted in his biography. More significantly, his approach to the instrument, its technique, and its history reflected a nineteenth-century mind very much attuned to a scientific and technological methodology that strove not just to understand the world but to control it.[7]

Foden's long disquisitions about the minutiae of technical subjects—especially right-hand technique, touch, and tone control—indicate that he, perhaps more than any other American guitarist, could have best appreciated the significant technical developments occurring in Europe in the early decades of the twentieth century. His preoccupation with tone quality and description of an oblique stroke with the "sides or corners" of the fingers conform generally to techniques developed and taught later throughout the twentieth century.[8] Nonetheless, when presented with a new development in right-hand technique—the *apoyando* or rest stroke—Foden dismissed it in a *Crescendo* column as "not of sufficient value to spend any time on." Despite his active embrace of Europe's earlier masters, their music, and techniques, Foden's quick and negative appraisal of a new European approach to the guitar points up his strong ties

Ethel Lucretia Olcott, aged 19. (*American Music Journal*)

to the nineteenth century and his inherently conservative attitudes. As will be seen in a later chapter, it fell to Foden's student, George C. Krick, to bring the changes in technique and repertoire to the attention of America's guitarists.[9]

When Foden first achieved national recognition with his 1904 Carnegie Hall appearance, he was forty-four years old, a member of a generation firmly based in the values and traditions of the mid-nineteenth century. That same year a nineteen-year-old who was to prove Foden's closest competitor for the role of America's premiere guitarist made her first appearance in the BMG magazines. Ethel Lucretia Olcott (1885–1980) was born in Sandusky, Ohio, but by the mid-1890s her family had settled in the Los Angeles area, where she began her guitar studies at age eight or nine. As an adolescent, Olcott played for Manuel Y. Ferrer, the noted California guitarist and teacher, who invited her to live with his family in the San Francisco area. She worked with Ferrer for about a year, but his sudden death in 1904 ended her formal studies. A busy performer from her youth, Olcott concertized in the Los Angeles area, presenting recitals that featured her as a solo guitarist. Although most reports document her West Coast activity, she appears to have attended the 1906 convention of the American Guild of Banjoists, Mandolinists and Guitarists held in Springfield, Massachusetts, where she met multi-instrumentalist, ensemble director, and pedagogue Myron Bickford (1876–1961). Drawn to each other musically and personally, the two apparently created a scandal at the convention because Bickford had a wife and family in Springfield.[10]

Olcott returned to the West Coast, touring as a soloist and director of a women's ensemble, La Bandurria Guitar Trio. Her recital notices identified her as a player with an advanced technique as well as a new sense of programming. Olcott's importance as a performer in the early decades of the twentieth century derived not only from the frequency with which she performed and the literature she played, but also from the type of recital she presented to the public. Prior to 1915, when she and Myron Bickford began playing steadily as a duo, many of Olcott's performances were solo recitals or recitals in which her solo guitar worked dominated. Although other guitarists had been heard in solo recital formats, Olcott-Bickford's insistent use of this format as a young performer put her in the vanguard of the BMG community and contributed to a change in expectations for the American guitarist.[11]

While operatic arrangements dominated many of Olcott-Bickford's programs, she expanded the range of American concert repertoire to include music by Fernando Sor as well as new works by the contemporary Spaniard Francisco Tárrega (1852–1909). She regularly offered solos from the mid-nineteenth century by Mertz, Ferranti, and Legnani on her programs, but also performed pieces by late-century and contemporary player/composers like Ferrer, Romero, and Foden. Her contemporaries recognized her contributions, too, and a 1917 biographical sketch in *Cadenza* reflects how the BMG community regarded her: "Though much younger than other guitar soloists before the public, it is said that she has appeared in more cities and states and has given more complete recitals than any other guitarist. . . . It is doubtful if any guitarist before the public has a more extensive repertoire than Miss Olcott . . . since she has at her immediate command practically the entire literature of masterpieces for the guitar of all schools."[12]

The long-distance relationship with Bickford became permanent when Olcott toured the Eastern United States in 1914. That year she moved back to her native Ohio, teaching and performing there with Bickford. They married in 1915 and soon settled in New York City to perform and teach. In addition to their musical activities the Bickfords closely followed astrology, and in New York each adopted a new name appropriate to these interests. Ethel Lucretia became Vahdah Olcott-Bickford and her husband added Zarh to his moniker. Unlike most women in the BMG community who partnered in music and marriage with men, Olcott-Bickford never lost her individual identity on the pages of the magazines and was only occasionally identified as "Mrs. Bickford."[13]

The Bickfords were masters of promotion and maintained high profiles in New York and in the BMG magazines. He had been an active contributor to the magazines for years; her first articles appeared in *The American Music Journal* as early as 1906. Each sustained a regular presence in the magazines with letters, articles, concert programs, and columns. These included such items as a photograph of themselves costumed as gypsies for their musical roles in the production of a Shakespeare play or Olcott-Bickford's reports of her work as the live-in guitar instructor (and perhaps astrologer) for the Vanderbilt family in the late teens and early twenties. Her early articles and concert programs especially set the stage for Olcott-Bickford's role as a guitar authority in her later monthly columns, first in *Crescendo* (1912–17 and 1927–29) and then in *Cadenza* (1916–22). When she took responsibility for "The Guitarist" in *Cadenza*, she highlighted her position in America's guitar community, adding the title "Premiere Guitariste" to her byline.[14]

In both of her columns Olcott-Bickford created a forum for guitarists that treated a broad range of subjects with musical maturity, sincere enthusiasm, and professional authority. Her authority derived not just from her training under a revered master but also from her extensive experience as a touring concert artist and a dedicated teacher. Olcott-Bickford's columns were significant because they brought the discussion of the guitar in America's BMG periodicals into the twentieth century. She clearly respected, played, and taught works from early eras, but she chastised teachers who unquestioningly handed on inadequately written "heart-rending 'parlor pieces.'" Unlike some progressive critics who rejected old music primarily because it was old, Olcott-Bickford embraced all well-written music, citing works by Bach, Haydn, Beethoven, and Giuliani as examples. At the same time, she encouraged teachers and players to search out the new "progressive" pieces as well as the master works of Mertz and Ferranti. When questioned about studies and methods, Olcott-Bickford suggested exercises by early-nineteenth-century guitarists like Carulli, Carcassi, Sor, and Giuliani as well as Justin Holland's more recent American method (1874). Olcott-Bickford respected the guitar music of earlier eras for the musical and technical foundation it provided but still looked to contemporary players and composers to create an appropriate modern repertoire. Both Zarh Bickford and Olcott-Bickford composed works for the guitar, mostly small and lightweight works suitable for student performances. Olcott-Bickford aggressively promoted her husband's "Concerto Romantico," a large work for guitar and piano written for her, as a prime example of a well-composed modern piece, though it achieved little recognition outside of her columns. Like so many BMG advocates, Olcott-Bickford's calls for a new repertoire were grounded in the spirit of progressive modernism. In that spirit, she eventually produced her own method in 1921, arguing in its foreword that "it has been a matter of regret among progressive teachers of the guitar that there is no method before the public which is a truly thorough, musicianly method, other than the various 'editions' of the Carcassi Method or some few other methods of the masters. . . . The style in guitar playing now is *not* that of the time of Carcassi and Carulli, though many of their studies are still *invaluable*." Her *Method* includes a number of original

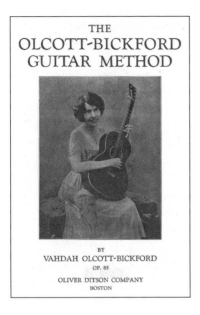

THE
OLCOTT-BICKFORD
GUITAR METHOD

BY
VAHDAH OLCOTT-BICKFORD
OP. 85

OLIVER DITSON COMPANY
BOSTON

Vahdah Olcott-Bickford from the cover
of her method book. *The Olcott-Bickford
Guitar Method* (Boston, 1921)

compositions and arrangements by both Bickfords but includes a greater number of studies and exercises by Carcassi, Sor, Giuliani, Carulli, Mertz, and others. Like so many BMG advocates who wrapped themselves in the progressive banner, Olcott-Bickford neither articulated what the modern and progressive guitar repertoire or techniques might be nor did she explain where they differed from those of the nineteenth century.[15]

On the other hand, Olcott-Bickford did articulate her expectations for the modern guitarist. As noted in chapter 5, Olcott-Bickford strenuously argued that technique alone did not make a musician. For her, musical competency demanded quality sound, good taste, and musical intelligence coupled with technical accomplishment. "It is the personal opinion of this writer that too many of our guitarists have aimed for a showy technic as the acme of perfected art, that too many of them have relied on mere digital dexterity. . . . [Guitarists] will have to play a grade of music that is worthy of the instrument at its best, and such as their contemporaries on the violin or piano would be glad to play. They will also have to bring to these numbers the richness and beauty of tonal quality of which the instrument is capable, and charming and expressive interpretation." She devoted an entire column to the subject of "Musicianship Versus Technic," and in an earlier column she snidely noted: "Anyone with average intelligence and persistence to practice can acquire digital dexterity that is amazing, granting they aim for finger-dexterity above all things in music. In fact, people of inferior intelligence have been able by years of constant practice to astound people with their mastery of the mechanics of their instrument." Olcott-Bickford assumed in the professional guitarist a formidable technique based on the foundational work of the earliest generations of players and teachers. Additionally, she required that this player put his or her technique at the service of the art of music, expressively interpreting music from a range of periods and styles as the composers indicated. Olcott-Bickford was calling, in fact, for a new breed of guitarists/musicians.[16]

When asked to identify some of this new breed of player, Olcott-Bickford demurred, turning to the previous generation. In response to a query about the country that "possesses the greatest number of good guitar soloists," she put Spain and the United States at the top of the list. She listed the most prominent players of each country, identifying Francisco Tárrega and her own teacher, Manuel Y. Ferrer, as the greatest of the "modern masters" for each country, despite the fact that Tárrega had been dead eight years and Ferrer thirteen. Other Americans noted in her response were Justin Holland, Luis T. Romero, and Charles de Janon. Olcott-Bickford recognized Holland for his pedagogy, and Romero and de Janon for their playing and composing. These were the only American guitarists she listed.

Olcott-Bickford pointedly overlooked William Foden, regarded by many in the BMG community at that time as America's most important guitarist. In fact, these two guitarists—the most important American players and apologists for the guitar in the first half of the twentieth century—virtually ignored each other on the pages of the BMG magazines. Despite their similar work for the periodicals; their concert appearances for the American Guild of Banjoists, Mandolinists and Guitarists; the proximity of their names in advertisements and articles; and their choice of the New York metropolitan area as home, neither William Foden nor Vahdah Olcott-Bickford acknowledged each other in their columns. Olcott-Bickford had occasionally performed works by Foden very early in her career and even listed two of his pieces in an early article on repertoire, but she never recognized him as one of America's notable guitarists. Her unceasing critique of the merely "mechanically dexterous" player may well have been meant or taken as an attack on Foden and his approach to the instrument. Zarh Myron Bickford offered a cryptic evaluation of Foden in his "Problem Prober" column, an estimation with which his wife undoubtedly agreed. Responding to a reader's question about guitarists active in the teens, Bickford ignored Foden's work as a performer and composer, noting that Foden had been a prominent teacher in St. Louis for many years and continued in that role in New York. In light of Olcott-Bickford's words, her husband's estimation of Foden—"one of the greatest guitar technicians of the present day"—reads as damning praise. Clearly, the Bickfords saw themselves on the progressive side of a yawning divide that separated them from the old guard, personified by Foden.[17]

Although William Foden continued to be identified as America's premiere guitarist, Olcott-Bickford certainly challenged his standing. In addition to her solo work, she and her husband regularly performed duets for mandolin and guitar and piano and guitar. *Crescendo* also documented Olcott-Bickford's pioneering efforts to extend the guitarist's repertoire through nineteenth-century chamber music. In the early 1920s, Olcott-Bickford played with string quartets (nearly all involving her husband, a violist as well as mandolinist and pianist), presenting works by Mauro Giuliani and Niccolò Paganini.[18]

While not the only American guitarist involved in chamber music, Olcott-Bickford was probably the most visible. Her high-profile chamber work supported the traditional BMG goal of increasing the status of plectral instruments in America's wider musical culture. The association of the guitar with elite chamber ensembles, especially string trios and quartets, enhanced its cultivated cachet and brought it to the attention of a wider classical music audience. Olcott-Bickford's performances of chamber works by Paganini, Boccherini, and others encouraged guitar apologists to recall the guitar's long association with the finest of Europe's prized composers. For the BMG community the guitar's appearance on the same platform as a string quartet transcended any other setting for the instrument, while even polite nods from classical critics or a refined audience validated its worth as a legitimate instrument.

At the same time, despite commitments to the American BMG gospel by many guitar apologists (including Olcott-Bickford), advocacy of chamber music performances encouraged their guitarist/readers to return to the guitar's European roots, abandoning America's mandolin and banjo ensembles. Such performances helped widen the split between popular and elite music by defining refined European chamber music as the realm of the real musician and the goal of all serious guitarists. Such advocacy encouraged American guitarists, amateur and professional, to see themselves more as members of a worldwide guitar community grounded in Europe's traditions and less a part of America's progressive BMG community, tied to the mandolin orchestra. This elite–popular divide, coupled with the Old World–New World split, contributed to a redefinition of the guitar and its role in American music-making. Although devoted to American musical culture, Olcott-Bickford's chamber music activity helped point up these musical and cultural divides.

As might be expected of musicians who promoted themselves as up-to-date, the Bickfords spent time in the recording studio in the 1920s. Their first two sides on the ZarVah label were announced in *Crescendo* late in 1921 and quickly were followed by four more releases early in 1922. The recordings, featuring Zarh's compositions and Vahdah's arrangements, consist principally of duets. While Olcott-Bickford's playing is generally clean, she comes across as a bit stilted, perhaps intimidated by the studio technology or trying too hard to make everything perfect. As would be expected, the sound is somewhat thin and does not hold up particularly well when compared with recordings from even a few years later. Nonetheless, few, if any, other commercial recordings of American guitar soloists survive from this period and, despite their limitations, these recordings stand as an important artifacts of the era.

In 1923 the Bickfords left New York for Los Angeles, where she continued her activities on behalf of America's guitar community as a performer, arranger, teacher, and musical authority. Zarh established important contacts in the movie studios and a later observer has noted that anytime a mandolin or banjo was heard in a Hollywood movie from the late 1920s and 1930s, one of the Bickfords was undoubtedly playing.

Despite her mandolin playing and forays with the ukulele, Olcott-Bickford's instrument remained the guitar and she devoted herself to its promotion. *Cadenza* had ceased publication in 1924; Olcott-Bickford remained a persistent presence in *Crescendo* even though she had no official capacity with it, submitting reports about her performances and her publications as well as articles about a variety of guitar-related matters. Even when she reprised her role as a featured columnist for *Crescendo* (1927–29), Olcott-Bickford often contributed long articles in addition to her monthly column. Her contributions ranged from items as diverse as an article titled "Fairy Music for Guitar" to both a letter and an article decrying the BMG community's focus on music as a business.[19]

Olcott-Bickford's most important contribution to America's guitar community in these years was her creation of the American Guitar Society (AGS) in Los Angeles in late 1924. By the middle of 1925 announcements about the activities of the organization ran in *Crescendo* almost monthly. These announcements included details about AGS meetings and performances as well as Society publications (all edited, arranged, or composed by Olcott-Bickford). In 1925 Olcott-Bickford instituted a unique series of lecture-recitals, each focusing on the works of one guitarist/composer. Some programs featured well-known guitarists like Fernando Carulli and Leonard de Call, while others presented the works of obscure historical figures like Franz Bathioli and Francesco Calegari and the contemporary master Heinrich Albert.[20] These programs often reflected Olcott-Bickford's interest in chamber music by including ensemble pieces as well as solo works. In fact, after her move to Los Angeles she became even more active in chamber music, joining the Zoellner String Quartet in 1924 for performances of works by Luigi Boccherini and Paganini. In 1926 Olcott-Bickford offered *Crescendo* readers a long article on the use of the guitar in ensembles, devoting several paragraphs to the guitar with bowed strings and flute, among other combinations. In 1928 she extended this subject into the past with a rambling three-part explication of the guitar's history as a chamber instrument.[21]

In the late 1920s Olcott-Bickford reported that she had taken up the lute. Nearly all guitar apologists of this period subscribed to an evolutionary history for the lute and guitar, understanding the guitar to be the hardy, surviving descendant of the lute. Olcott-Bickford's 1928 serial article "The Guitar in the History of Chamber Music" stands as a particularly good example of this point of view, with her historical elision of the medieval and renaissance lute into the guitar. Despite her recognition of the guitar as the more developed instrument, Olcott-Bickford acquired a "fine old Elizabethan lute of rare beauty," using it to accompany a vocalist in a 1928 recital and performing Bach on it in 1930. Through that year, Olcott-Bickford played this instrument in a variety of settings including radio broadcasts with a vocalist "who sang fascinating old French songs," playing lute duets with her husband, as well as a performance with the Burbank Symphony Orchestra of an arrangement of a Palestrina work for vocal quartet and lutes. The following year she identified herself on a program as "guitarist and lutist," performing Heinrich Albert's "Suite for Lute in C" and several movements from his "Suite in Olden Style." In a *Crescendo* featuring a cover portrait of Olcott-Bickford with her lute, an article declared her "America's Only Lute Exponent." This magazine cover showed a hybrid instrument with a lute's body and a guitar's six-string bridge and frets embedded in the fingerboard. A carved headstock resembling that of a viola da gamba fitted with mechanical tuners completed this "old-new" instrument. Neither lute nor guitar, this instrument was especially popular in the German "Wandervogel" movement between the wars.[22]

The Bickfords maintained active careers in Los Angeles. In the fall of 1927 Olcott-Bickford noted that, in addition to their work with the American Guitar Society, both she and her husband taught at the Zoellner Conservatory. He also played with the Burbank Symphony Orchestra and coached instrumental ensembles at the University of Southern California. In the early 1930s both Bickfords wrote for the *Serenader*, a BMG journal published in Sioux City, Iowa. Olcott-Bickford promoted her American Guitar Society in the *Serenader* and in 1932 she announced that the periodical had become the official organ of the Society. The magazine included accounts of meetings and promotions for her publications from the Society. Only a few of Olcott-Bickford's articles for the *Serenader* survive; but they pick up where she left off in *Crescendo*, defending the traditional six-string guitar against hybrid instruments and decrying the popularity of jazz.[23]

Despite a significant number of women involved in BMG ensembles and a large number of female teachers, men led America's BMG community. Olcott-Bickford's amazing success and notoriety within the male-dominated BMG world rested principally on her reputation as a performer and her incessant public activity on behalf of the guitar, an activity that kept her constantly in the BMG community's eye. But her success derived as well from her creation and promotion of a public image that not only tied her closely to the guitar but also embodied specific cultural themes about the guitar and women musicians. Conventional attitudes within the BMG community would have assigned to Olcott-Bickford the natural (female) emotions and sensitivity that allowed her to appreciate and highlight the guitar's expressive nature. Indeed, in her numerous articles, columns, and letters, Olcott-Bickford often challenged the BMG community's valorization of technique, attacking technically brilliant but dry playing. She touted the guitar's expressive nature, regularly reminding guitarists of their responsibility to play with emotion and expression. Her insistent promotion of the expressive capabilities of the guitar aligned Olcott-Bickford with the perceived sensual, feminine side of music-making, opposing her to a more masculine, scientific, and technical approach.[24]

But her image as a guitarist extended beyond such essentialist conventions as a gender-based attention to musical expression. In her biographical sketches and columns, Olcott-Bickford tied herself to a past generation and to the Spanish roots of the guitar through her studies with Manuel Ferrer, a relationship depicted as an act of musical adoption. Despite her midwestern roots and Anglo heritage, this adoption positioned her to inherit Ferrer's Spanish mantle. This connection reinforced her emphatic calls for musically expressive playing by associating her with a people regularly portrayed as emotional and expressive musicians. Olcott-Bickford wore this Latin mantle well, in one case outplaying a contingent of foreign guitarists to win a gold medal in a New York competition.[25]

Olcott-Bickford's connection to Latin players and musical expression was only one means of emphasizing the exotic nature of the guitar. Her astrological activities (including her star-guided name change), coupled with her discussions of "fairy music" for the guitar, reinforced the idea of the guitar as an exotic instrument. Her adoption of the lute linked her to an ancient mythical era. Olcott-Bickford had a penchant for the dramatic and employed various methods to emphasize the exotic nature of her instrument and her role in its promotion, including the emotional, racial, sensual, and mythic associations of the guitar.[26]

Olcott-Bickford's emergence in the early years of the twentieth century coincided with the appearance W. L. Hudson's BMG girls on *Cadenza*'s cover. It would be farfetched to suggest that one was modeled on the other, but in many ways Olcott-Bickford embodied the attributes of the Hudson girls. She was a modern woman, and articles, biographical sketches, and photographs in the BMG magazines reinforced this status by emphasizing her perky self-confidence, direct and friendly gaze, and fashionable dress. Olcott-Bickford exuded a girlish enthusiasm and charm, characteristics that appealed to male readers or listeners and inspired females.[27] Her work took place outside the home, dissociating her from past expectations of women to contribute to the well-being of her home and family. In this period of societal and cultural transition, Olcott-Bickford not only embraced new roles for women but also personified these significant changes for the BMG community.

Olcott-Bickford has been recognized in the years since her death in 1980 as an important figure in America's classical guitar world, principally for her work with the American Guitar Society. She still stands behind William Foden, however, whose reputation as a performer, pedagogue, and composer have marked him as America's *only* guitarist from the 1880s to his death in the 1940s. That she is remembered principally for her work as a supportive and nurturing figure ("The Grand Lady of the Guitar") and he for his technical accomplishments ("The Wizard of the Guitar") may perhaps be yet another demonstration of the conventional gender-specific roles assigned to men and women in the BMG movement.

A close reading of the extant BMG periodicals indicates, however, that until the arrival of Andres Segovia and other European guitarists, Olcott-Bickford and Foden shared the BMG spotlight on the pages of *Cadenza* and *Crescendo* as America's foremost guitarists and guitar authorities. Foden's position rested on his realization of the precepts of "scientific music" as a virtuoso performer, composer, articulate pedagogue, and informed historian. During the teens and twenties, members of the BMG community recognized Olcott-Bickford as an equally accomplished performer, pedagogue, and historian. Although she received less notice for her original compositions, her numerous arrangements and anthologies were well-publicized and probably competed well with Foden's compositions in sales.

Despite Ronald Purcell's biographical work on her behalf, Olcott-Bickford remains a curiosity in the history of the guitar in America, noted principally for her astrological activities and her more outlandish pronouncements ("Fairy Music for Guitar"). That she was capable of challenging Foden, twenty-five years her senior and firmly established as America's premier guitarist long before her first notice in the magazines, indicates that her posthumous reputation recognizes little of the ambition, drive, and savvy manipulation of her public image displayed in the BMG journals. Olcott-Bickford stood shoulder to shoulder with Foden on the pages of *Cadenza* and *Crescendo* and in the eyes of much of the BMG community. She accomplished this remarkable climb to the top of the BMG world in part by creating and maintaining a public persona and image that played on the BMG community's expectations of the guitar and a woman. She combined her role as a female musician (expressive, sensual, mysterious, and nurturing) with the positive aspects of the guitar (emotionally and musically expressive, intimate, exotic, and charming), essentially embodying the instrument for the BMG community.

William Foden's overwhelming technical mastery of his instrument served as an awe-inspiring model for America's guitarists, a confirmation that the instrument and its music were as musically sophisticated and technically demanding as any other elite instrument or repertoire. Vahdah Olcott-Bickford's sensitivity, artistic flair, and enthusiasm confirmed for the same guitarists that their instrument met the highest aesthetic standards of America's musical culture. Despite their undisputed primacy as America's foremost guitarists at the start of the twentieth century, however, neither Foden nor Olcott-Bickford could successfully negotiate the new topography of America's musical culture, especially as it related to the guitar. As America's highbrow/lowbrow split widened to a cultural chasm, musicians like Foden and Olcott-Bickford found themselves marginalized. While the guitar gradually eclipsed the banjo and mandolin in the United States, it was not the gut-strung classical guitar championed by these two BMG heroes but the steel-strung plectrum guitar. The next chapter documents the final challenge to the BMG community in which Foden and Olcott-Bickford flourished: a new generation of European guitarists led by Miguel Llobet and Andres Segovia.

Chapter Nine

THE OLD WORLD RECLAIMS ITS INSTRUMENT

For much of the BMG era, players had prided themselves on their ability to play several (if not many) of the plectral instruments, but through the teens other BMG promoters followed Vahdah Olcott-Bickford's lead, encouraging musicians to focus their energies on one instrument.[1] This specialization eventually extended to the multiple forms of the guitar, and although some American guitarists played both classical and plectrum guitar, by the mid-1920s the two instruments and their repertoires were recognized within the BMG community as distinct. This divide between plectrum players with steel-strung guitars and fingerpicking classical guitarists with gut-strung instruments mirrored the growing chasm between the popular and elite American audiences. As plectrum guitarists increasingly turned to the American vernacular of jazz and popular music, classical guitarists remained committed to a nineteenth-century technique and musical sensibility.

The BMG journals document not only the classical players' rejection of jazz and jazz-inflected popular music but also their increased exposure to the influence of European guitarists. As early as 1908 European players offered America's BMG community a glimpse of the guitar's future, when Spanish guitarist Arturo Santos presented a New York audience with a solo program that included arrangements of Haydn, Schubert, and Puccini as well as original works for guitar by Mertz and Francisco Tárrega. While his performance created little apparent stir, *Crescendo* noted not only his technique but also the special effects of modern Spanish guitar music: "Senor Santos is undoubtedly one of the world's great guitarists. His technique is marvelous and in his rendition of some of the Spanish pieces he produces various effects which probably have never been heard in this country before."[2]

Four years later another Spanish virtuoso provided a select American audience notice that Santos's recital had not been an isolated event. Miguel Llobet's hastily organized and informal appearance in Boston in 1912 registered a bemused respect from *Cadenza*'s staff. A notice of the performance observed that something very special had occurred, but the reporter appeared incapable of identifying it precisely:

> Between "incident" and "event" there really is a broad differentiation. The first may effectively color the trend of life, thought or action, but the second effectually changes it. To hear a virtuoso exploit on an instrument is an intellectual incident, while to listen to a king of virtuosi disclosing the hidden secrets of the same instrument becomes a revealing event, and revelation is the unseen boundary line of intellectuality. . . . Mr. Paul Eno of Philadelphia was in Boston on Monday, October 7th, and . . . presented Senor Miguel Llobet, a Spanish guitarist on his way from Chili [*sic*] to France, who graciously played three solos for a small audience of invited guests. To treat of Senor Llobet's performance technically would be criticism trite and effete, though perhaps an easy way out. But to tell of his perfect tonal production, wonderful dynamics, confusing rapidity of execution and strange and bizarre effects would be well nigh impossible. Suffice it to say, that to The Cadenza it was an event, if not an epoch.[3]

Members of *Crescendo*'s staff also attended this recital and attempted to explain what they had seen and heard:

> Signor Llobet played three times, the third number being one of his own compositions, a Spanish fantasia. He is undoubtedly a great artist. His command of the instrument is wonderful. His fingers, being long and tapering, are particularly adapted to the instrument and his command of the fingerboard is very remarkable. In the Fantasia he gave an exhibition of left hand playing which was the finest piece of work of this kind we have ever heard. He played intricate runs, harmonic effects and chords entirely with the left hand. In this piece he also introduced right hand harmonics. Of course he played a guitar with gut strings as all good guitarists do, and he has a peculiar faculty of using the vibrato with the left hand in such a way that the guitar tone carried more than is usual with many of the soloists. His interpretation was musicianly. . . . He shows more temperament than most guitar soloists and he undoubtedly ranks on the guitar as does Kubelik on the violin. He is a wonderful performer, a complete master of brilliant technic and a thorough musician.[4]

At the end of that same month, Llobet offered a more formal recital in Philadelphia, presenting a select audience impressive renditions of original solo works by Napoleon Coste, Fernando Sor, Francisco Tárrega, and Llobet himself, as well as his own arrangements of Bach, Beethoven, and Chopin.[5] Llobet's brief appearance in America may have mystified some auditors, but others in the BMG community undoubtedly recognized a different approach to the guitar, in which virtuoso technique supported an elegant and expressive musicianship. Over twenty-five years later, George C. Krick (who attended Llobet's Philadelphia performance) observed:

> Before Llobet came upon the scene the guitar was heard frequently in concert halls, but failed to attract the general musical public, neither did the music critics think it worth while to attend a guitar recital. The remarkable technic and rare musicianship displayed by Llobet brought about a change in their attitude toward the guitar and it was his rendition of the classics that convinced everyone within his hearing that this instrument was capable of producing musical effects that equaled, and in some instances surpassed, those one is accustomed to associate with the violin, piano or violoncello.[6]

The BMG periodicals do not document a direct impact on American guitarists by Llobet's appearance, but later that same year Ethel Lucretia Olcott not only called for more modern music on American guitar recitals but also included Tárrega's cutting-edge "Capricho Arabe" on a program.[7] From her bully pulpit as a regular columnist first for *Crescendo* and then for *Cadenza*, Olcott championed both a new repertoire and a new sort of performer:

> [I]t is sad but true that a large number of professionals are mechanical musicians only . . . for they might be a clever technicians [*sic*] and understand their instrument well, as far as the pure mechanical goes. They may understand theory and be wizards of pyrotechnics. All this does not make them true musicians. To be a true musician one must have the mechanics, the theory and **more** . . . Cultivate a splendid technic merely for the purpose of better expressing your music. . . . If ever any instrument was created for the soul qualities in music, the guitar is one of them. . . . Study for a technic that is adequate to play satisfactorily the compositions of the masters of the instruments, but **do** not make technic your goal.[8]

As described in Chapter 5, Olcott's comments from 1914 directly challenge the old order represented by America's most famous guitar virtuoso, William Foden. Her carefully chosen words could refer only to Foden, whose advice columns in *Cadenza* in the early teens often focused on the basics of music theory and whose astounding technique had earned him the nickname "The Wizard of the Guitar."

In this period, Olcott slowly moved toward a new repertoire that demanded an excellent technique in support of expressive music-making rather than pyrotechnic showboating. She also looked to Europe for new repertoire, incorporating other works and arrangements by Tárrega as well as solos by the Spaniard Julian Arcas (1832–1882) and the Pole J. N. de Bobrowicz (1805–after 1857) into her programs.[9] Her gradual adoption of this new solo repertoire and her activity as a chamber player seemed to offer the BMG community a new model of a professional classical guitarist, but despite her calls for new works, after her marriage most of Olcott-Bickford's new repertoire was penned by her husband, while her chamber repertoire reflected a growing interest in nineteenth-century composers.

It fell to George C. Krick (1872–1962), William Foden's most accomplished student, to introduce America's BMG community to the significant activity in Europe's guitar circles of the teens and twenties. A native of Germany, Krick came to the United States in his late teens. In 1924, Krick returned to Europe for a three-month visit, much of it spent in Germany, and late that year *Crescendo* ran Krick's report of his trip, "The Mandolin and Guitar in Europe." The bulk of this article reflected the interests of America's BMG movement, focusing on the growing popularity of the mandolin in Germany. Of greater historical significance, however, Krick documented the domination of the European guitar scene by three Spaniards: Miguel Llobet (1878–1938), Emilio Pujol (1886–1980), and Andres Segovia (1893–1987). He reported the Munich-based German Guitar Society's efforts to promote the guitar to wider public audiences by scheduling concerts across Europe for the Italian Luigi Mozzani (1869–1943) as well as Llobet and Segovia. "In November and December there will be thirty recitals by Llobet, and the same number by Segovia in the largest German cities, and these two guitarists have been acclaimed by the press and public for their wonderful performances. I am told that at the last Segovia recital in Munich scenes were enacted only comparable to a Paderewski or Kreisler recital,—people refused to leave the hall until Segovia played a dozen encores after his regular program."

Krick's column, the first notice of Andres Segovia in a BMG periodical, set the tone for *Crescendo*'s enthusiastic reportage of the Spaniard's activities. Just as earlier American auditors had heard something special in the playing of Llobet, Krick observed a different approach to the instrument by guitarists he heard in Europe. He closed his article with a call to American players that echoed Olcott-Bickford's earlier words: "In conclusion, I would like to mention one more impression gathered listening to some of the soloists, something for our ambitious guitarists and mandolinists to ponder over: in Europe today technique is accepted as a matter of course; musicianship and individuality in the rendition of a program are the qualities that count with the audience, and distinguish the artist from the player." [10]

Krick's reports became a regular column and established him as America's foremost expert on European guitar music. By early 1925, he had parlayed his European musical connections into a business venture, offering the BMG community direct access to the new music of Europe as well as the works of earlier generations and American favorites. Although Krick's advertisement ran in *Crescendo* on the same page as William Foden's "Guitarists Round Table" column, Foden's name eventually disappeared from the list of modern composers whose music his former student sold. The only American composer to remain on Krick's list was Manuel Ferrer, still remembered as an American composer/guitarist "of pure Spanish heritage." By mid-1925, Messina Music of Brooklyn, New York, also offered guitarists and mandolinists solo and ensemble works from European sources. An advertisement from Messina Music in 1927 identified "a modern school" including "such outstanding figures as Segovia, Mozzani, Tárrega, Llobet, Pujol, etc, who today are feted in Europe as were their predecessors of 100 and more years ago." [11]

In the early 1920s Krick and others recognized Llobet as the guitarist most responsible for the instrument's newfound popularity in Europe. But Andres Segovia surpassed Llobet's initial predominance, eventually establishing himself as the most influential classical guitarist in Europe and the Americas. Krick's columns and other reports from Europe offered fair warning, and in the months before Segovia appeared in this country *Crescendo* ran several articles indicating that some of America's guitar apologists recognized the increased activity in Europe as a challenge to their perception of America's preeminence in the guitar and mandolin field. [12]

In 1927 Olcott-Bickford returned to the pages of *Crescendo* as a monthly columnist. The title of her first column rhetorically asked "Why Is the Guitar More Popular in Europe Than in America?" She proposed three answers to the question. First, Americans were not serious about anything difficult; second, the steel-strung Hawaiian guitar distracted potential students from serious study of the classical guitar; and third, because Europeans had more call for guitarists, more guitarists were in Europe. Olcott-Bickford offered no supporting evidence and, following the lead of many editorialists in the BMG magazines, assumed her claims to be self-evident to her readers. In response to these widely disparate challenges to America's guitarists, Olcott-Bickford proposed but one solution: membership in her American Guitar Society. Optimistically promising to hold conventions with lectures and concerts "as soon as the membership is sufficiently large," she reported that her local group was not only prepared to accept at-large members from outside Los Angeles but was also willing to "form branches all over America." [13]

Several months later, a lead editorial in *Crescendo* called for a community-wide effort to increase the guitar's popularity. Also a response to reports from Europe about the performances and popularity of Spain's celebrated guitarists, the editorial sounded a typical theme for the BMG community: the responsibility of each BMG teacher to polish his or her guitar skills, inspiring students and the public at large to take up the instrument.

It is up to every teacher, and every student as well, to demonstrate what can be done with the guitar before you can expect the multitude to "go wild over it." It is the individual effort of each teacher that counts. There is nothing that will stimulate the efforts and ambitions of a good pupil more than listening to a finished concert. . . . If everyone of us take it upon our shoulders to acquaint the public with the great beauties and advantages hidden in the guitar there can be brought about a change in the public sentiment that will again pay homage to this most beautiful of fretted instruments—the guitar.

In a prelude to this call, the anonymous author presented a typical overview of the guitar's ancient, courtly, and refined history and repertoire, including a list of past individuals associated with the guitar. His survey decried the paucity of active players capable of impressing an audience, citing as contemporary examples only the Americans William Foden, the sixty-seven-year-old technical wizard grounded in the nineteenth century, and Johnson Bane, the itinerant master of the open-string Saxton tuning. Echoing a commonly held attitude of non-guitarists in the BMG community, this contributor acknowledged that the guitar "is not more universally studied . . . because of the necessity of real hard study to master it." Despite this technical challenge, however, the author implied that every BMG teacher, with "individual effort," could master the guitar well enough to concertize and draw new students into the fold.[14]

This editorial shared the same page with another article, "Spain and the Guitar," comprised of two citations from other periodicals. The more significant citation quotes a Spanish music critic for Madrid's *El Sol*, who rhetorically wondered about Segovia's impact on their nation's music:

What will this happy appearance do for Spanish music? An artist of the first order appeared playing the guitar as his chosen instrument—the national musical instrument of Spain. We all know what Casals did on the cello; by virtue of his technique. Segovia has done as much on the guitar, and more: he has enlarged the field of expression beyond what has been produced on it before, so that in his hands it expresses every shade of feeling conceived by modern music. . . . Spanish composers of modern times have already contributed to the special literature for the guitar, and the famous Falla at their head has written a beautiful elegy which seems an example of the highest in Spanish music.[15]

Crescendo's editor undoubtedly intended these lead articles to rally America's BMG teacher/players to brush off their guitars. But the first ignored the activity in the European guitar community, holding up only two Americans who were clearly out of step with Europe's contemporary guitar masters; additionally, it reiterated typical BMG themes: an emphasis on music as a business, a fear of the guitar's technical challenges, and a promotion of the multi-instrumentalist paradigm. The second article noted that Segovia had single-handedly resuscitated Spanish music, popularizing it throughout Europe. Clearly *Crescendo's* editor wanted readers to conclude that America's BMG enthusiasts could do the same for this country's music by creating an American music for the guitar. Juxtaposed as they were, these articles attempted to rally America's BMG teachers, still principally mandolinists or banjoists, to create not just a groundswell of guitar popularity, but to inspire a new American literature for the instrument, modeled on the compositions and examples of Foden and Bane.

Together with Olcott-Bickford's passionate but self-serving call to action, these articles demonstrate the American BMG community's myopic convictions that the business-driven American model of a musical community would prevail, that American musicians stood at the pinnacle of the world's plectral community, and that the BMG multi-instrumentalist paradigm remained viable. Although Olcott-Bickford often sounded as if she were battling the commercial status quo, her call to teaching professionals to rally around the banner of her American Guitar Society confirmed her savvy recognition that the BMG community's power and influence lay in the organization of its mass-market reach through local teaching studios and music stores. In addition, these three examples from *Crescendo* underscore the American BMG community's misapprehension of the significance and the depth of the powerful Spanish-led revolution in Europe's guitar world. They confirm that, despite reports by Krick and others, many in the American BMG community had no idea what to expect when Segovia finally appeared here.

Later readers recognize that Andres Segovia's debut in New York and his subsequent American tours remain the single most important story reported in *Crescendo* in its nearly thirty years. The staff of the magazine presciently appreciated its significance, too, and gave prominence not only to a portrait of the guitarist on *Crescendo's* cover but also to a long lead article that included an extensive citation from Lawrence Gilman's January 1928 review. The cover portrait tied Segovia directly to the BMG movement by framing the guitarist with the silhouette of a mandolin orchestra. While program details, even of the best performers, were regularly shunted off to *Crescendo's* back pages or listed beside those of student ensembles in a "Programs of Concert and Recitals" column, Segovia's January 8, 1928, New York program dominated the first page of the lead article.[16]

Following this high-profile debut in *Crescendo*, Segovia's name appeared regularly that year in guitar-related articles and columns as well as in advertisements. These include readers' inquiries to the "Guitarists Round Table" as well as promotions from American music distributors offering pieces from Segovia's

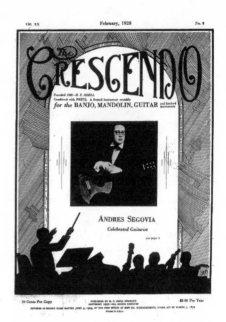

Segovia on the cover of *Crescendo* with a
BMG orchestra in the foreground.

repertoire.[17] More surprising, and more indicative of his impact within the
BMG community, non-guitarists cited his success, artistry, and repertoire as
models for all plectral players. In fact, after hearing him play, some enthusiastic fans in the BMG movement attempted to link Segovia's success with the
guitar directly to BMG movement's mandolin orchestras. As a result, when he
returned to the United States in early 1929 for a second tour, the American
Guild of Banjoists, Mandolinists and Guitarists was ready for him with "the
American Guild's first honorary membership and token." *Crescendo*, as the
Guild's official publication, featured yet another front-cover portrait of Segovia
as well as lead-story coverage of the award ceremony. This event, attended
principally by representatives from the music industry, opened with a recita-
tion of the history of the guitar and a review of Segovia's accomplishments to
that date. Following the award of a gold medal, a Guild leader outlined the
organization's history and goals, as well as its role in a new promotion of fretted instruments by the National Bureau of Music. *Crescendo*'s report noted
that the American speakers frequently referred to all fretted instruments,
while Segovia reiterated his focus on the guitar alone. Segovia's ignorance of
the American BMG movement's plethora of instruments seems to have disappointed some BMG apologists. Walter Kaye Bauer, at that time publicity director for the Guild, reported that Segovia "evidenced much interest in the future
Mrs. Bauer when informed that she was a mando-cellist." But Bauer added,
with a touch of disappointment, "[t]his instrument seems to be somewhat hazy

CRESCENDO

Founded 1908 by H. F. Odell
Combined with *Frets*

Published Monthly by the H. F. Odell Co., 157 Columbus Ave., Boston

Vol. XX   BOSTON, FEBRUARY, 1928   No. 8

ANDRES SEGOVIA
Celebrated Guitarist

FIRST, let us scan the early history of the guitar and its capability of expressing the highest musical sentiment. The guitar has an aristocratic and ancient pedigree, and according to Ernst Biernath its origin dates back to 3000 B. C. During religious ceremonies it is said that the Babylonians, Egyptians and Hebrews used instruments very similarly shaped to the guitars of today, and that the chief musician was held in high regard and esteem by the entire nation.

The guitar found its way from Asia Minor into Greece and Rome, then later to Spain, Italy and Germany. Through the Medieval Ages it continued to capture the heart of the troubadour and minnesinger, king and peasant, rich and poor, reaching the height of popularity in the nineteenth century. Garulli, Carcassi, Sor, and Giuliani showed to the music loving world the wonderful possibilities and beauty of the guitar. Such famous composers as Beethoven, Mozart, and Hayden, also played this captivating instrument, and the great Paganini wrote many remarkable duos for the guitar and violin, and performed them in concert. Today there are but a few eminent artists who can say they have appeared before the public as celebrated guitarists. Among them is Andres Segovia, who the past six or more

PROGRAMME

1. (a) Andante et Allegretto)
   (b) Thème varié .... Sor (1778-1839)
   (c) Serenata .... Malats
   (d) Danza .... Malats
   (e) Etude .... Tarrega
2. (a) Prélude
   (b) Allemande
   (c) Fugue
   (d) Courante .... J. S. Bach*
   (e) Sarabande
   (f) Gavotte
   (g) Menuet .... Haydn
3. (a) Sonatine (dedicated to A. SEGOVIA) ...... Torroba
       Allegretto   Andante   Allegro
   (b) Danza .... Granados
   (c) Legenda .... Albeniz

years has been exciting the music public of various European capitals by his guitar performances. His recitals in Paris have become a musical rage and his London debut last winter evoked lavish praise from the musical critics, one of them stated that "Here is an artist who, without doubt, stands in relation to the instrument of his choice as Casals does to the cello, or Kreisler to the violin." Senor Segovia was born in 1896 in Jaen, a small village near Granada, Spain, and has been playing as a guitar soloist, professionally, ever since he was fifteen.

On January 8 in the Town Hall, New York, he made his American debut and this first appearance will scarcely be his last, for, at Lawrence Gilman of the new York *Herald* says, "we make no bones about saying that Mr. Segovia is one of the most consummate masters of any instrument now before the public. He has made the guitar a thing to be spoken of in the same breath with the harpsichord of Landowska, the cello of Casals, the violin of Heifetz, the piano of Gieseking."

In appearance Senor Segovia exactly resembles the autographed portrait of him, painted by Miguel del Pino, a reproduction of which appears on the front cover of the Crescendo—many have suggested the likeness to Frans Schu-

(Continued on Page 8)

Page one placement of Segovia's 1928 New York concert program. (*Crescendo*)

in [Segovia's] mind." Segovia's unswerving devotion to the traditional six-string Spanish guitar was an essential part of his personal crusade and became legendary, but to representatives of an industry and community led by mandolinists and banjoists an unwillingness to share his spotlight (and his market) with these other instruments surely proved confusing if not frustrating.[18]

Despite Segovia's confusion about the mando-cello, Walter Kaye Bauer remained an enthusiastic admirer, often citing Segovia as an example for America's plectral players, especially in his choice of recital repertoire. Bauer responded positively and perceptively to the guitarist's musicianship, but also interpreted Segovia's American success as a business lesson for American musicians, acclaiming his performances of Bach as a savvy publicity maneuver:

I say, therefore, give the best music at your concerts and you will aid the mandolin orchestra in the future and incidentally help the publisher who has invested thousands of dollars in the publication of great masterpieces for these instruments. The lighter pieces can be interspersed with the heavy numbers in a judicious manner and can also be used for training purposes, but above all things give the public the best in music at your concerts. Publishers have great quantities of classics that will do this. When Andres Segovia made his sensational New York debut, he was heralded as "the virtuoso who plays Bach on the guitar." The skeptical critics saw and heard and were convinced. If this great artist had attempted to perform anything of lighter vein you can well imagine the comment of the fickle press. I call your attention also to the recent investigation conducted by the National Broadcasting Company . . . [that] determined that 85% of the radio audience wanted more high class concert music and less jazz and freak novelties.[19]

Even BMG apologists like Bauer, who appreciated the innovations of Segovia and his peers, instinctively evaluated such a musical talent based on commercial viability. At the same time, a jingoistic suspicion led many, including Bauer, to see a foreigner's American success as a public-relations ploy capitalizing on the exotic. He described Segovia and other European guitarists as "importations which always has a great influence in showmanship."[20] As a business observation, Bauer's identification of Segovia's ethnicity as a publicity tool should also be considered in light of the underlying xenophobia running through much American BMG literature. America's BMG apologists had consistently denied the African roots of the banjo and disparaged Italian and Spanish mandolinists and guitarists as dark and dangerous Latins. Such comments about ethnicity confirm that even the most open-minded of America's BMG enthusiasts remained suspicious of foreign musicians and could not easily relinquish the idea that American instruments and players were the world's best.

Many American guitarists had additional difficulty recognizing the Spaniard's impact because Segovia's repertoire differed significantly from that of America's guitar soloists, who favored virtuosic showpieces. By his 1928 American debut, Segovia's repertoire had been shaped through his constant touring. This repertoire rested on a foundation of transcriptions of suite movements by J. S. Bach, Spanish music including original pieces by Francisco Tárrega and arranged works by such Spanish nationalists as Isaac Albeniz and Enrique Granados, and new compositions written for Segovia. He augmented this foundation with transcriptions of early music for vihuela and Baroque guitar and selected works by Fernando Sor and Mauro Giuliani. Graham Wade's exhaustive examination of Segovia's repertoire documents the composition, premiere, and publication dates of many works written for the guitarist. Wade notes that Segovia's principal contributions to this new repertoire for the guitar consisted of his Bach transcriptions and the new pieces he inspired or cajoled from such composers as Manuel Ponce, Joaquin Turina, and Heitor Villa-Lobos. A list in Wade's study, documenting works edited by Segovia for publication by the German publisher Schott, includes seventeen new works written for Segovia as well as three collections of transcribed dance movements by

Bach, all published prior to his appearance in the United States. His Town Hall program, cited above, included compositions for the guitar by Fernando Sor, Francisco Tárrega, Joaquin Malats, and Federico Moreno Tórroba as well as arrangements of pieces by Bach, Haydn, Granados, and Albeniz.[21]

This program reflected developments in guitar repertoire instigated by Segovia, Llobet, and Pujol through the 1920s. These three recitalists strove to demonstrate the versatility, the historical roots, and the musical profundity of the guitar. Versatility was displayed in wide-ranging programs that crossed style periods from the sixteenth to the twentieth centuries. Transcriptions of music by sixteenth-century vihuelists such as Luis Milan and Luys de Narvaez and seventeenth-century Baroque guitarists including Robert de Visée, as well as Classical-era works by Sor and Giuliani, linked the guitar to Europe's musical past. More importantly, transcriptions of pieces by the universally recognized master Bach associated the guitar with the Baroque lute, confirming not only its historical relevance but also its musical depths. In response to a reader's question, Vahdah Olcott-Bickford endorsed Segovia's programming of Bach transcriptions, noting that Bach's music drew critics and a wider audience to guitar concerts because "to see 'the Father of Music' so well represented on a guitar program at once intrigued their interest as perhaps no other composer would have. That made them come to the concert with a different feeling of the importance of the guitar before they even heard a note,—and after they heard the fascinating way in which Segovia played the Bach numbers they had a higher opinion of the instrument, as is attested by the fact that every one of the critics dwelt especially on the Bach numbers."[22] While earlier players had occasionally programmed individual dance movements or theme and variation sets by Sor, Segovia added large-scale works, grouping dance movements by Bach as if they were suites, performing entire baroque dance suites by de Visée and, significantly, premiering newly composed extended works like Tórroba's "Sonatina" or Manuel Ponce's sonatas. Segovia's programming of these works conveyed to American listeners and critics a musical gravitas not usually associated with the guitar.

Crescendo regularly cited reviews of Segovia's concerts in articles and announcements, featuring passages that compared the guitarist and his repertoire with other musical notables such as Pablo Casals, Fritz Kreisler, or Wanda Landowska. Segovia and his contemporaries put the guitar—as other virtuosi regularly did with piano, cello, and violin—at the service of musical history and the expressive interpretation of composers' creations, drawing the attention of serious music critics and general audiences. The self-serving programs of America's best players, often comprised of virtuoso showpieces and vapid bonbons, held little weight next to Segovia's more musically substantial repertoire. America's best guitar music, Foden's theme and variation sets, stood on the cultural, aesthetic, musical, and technical values of the mid-nineteenth century. Segovia and his peers brought a new aesthetic, a new technique, a new sound, and a new repertoire to America that, in the end, transcended the BMG community's musical value system.[23]

In early 1929, Sophocles Papas (1893–1986) replaced Vahdah Olcott-Bickford as *Crescendo*'s advice columnist for the guitar. The column's title became "The Guitar and Steel Guitar Round Table," reflecting the BMG community's desire to encompass all plucked-string activity. Despite his assurance that "the Hawaiian guitar will receive equal attention and consideration as the Spanish," Papas's column actually confirmed the ever-widening gap within the American guitar community between classical guitarists and those playing steel-strung instruments.[24]

Papas, Segovia's greatest champion in the BMG community and eventually his most devoted disciple in America, had immigrated to this country as a young man. He arrived in the United States in 1914, intending to return to his native Greece after study at a New England agricultural college. His father had provided Papas's earliest musical training and he had acquired further skills on the piano, guitar, and mandolin as a youth in Cairo, Egypt. A stint in the United States Army during the First World War led to American citizenship, and by the early 1920s Papas had abandoned agriculture for music. He settled in Washington, D.C., working as a part-time musician, playing guitar in a trio with two mandolinists. Papas's early professional successes in the capital region came in live radio performances and, like nearly all BMG professionals of the era, he also played and taught various fretted instruments including the tenor banjo, Hawaiian guitar, and ukulele. In addition to guiding his own professional ensembles, Papas conformed to the role of the BMG teacher, directing several larger ensembles of student players. Essentially self-taught, Papas began guitar lessons with William Foden, but quit after only three lessons, dissatisfied with Foden's attitude and music. George C. Krick proved more approachable, introducing Papas to much of the guitar's serious literature. After teaching in several music studios, Papas eventually established his own studio in Washington.[25]

Papas traveled to New York in January 1928 for Segovia's American debut and the two men forged an immediate friendship instigated by Papas's language skills (besides Greek and English, he spoke French and had more than passing acquaintance with Arabic and Italian). Segovia invited Papas to coffee the day after his New York premiere and Papas later related that the Spaniard "seemed glad to know someone who could help his career."[26] Although he was instrumental in eventually securing Segovia concerts in the capital, Papas's most immediate support of Segovia appeared on the pages of *Crescendo*.

Papas inherited *Crescendo*'s guitar-advice column within a year of Segovia's premiere and, despite the promised inclusion of the Hawaiian guitar as an equal subject, immediately devoted significant column space to the classical guitar and his Spanish friend. In his opening column, Papas credited Segovia with reviving worldwide interest in the instrument and establishing even higher technical and musical standards for players. He recognized that the Spaniard had fulfilled the long-standing goal of the BMG community to render "high class music" on a plucked instrument, and encouraged American guitarists to adopt parts of this new repertoire.

Now that we are so fortunate as to have one of the greatest artists in the world touring the country, playing our beloved instrument, there is an ever greater demand for the better class of music, even for the works of so strict a classicist as Bach. This, of course, is due directly to Segovia who, with his marvelous interpretations has made the public better able to understand and appreciate the works of this great composer. . . . The Segovia arrangements [of Bach] are such that the guitarist is able to interpret their works correctly and with proper effect, and many of them are not technically difficult.[27]

Papas devoted much of this opening column to an analysis of Fernando Sor's "Variations on a Theme of Mozart," a staple of Segovia's recitals. While Papas's examination of the piece dealt with technical matters—articulated slurs, vibrato, and right-hand fingerings—he presented these techniques within the context of the musical performance of an entire piece. Earlier technical columns by Olcott-Bickford and Foden had generally focused on overcoming specific limitations, not necessarily on playing a piece of music. Foden, especially, often gave the impression that musical works were merely strings of technical challenges to be negotiated. Papas, on the other hand, emphasized a big picture view of Sor's variation set. Guided by Segovia's interpretation, Papas highlighted specific technical points to enhance the inherent beauty of the piece—vibrato lends drama to a slow variation, articulated slurs add grace to a line, appropriately placed rubato and accelerando contribute to the phrasing of a melody. At the end of his variation-by-variation dissection, Papas encouraged readers to listen to Segovia's recent recording of the Sor "Variations," but unlike other writers who endorsed this new medium, Papas explained why and how to listen. Papas encouraged students to approach and understand the piece "as a whole," clearly identifying what an auditor should listen for in Segovia's recording—musical subtleties like tone production and tempi, as well as the nuanced variation of each. While earlier guitar apologists like Olcott-Bickford and Krick had encouraged artistic, expressive playing, they neither offered concrete examples nor explained how it was accomplished. Papas—in the right place at the right time—could do both, having both Segovia's edition (with fingerings) and his recorded interpretation as illustrative examples. As importantly, Papas, by all accounts a master teacher, proved capable of identifying and articulating the expressive elements of Segovia's playing and linking them to specific supporting techniques.[28]

Despite his devotion to the classical guitar, Papas's role required him to deal with the steel-strung instrument. His predecessors—Foden, Krick, and Olcott-Bickford—had generally ignored steel-string guitarists in their columns, avoiding confrontational language while encouraging readers to use gut strings, a technique derived from the European classical tradition, and a repertoire of older classics and more contemporary, lighter fare. Papas, whose musical training, performing experience, and teaching expertise crossed both realms, appeared an ideal candidate to write a new column devoted to the gut- and steel-strung instruments, capable of respecting and responding to each faction. In the main, Papas addressed correspondents' questions about the Hawaiian guitar politely and thoroughly, eventually offering these readers a long article about their instrument independent of his regular column.[29]

In a rare display of impatience, however, Papas revealed that his polite demeanor to the steel-string guitarists camouflaged an air of condescension. When a reader wrote to remind him of the accomplishments of popular plectrum players like the singer/guitarist Nick Lucas, Papas caustically clarified the divide between the popular and the elite.

> It is true that Segovia could not take Nick Lucas' place and make people mushy, anymore than Kreisler or Rachmaninoff could. It is amusing to me that a man of your experience should be so lacking in judgment as to attempt to class Segovia with Nick Lucas, and to say that "he would have to go some to play his stuff." Segovia's technique is transcendent, and this means beyond criticism. . . . With an artist, technique is taken for granted, and it's only his musicianship which determines his greatness. If you want to get an idea of Segovia's technique, hear some of his records and then buy some guitar music of the modern Spanish composers and see how difficult it is to play. . . . if we may have only one Segovia, there are many who have the same artistic standard, regardless of whether they are able to attain it or not. There are several great guitarists giving concerts in Europe today, but even there, according to the critics of England, Germany, Spain, France, Italy and Austria, Segovia is something unique, not only among guitarists, but the great artists of all instruments.[30]

Papas's stint as a guitar columnist for *Crescendo* lasted only through November 1929, but in his short tenure he helped set the stage for Segovia's eventual domination of America's classical guitar community.[31] Unlike other BMG apologists, Papas made no attempt to tie Segovia and his success to the mission of the Guild or to other instruments. In his response to the Nick Lucas fan, Papas not only articulated the divide between popular and cultivated music that the BMG movement had tried to negotiate for nearly fifty years, but also invoked this gap against purveyors of "mushy" popular music. Papas saw it as his duty to confirm for America's BMG community that the future of the guitar as a refined classical instrument lay with a European musician performing European music on a European instrument. Papas credited Segovia with establishing the guitar's "proper place in the musical world"; for Segovia (and eventually for many of his disciples in the United States) this "proper place" was independent of America's BMG industry as well as the mandolin and banjo. As importantly, Papas encouraged American guitarists to follow Segovia's model, a model that had no use for mandolins, banjos, and ensembles of these instruments.

From 1928, when Segovia first visited the United States, to early 1934, when *Crescendo* ceased publication, Spanish music and musicians dominated its pages devoted to the guitar. America's best-known guitarists, William Foden and Vahdah Olcott-Bickford, as well as lesser lights like Johnson Bane and C. W. F. Jansen, continued to appear in the magazine, yet none could compete for the excited attention and extravagant praise lavished on Segovia, Llobet, and other European players. Olcott-Bickford's repertoire in these years came to focus on historical lecture-recitals sponsored by her American Guitar Society as well as her lute performances. Foden appeared in advertisements as a composer and in articles principally as a revered teacher and former performer.[32]

A *Crescendo* article from 1931 admitted that "Since the Armistice, the great stream of music has continued to flow through our land ... [y]et it seems, instead of moving along with the current, our own activities have drifted off into a backwater, where they have swirled about like an eddy, without making any great amount of headway."[33] Several months later George Krick put a brave face on the situation, but admitted to the contemporary dominance of the guitar world by the Spaniards.

> Luis Romero, Johnson Bane, William Foden, in New York, whose fine arrangements and original compositions are known the world over, [this] writer in Philadelphia, Papas in Washington, all these men have kept alive the spirit of the guitar in this country.... It is to Spain, however, that we are indebted for the present revival of the guitar, and the man primarily responsible is no less than Francisco Tárrega.... Too modest to travel as a concert artist, he sent out into the world Llobet, Pujol, Fortea, Sainz de la Mazza and others.... Andres Segovia now appears on the scene and what words can describe the impression he makes upon one, with his wonderful technique, beautiful tone and great musicianship. No one can fail to fall under the spell of the guitar in Segovia's hands and the most prejudiced critics are forced to pay tribute to the great artist and his instrument.[34]

Despite such enthusiasm, some American guitarists resisted the Spaniard's spell. Olcott-Bickford's increased chamber music activities and forays with the lute can be seen as an attempt to chart a new course that would not compete directly with the Spanish guitarist. Foden registered a tepid response to Segovia's early American concerts, but even he eventually succumbed, imitating Segovia's Bach arrangements and resuming work on a large-scale guitar solo similar to the modern repertoire performed and recorded by Segovia.[35]

Although Segovia's artistic interpretations of a new and varied repertoire eventually drew the attention of BMG advocates, most still misunderstood his significance because the American BMG community remained incapable of understanding music-making outside its business/organizational framework. America's most important BMG musical figures—including guitarists William Foden, Vahdah Olcott-Bickford, and George Krick; banjoists Frederick Bacon and Alfred Farland; mandolinists Giuseppe Pettine, Valentine Abt, and Samuel Seigel—made their livings principally as teachers, remained active in ensemble work as performers or directors, and often played and taught instruments other than their principal one. Most importantly, these individuals, like the rest of the BMG community, were committed to large-scale organizations; the symphony orchestra remained the ideal musical model, while large corporations financed and guided the overarching Guild in its efforts to standardize and control technical skills, teaching policies, and business dealings. The individual American artist remained a company man (or woman), vying for corporate endorsements, eagerly embracing Guild or Guitar Society performances and guidelines, and arguing about how many guitarists should play in mandolin or plectrophonic orchestras.

BMG articles, reviews, and editorials acclaimed the single-minded, heaven-inspired virtuoso whose art lifted him above and freed him from society's conventions, but America had never seen a guitarist (or banjoist or mandolinist, for that matter) who could truly play that role. Segovia played it to the hilt, remaining consistently focused on his role as the artist/performer, fulfilling a divinely ordained mission. In his later career, Segovia mentored promising young players and taught master classes, but he was not, especially in his early years, primarily a teacher. He had little or no interest in other instruments (especially "folk" instruments like banjos, mandolins, or steel-strung guitars), to the point of seldom sharing the stage with other non-guitarists in chamber music. Although recognized by many musical organizations with awards and honorary lifetime memberships, Segovia neither actively participated in nor ever put himself under the control or guidance of any such organization.[36] Segovia's technique, repertoire, and musicianship created a new and (eventually) comprehensible paradigm for America's guitarists, in part because, as revolutionary as they were, they were rooted in a shared musical/technical history. But Segovia's role as an artist remained incomprehensible to the BMG world of musical business, for he effectively undermined the paradigm of the "BMG artist"—the multi-instrumentalist, teacher, publisher, conductor, composer, and businessman. Segovia demonstrated to America's BMG community how a performing artist worked, and his model shared no correspondences with the work of BMG entrepreneurial player/teachers.

Segovia's legacy in America is two-part. First, he established new criteria of technique and musicality with a new repertoire; second, he offered America's classical guitarists a new model of the solo guitarist, independent of the rest of the BMG community. Vahdah Olcott-Bickford and others called for BMG players to focus exclusively on their individual instruments, but never removed themselves or the guitar from the BMG movement. Segovia, with no ties to this movement, demonstrated to guitarists how their instrument might truly stand apart from the mandolin and banjo, eventually giving many American players and teachers a renewed impetus to move away from the BMG ideals and the BMG ensembles. In short, Segovia encouraged the liberation of the guitar from the mandolin and banjo orchestra in America, contributing significantly to the weakening of the BMG movement.

Nearly fifty years after American banjoists and mandolinists adopted the gut-strung guitar as a cultivated prop and model for their instruments, it was reclaimed by a new generation of European guitarists. Independent of the BMG community and industry, these players liberated the guitar not only from America's mandolin and banjo ensembles but also from the musical and social constraints that had relegated the guitar to roles and repertoires based on late-nineteenth-century prejudices, techniques, and repertoires. American musicians played the new steel-strung mandolin-guitar, creating a new technique for a new popular repertoire, while European guitarists, endowed with a sophisticated and powerful technique, recreated the Old World's guitar, bringing America a new solo repertoire for a truly modern instrument.

Chapter Ten

SUMMARY AND CONCLUSIONS

*C*rescendo celebrated its twenty-fifth anniversary in 1933. A number of guitar-related articles appeared in the magazine that year, including a full-page biography of William Foden, a testimonial to the instrument and Segovia by a French correspondent, and ongoing reports by Vahdah Olcott-Bickford about her activities with the American Guitar Society. Enthusiastic articles and reviews documented the American premiere of the young Viennese virtuoso Louise Walker and announced a new American tour by Segovia. The magazine reported the death of jazz guitarist Eddie Lang, continued to address readers' questions about the Hawaiian guitar and plectrum guitar techniques, and noted the many former students of William Foden playing plectrum guitar with popular bands led by Rudy Vallee, Paul Whiteman, and others. Also in 1933, *Crescendo* offered a series of articles about electric amplification and published several plectrum guitar solos, including a blues.[1]

By this date, the community of guitarists in America had split on the issues of instrument, technique, and repertoire, and in its final year of publication *Crescendo* documented this division in its ongoing promotion of both the classical and plectrum guitar. Walter Kaye Bauer continued to encourage banjoists to play both plectrum and finger-style, but reflecting the divisive guitar world, noted that guitarists had to choose. "In the case of the guitar, we might look at it from a different angle [than the banjo], since most advocates of plectrum playing will buy the arch top style of guitar in order to use heavy wire strings and gain the utmost volume. If we wish to learn the guitar in finger style, however, such a type of guitar is out of the question as it is not possible to string it with gut strings. . . . For finger style of playing, there is only one style of guitar, and that is the flat top with thin sensitive sounding board, and strung with three gut and three silk wound strings." Many guitarists and guitar teachers, of course, still adhered to the BMG tradition of playing and teaching multiple instruments and undoubtedly owned several guitars, including at least one steel-strung instrument for plectrum or Hawaiian style and one traditional guitar for the classical repertoire. Yet the professional guitarists who contributed to *Crescendo* universally preferred the latter and continued to encourage readers to choose the higher road of the classical guitar.[2]

Despite this professional advocacy for the classical guitar at home and a worldwide enthusiasm for the instrument, the country's BMG leadership remained resolutely dedicated to mandolin and banjo ensembles. Two articles celebrating the magazine's silver anniversary identified highlights in BMG history, confirming that at the end of its golden age the BMG movement's focus remained on business, the banjo, and the mandolin. Notable moments included "entry into the fields of manufacturing and publishing by several very worthy firms," as well as "marking all music at net selling price." Other important items were the development of families of mandolins and banjos, debates about notation for mandolins and banjos, the introduction of new instruments like the ukulele and taro-patch, and the standardization of the "plectrophonic plan" for mandolin orchestras. The introduction of three new guitar types—steel (Hawaiian), tenor, and plectrum—was noted, as was the introduction of electrically amplified instruments. But neither article observed that *Crescendo* had been witness to the most significant change in the BMG world, the reclamation of the classical guitar by Europe's virtuosi guitarists, musicians little interested in this country's plectral orchestras.[3]

Almost fifty years earlier, America's banjo players and manufacturers began a crusade to strike a balance with and to declare independence from Europe's musical hegemony by cultivating instruments and a repertoire both derived from and independent of the Old World. Despite their efforts and those of the leadership of the new BMG movement, however, the cultivated repertoire of the solo mandolin and solo banjo, as well as that of the mandolin and banjo orchestras, faded from both the pages of America's music periodicals and from public consciousness. The banjo and mandolin, linked not with the violin but with the fiddle, became essential elements in America's string band and bluegrass traditions. Of the many plectral instruments promoted by the BMG magazines, only the classical guitar held a place in the elite and cultivated musical worlds of the mid- and late twentieth century. It did so, however, thanks not to the work of America's guitarists and composers, but to the overwhelming technique, musicality, and tradition of Segovia and his peers. In the end, America's BMG community abandoned its claim on the guitar as a cultivated instrument, allowing European players and composers to determine the instrument's standards of technique, musicianship, and repertoire.[4]

Of course, to consider only the classical side of BMG guitar activities is to miss the important developments surrounding the guitar in popular music and jazz, a number of which have a direct connection to the BMG movement. The creation of the plectrum guitar and the invention of electric amplification did, of course, appear on *Crescendo*'s list of significant events in its twenty-five-year retrospective. As outlined in an earlier chapter, the newly invented hybrid mandolin-guitar as well as the mandolinists' plectrum technique became the standard instrument and playing style for America's popular musics of the 1930s. With the advent of the electric guitar, that instrument became inextricably tied to the story of American popular music, especially in the hands of the country's black and white underclass following the Second World War. While the history of the amplified electric guitar falls outside the parameters of this study, it can hardly be ignored here, since some of its roots spring from the BMG movement. These include not just the overt connections to the mandolin (through the arch-top design and plectrum technique), but the approach to musical instruments as commercial products, the tradition of the BMG inventor extending the limits of design and technology, and the overblown rhetoric of BMG promotions, among others.

Many of the earliest experiments with amplified guitars focused on the Hawaiian steel guitar, an instrument very actively promoted within the BMG movement. As a result, in the mid-1930s when manufacturers finally created an electric guitar that achieved some commercial success, they promoted it as a "Spanish guitar" (to distinguish it from their "Hawaiian guitars"). In the spirit of the BMG industry, the Gibson Company brought their EH (Electric Hawaiian) and ES (Electric Spanish) guitars together by publishing music for mixed ensembles of these instruments. These Gibson music folios, like the BMG magazines, featured photographs and biographies of amateur and semiprofessional ensembles playing Gibson's amplified Hawaiian and Spanish guitars.

In reality, Gibson's ES-150 ("Electric Spanish"), the first really successful six-string electric guitar, was Spanish in neither design nor playing technique but rather a hybrid arch-top guitar fitted with an electric pickup and played with a pick. Advertising chutzpah and a desire once again to link a hybrid BMG instrument to the Old World classical guitar led Gibson's promoters to identify this instrument as a "Spanish guitar." Nonetheless, in the hands of numerous players but especially Charlie Christian, this new instrument became the voice of the jazz guitarist. In an article from late 1939 ascribed to Christian, he rallied guitarists, assuring them that "Electrical amplification has given guitarists a new lease on life. . . . [Y]ou play damned fine music, but now you've got a chance to bring the fact to the attention of not only short-sighted [band] leaders but to the attention of the world."[5] Many later writers see Christian's adoption of the electric guitar as the beginning of the modern guitar and even America's modern music. And clearly none of the important popular modern American musics that developed following World War Two—urban blues, country and western, rhythm and blues, and eventually rock and roll—could have done so without the electric guitar. But just as we find the roots for each of these musical styles in the first half of the twentieth century, so too should we recognize the roots of America's new electric instrument and its new electric musics in that same era.

The BMG movement did not end, of course, with the demise of *Crescendo* in 1934 or with the successful marketing of electric guitars in 1936. Other periodicals carried on through the 1930s and spokesmen for the movement continued to promote the activities of the American Guild of Banjoists, Mandolinists and Guitarists. The Guild sponsored well-attended conventions through the 1940s and BMG advocates continued to found and direct large ensembles, some of which performed into the 1950s.[6]

Of the important guitar advocates in the BMG movement, George Krick maintained one of the highest profiles, penning a column about the plectral instruments from late 1937 to 1943 for *Etude*. In *Etude*, Krick continued to highlight the values of the BMG movement: a strong commitment to amateur banjo and mandolin ensembles; an equally strong commitment to the commercial promotion of new technology (including amplification), focusing principally on steel-strung hybrid instruments; a pedagogical philosophy based on business plans, articulated in the by-laws of the American Guild of Banjoists, Mandolinists and Guitarists; and the grateful recognition that musical instrument manufacturers (active and influential members of the Guild) powered the BMG movement.

Krick's columns confirm the continuity of the BMG mission yet also demonstrate that the gaps between America's elite and popular musics and between the classical guitar and the popular steel-strung instruments within the BMG movement, opened in the early years of the new century, continued to widen. Despite his encouraging words about the Guild, tenor banjos, plectrum guitars, mandolin orchestras, and other manifestations of the BMG movement, Krick consistently promoted the classical guitar as the instrument of artists, as the "standard" guitar by which others should be evaluated. Like Sophocles Papas before him, Krick supported the steel-string guitar, but when pushed, he aggressively pointed out its inferiority to the classical guitar.

THE CLAIM that the plectrum guitar is an improvement or a modern version of the classic guitar is not based on facts; it should be called the noisy brother to that romantic, aristocratic and highly cultured member of the guitar family. It was invented to compete with the trumpet and saxophone in the dance band, where it is primarily used to strum chords as a rhythmic background for the melody instruments. It is true that the shape is the same and it has six strings tuned in a like manner. However, the strings are made of steel wire and played with a heavy plectrum, in order to get quantity of tone. The difference in tone quality is so pronounced in favor of the classic guitar that there is hardly a division of opinion amongst those who have made a thorough study of both instruments.[7]

Krick carried this distinction over to his reports about popular music, which he clearly held to be inferior to elite concert music. He regularly devoted columns to significant contemporary players of the classical guitar, highlighting their repertoire and identifying their special contributions, yet he never singled out any plectrum or Hawaiian guitarist by name for any distinction.[8]

With Miguel Llobet's death in 1938, Andres Segovia became the undisputed Spanish master of the guitar, maintaining a nearly worldwide hegemonic hold on the instrument's repertoire, techniques, and performance practices until his death in 1987.[9] In the same years, the new American guitar—electric or acoustic, flat-top or arch-top, but certainly steel-strung—became the dominant instrument in this country's vibrant popular musical culture in the hands of musicians like Charlie Christian, Merle Travis, Les Paul, Chet Atkins, Muddy Waters, Chuck Berry, Freddie Green, B.B. King, and others, who redefined the instrument in the musical languages of country and western, jazz, blues, and rock. Among America's legendary guitarists, some dabbled with the classical guitar, even going so far as to play for Segovia, whose Old World manners did little to hide his palpable disdain for the steel-string and electric guitar.[10] Little wonder that when guitar historians like Harvey Turnbull or Frederic Grunfeld wrote about the instrument, they either ignored America altogether (it had no classical guitar tradition) or they focused on America's guitar-playing cowboys or bluesmen (romanticized and visible icons of the country's popular music roots).

This study demonstrates that such simplistic assumptions have distorted the history of the guitar in America. It suggests that any future history of the instrument in this country must seriously consider the complexities of America's musical culture and must attempt to create a context for the guitar within those complexities. It also suggests that the guitar, now viewed principally as a popular or folk instrument, may deserve greater visibility in future narratives of America's broader musical history.

The conclusions of this study may be summarized as follows. Until the last decades of the nineteenth century, many Americans who played the guitar approached the instrument as others approached the piano; both were cultivated instruments, suitable for the parlor and especially appropriate to accompany the voice. The guitar, overshadowed by the popular banjo and lower-priced pianos at mid-century, achieved a new popularity beginning in the 1880s partly as the result of a conscious effort by banjo and mandolin manufacturers and enthusiasts to associate their instruments with the guitar. Banjoists and mandolinists raised the standing of their instruments by drawing on the guitar's refined history, established technical and pedagogical traditions, and elite status. Musical instrument manufacturers created new, hybrid instruments—especially the steel-strung plectrum guitar—which drew the instrument closer to the banjo and mandolin and gradually displaced the traditional Spanish or classical guitar in America's musical culture. By the 1930s America's guitar community was torn in two directions—toward this country's new popular musical idioms (which utilized the plectrum and, eventually, electric guitar) or toward the classical guitar's traditional European repertoire, championed by Andres Segovia.

At the same time, this study has touched on specific issues about the guitar and America's musical culture. The BMG community's attempts to bridge the gap between the world of popular and fine art music reflect the debate carried on in America's wider musical culture as the twentieth century began. BMG advocates failed to convince America's elite musical leaders that the banjo, mandolin, and guitar deserved a position on the concert platform with standard orchestral instruments. Likewise, they failed to create either a repertoire or an ensemble that transcended accessible popular music to attract a sophisticated and elite audience. The BMG movement's failure to reconcile the popular and the elite, coupled with its recognition that commerce and advertising played significant roles in America's musical world, resonates even a century later. While the actual music of the BMG magazines and movement warrants little technical or compositional notice, it serves as a reminder of how hard America worked to create art that distinguished itself from, yet remained indebted to European culture. The BMG magazines also reflect this country's conflicted attitude toward music-makers—eyeing the professional performer with a mix of awe and suspicion, offering the devoted teacher grudging respect (but not necessarily a living wage), and enthusiastically encouraging the dedicated amateur to follow his or her muse (but not too seriously). Both consciously and unconsciously, the BMG movement drew on ancient and powerful mythologies, traditions, and images to promote its members' understanding of the roles of minorities and women in America's musical life as well as its wider culture.

The value of focused musicological research derives in part from its relevance to the wider field of cultural history. This study developed from and has been driven by two important ideas about America and music, points articulated nearly a century ago by Oscar Sonneck, the father of American music history. The first idea reflected Sonneck's dedicated work as a librarian and bibliographer. In numerous articles and papers, he bemoaned the many gaps in the bibliography of America's musical history and called for scholars to dedicate themselves to discovering and organizing America's source material before it was irretrievably lost.[11] The second idea propelling this study was Sonneck's perceptive evaluation of America's relationship to music.

> The distinctive characteristic of American musical life is and always has been private enterprise. The European who overlooks this fundamental fact will never be able to understand the situation with its weaknesses and its strong points, and if an American makes the same mistake he will understand only up to a point. . . . The

American views music as a business—not, of course, as a trade that like a butcher's caters to the body, but rather one that caters to the esthetic sense. . . . The heart of the matter is that the American musician views the business side of musical activity not as a necessary evil but, on the contrary, as the artist's only healthy and artistically appropriate means of changing cause into effect.[12]

Sonneck included periodicals in his discussion of America's musical life, and may well have been referring to the BMG magazines when he criticized contemporary journalistic puffery in 1909. He pointed up the false picture of America's musical culture such magazines created, but also shrewdly observed that puffery had its role in business.

[European immigrant musicians] see American musical life only as mirrored by certain musical magazines that to a degree engage in unabashed puffery and only in puffery. These magazines, however, do not give a true picture of American musical life and of Americans as musicians, insofar as the latter think of themselves as artists and not merely as artisans. The American artist regards these magazines with scorn and uses them, when he uses them at all, just as he uses the respectable ones—for puffery after all plays a natural part in every business. Thus he does not even notice the evil influence that systematic, garish, often childish, and sometimes dishonest advertising gradually exerts on his artistic conscience. . . . They console themselves instead with the thought that in the end it is better if the darker aspects are exposed to view rather than being glossed over, only to serve as hiding places for hypocritical idealism.[13]

Sonneck went on to sound a prescient warning about music as a form of commercial speculation, but he also recognized that American musicians, even great artists, participated in the hurly-burly of the country's day-to-day democracy.

In everyday life the distinction between the prosaic view of art as a business and the romantic view of art as a selfless mission narrows down to a precise point. From this crossing on, the two views separate again. . . . If only the profile of American musical life depended solely on the artists, then perhaps they would be able through the power of their idealism to control satisfactorily the threats posed by the problem of art as business. Such, however, is not the case, nor can it be. Even if in the end art exists only for artists . . . the fact remains that in everyday life art and artists rub shoulders constantly with the masses, the people.[14]

Sonneck did not specifically identify any "precise point" of intersection for art and commerce, but clearly, in the years when he was formulating these ideas about music in America, one of those precise points, a point where America's bifurcated appreciation and use of music manifested itself, was the guitar—a tool, a product, and an icon for America and its musicians.

⊰ NOTES ⊱

INTRODUCTION

1. A well-documented case of the guitar in America being put almost exclusively into the hands only of cowboys or bluesmen is Frederic V. Grunfeld, *The Art and Times of the Guitar: An Illustrated History of Guitars and Guitarists* (New York: Collier Books, 1969). Peter Danner cites Grunfeld's oversight in "The Guitar in 19th-century America: A Lost Social Tradition." *Soundboard* 22/3 (1985): 293. Tom and Mary Anne Evans also offer a consistently anachronistic view of the American guitar in *Guitars: Music, History, Construction and Players from the Renaissance to Rock* (New York: Paddington Press, 1977), 286–88. In its volume on the United States and Canada, the *Garland Encyclopedia of World Music* indexes the "non-electric" guitar sixty-five times but only one of these references documents a non-folk or non-popular setting. This one citation leads the reader to a short paragraph about the nineteenth-century African American guitar pedagogue, composer, and arranger, Justin Holland; *Garland Encyclopedia of World Music: Volume 3, The United States and Canada*, Ellen Koskoff, ed. (New York and London: Garland Publishing, 2001). In his recent study, Steve Waksman ignores the early history of the guitar in America, asserting (but not documenting) that "The guitar [like the banjo] similarly entered the American continent through the slave trade"; Steve Waksman, *Instruments of Desire* (Cambridge, MA: Harvard University Press, 1999), 17.

2. Waksman's study stands as a particularly good example of this celebration of the guitar as a tool of resistance and rebellion. He celebrates the musical achievements of many twentieth-century guitar icons but, drawing on the work of Jacques Attali, uses them as exemplars of transgressive creators of social and cultural noise that challenges and eventually overturns the status quo.

CHAPTER 1. THE GUITAR IN AMERICA TO 1880

1. See for example, Mike Longworth, *Martin Guitars: A History* (Cedar Knolls, NJ: Colonial Press, 1975); Jim Washburn and Richard Johnston, *Martin Guitars: An Illustrated Celebration of America's Premier Guitarmaker* (Emmaus, PA: Rodale Press, 1997); Robert Carl Hartman, *Guitars and Mandolins in America. Featuring the Larson's Creations* (Hoffman Estates, IL: Maurer & Co., 1984); or John Teagle, *Washburn: One Hundred Years of Fine Stringed Instruments* (New York: Music Sales, 1996). Waksman, 283–84, offers an evaluation of the vintage guitar movement as an

attempt to both idealize and reify the past. For a slightly more critical view of the vintage guitar market as well as the place Martin guitars hold in that market, see Timothy Brookes, "Martin's Millionth Guitar Is a Flash of Its Future," *Philadelphia Inquirer* (December 21, 2003).

2. *Guitar Review* and *Soundboard* remain the most important resources for scholarly work about the classical guitar in America. Articles from these periodicals have played a significant supportive role in this study and are cited throughout. Readers are encouraged especially to consider the work of Peter Danner and Douglas Back, two of the more productive researchers in this area.

3. Philip F. Gura, *C. F. Martin and His Guitars, 1796–1873* (Chapel Hill and London: University of North Carolina Press, 2003).

4. See, for example, Sonneck's paper, "The Musical Life of America from the Standpoint of Musical Topography" (1909), collected in *Oscar Sonneck and American Music*, ed. William Lichtenwanger (Urbana and Chicago: University of Illinois Press, 1983). For examples of Crawford's approach to America's musical story, see Richard Crawford, *The American Musical Landscape: The Business of Musicianship from Billings to Gershwin* (Berkeley: University of California Press, 1993) and *America's Musical Life* (New York and London: W. W. Norton, 2001).

5. Lawrence W. Levine describes this cultural divide in *Highbrow Lowbrow: The Emergence of Cultural Hierarchy in America* (Cambridge, MA: Harvard University Press, 1988), a book that has inspired numerous other studies. For a critique of Levine's conclusions see Ralph P. Locke, "Music Lovers, Patrons and the 'Sacralization' of Culture in America," *19th-Century Music* 17 (Fall 1993): 149–73. While Levine places this cultural division in the second half of the century, Michael Broyles describes three stages covering most of the nineteenth century in "Music and Class Structure in Antebellum Boston," *Journal of the American Musicological Society* 44 (Fall 1991): 451–93.

6. Richard Crawford examines early French and Spanish music-making on this continent, describing a seventeenth-century French ceremony as an example of both religious and political use of music. See *America's Musical Life*, 15–19. In the opening chapters of *A History of Music and Dance in Florida, 1565–1865* (Tuscaloosa: University of Alabama Press, 1991), Wiley L. Housewright documents numerous examples of sixteenth- and seventeenth-century European music-making in North America. Tim Brookes cites Housewright and other sources in his discussion of America's earliest guitarists; see Tim Brookes, *Guitar: an American Life* (New York: Grove Press, 2005), 17–22 and 27–35. James Tyler's *The Early Guitar: A History and Handbook* (London: Oxford University Press, 1980) offers an excellent introduction to the Baroque guitar, its music, and its players. A recent update of Tyler's book has expanded to include similar materials for the transitional guitar of the late eighteenth century; see James Tyler and Paul Sparks, *The Guitar and Its Music: From the Renaissance to the Classical Era* (New York: Oxford University Press, 2002).

7. See Oscar George Theodore Sonneck, *Early Concert-Life in America (1731–1800)* (New York: Musurgia Publishers, 1949), 29, 32, 76, 130–31, and 137, as well as Peter Danner, "Notes on Some Early American Guitar Concerts." *Soundboard* 4/1 (February 1977): 8–9 and 21. Danner's article draws primarily on Sonneck. See Crawford, *America's Musical Life*, 83ff., for an overview of colonial concert life, also based on Sonneck. For the guitar's connections to some of our colonial leaders, see Clinton Simpson, "Some Early American Guitarists," *Guitar Review* 23 (June 1959): 16, and Frank Mortimer, "Music for the Funeral Services for George Washington," *Guitar Review* 23 (June 1959): 14–15. In all likelihood, the instrument examined in these articles was the "English guittar," unrelated to the traditional "Spanish guitar."

8. Sonneck, *Early Concert-Life in America*, 130.

9. In *America's Musical Life*, 76ff., Richard Crawford describes some of the practices of America's early music teachers. In *Early Concert-Life in America*, Sonneck documents many performances by Henri Capron, principally as a cellist. In 1788, Capron announced that he intended to settle in New York as a teacher of "singing, pianoforte, violin and guitar"; *Daily Advertiser* (November 5, 1788), cited in Sonneck, *Early Concert-Life in America*, 226. A number of early guitar methods acknowledged the suitability of the guitar for song accompaniment and its attraction to amateur players. See Paul Cox, "Classic Guitar Technique and Its Evolution as Reflected in the Method Books ca. 1770–1850" (Ph.D. diss., Indiana University, 1978), 28–29.

10. Cox, "Classic Guitar Technique," remains the most thorough examination of early European methods for the classical guitar. For information on most of these methods see Aaron Shearer, "A Review of Early Methods," *Guitar Review* 23 (June 1959): 24–26; Danner, "The Guitar in 19th-century America," 295; or Peter Danner, "A Noteworthy Early American Guitar Treatise: James Ballard's 'Element' of 1838," *Soundboard* 8/4 (1981): 270–76. Danner singles out Ballard for his incorporation of sound European pedagogy and Gura discusses Ballard's method in some detail, citing Ballard's introductory notes as well as contemporary praise for the book. Gura identifies some of Ballard's musical sources, including Fernando Sor, Mauro Giuliani, Dionisio Aguado, and Johann Strauss; Gura, *C. F. Martin*, 24–29.

11. For more information on the English guittar, see P. Coggins, "'This easy and agreeable instrument': A History of the English Guittar," *Early Music* 15 (1987): 204–18. For a more concise discussion see Robert Spencer and Ian Harwood, "The English Guitar," *The New Grove Dictionary of Music and Musicians*, ed. Stanley Sadie (London, 2001). Even as late as the 1820s, methods for the English guittar were published in the United States. See, for example, Shearer, "A Review . . . ," who cites the title page of J. Siegling's 1820 method, which identifies the tutor as a "Complete Instructor of the Spanish and English guitar." Art Schraeder bases his argument about the English guittar in the colonies on iconographical evidence in colonial and Federalist portraits (many featuring a guittar in the hands of an upper-class woman) and on an examination of surviving sheet music. See Art Schrader, "Guittars and Guitars: A Note on a Musical Fashion," *American Music Research Journal* 1 (2001), 1.

12. For example, see Walter Carter, *The Martin Book: A Complete History of Martin Guitars* (San Francisco: Miller Freeman Books, 1995), 9ff. Through the Martin company archives, Gura documents this immigrant luthier's early dependence on and close business ties to partners or suppliers in Germany; Gura, *C. F. Martin*, 35–46.

13. See Tyler, *The Early Guitar*, and Tyler and Sparks, *The Guitar and Its Music*, for discussions of notational systems for the Baroque guitar and the transition to standardized staff notation. One of the first comprehensive investigations of the transitional guitar, its literature, and its notation can be found in Thomas F. Heck, *Mauro Giuliani: Virtuoso Guitarist and Composer* (Columbus, OH: Editions Orphee, 1995). This book is a reworking of Heck's dissertation, "The birth of the classic guitar and its cultivation in Vienna, reflected in the career and compositions of Mauro Giuliani (d. 1829)" (Ph.D. diss., Yale University, 1970). A more recent article by Richard Savino confronts some of the same material from a performer's point of view; "Essential Issues in Performance Practices of the Classical Guitar, 1770–1850," in *Performance on Lute, Guitar, and Viheula*, Victor A. Coelho, ed. (Cambridge: Cambridge University Press, 1997), 195–219.

14. See Danner, "The Guitar in 19th-Century America," 292–98 for a discussion of the antebellum popularity of the guitar. For a graphic demonstration of the development of the European classical guitar from the late eighteenth century through the first half of the twentieth, see *La Guitarra*

Española/The Spanish Guitar (Madrid: Opera Tres, 1993), the lavishly illustrated exhibition catalog from the Museo Municipal in Madrid and New York's Metropolitan Museum of Art.

15. See Carter, *The Martin Book*, 13–16, for a discussion of the simpler, more affordable guitar. Gura not only documents the physical changes to Martin's guitars in the mid-nineteenth century but also compares these instruments to those produced by James Ashborn and William B. Tilton; Gura, *C. F. Martin*, 109–42. Gura's book offers numerous color plates of all aspects of Martin guitars, including developments in the construction methods and bracing patterns. Dominga Lynch offers a contemporaneous account of her imported guitar's demise in *Stewart's* 11/6 (February-March 1895): 5. See also "The Guitar," in *Gatcomb's* 1/1 (September 1887): 1.

16. Danner, "The Guitar in 19th-Century America," 294. For examinations of the same theme, see Danner's, "The Meaning of American Parlor Music," unpublished paper, 1996 as well as his foreword to Antonio Lopes, *Instruction for the Guitar, Facsimile Edition* (Menlo Park, CA: Instrumenta Antiqua, 1983), iii–v.

17. Joseph Willson, *Sketches of the Higher Classes of Colored Society in Philadelphia* (1841), quoted in Eileen Southern, *The Music of Black Americans* (New York: Norton, 1997), 101.

18. For an examination of this early American guitar repertoire, see Danner, "The Guitar in 19th-Century America," 293. While antebellum American guitar solos survive in considerable numbers, most are available only in original editions in libraries or private collections. Some recent publications feature later-nineteenth-century guitar solos by American composers like Justin Holland, William Foden, Charles de Janon, and others, but Danner's 1978 anthology remains the best source for a broad sampling of earlier American solos: Peter Danner, ed., *The Guitar in America: A Historical Collection of Classical Guitar Music in Facsimile* (Melville, NY: Belwin Mills, 1978). For facsimile reproductions of Foster's songs with guitar accompaniment, see *The Music of Stephen Foster*, 2 vols., Steven Saunders and Deane L. Root, eds. (Washington and London: Smithsonian Institution Press, 1990). Although many of Foster's works were initially heard on the minstrel stage, none of the early publications of his songs—even his "Ethiopian" or "plantation" songs—were offered with a banjo accompaniment. Crawford, *America's Musical Life*, 221ff.

19. See, for example, Charles Converse, *New Method for the Guitar, containing Elementary Instructions in Music, designed for those who study without a master* . . . (New York: William Hall & Son, 1855) and two of Septimus Winner's several guitar tutors: *Winner's New School for the Guitar, in which the instructions are so clearly and simply treated, as to make it unnecessary to require a teacher*, . . . (Boston: Oliver Ditson & Company, 1870) and *Winner's Primary School for the Guitar; a Thorough and Complete Course of Instruction for the Guitar. Written and Arranged for Self-Instruction as well as for Teacher's Use* . . . (Cleveland: S. Brainard's Sons, 1872). In the course of his study of American guitar tutors from the early nineteenth century into the 1920s, Robert Ferguson has identified more than double the number listed in Shearer, "A Review . . ." and John C. Tanno, "American Guitar Methods Published from the Turn of the Nineteenth Century to the Present," *Guitar Review* 23 (June 1959): 28–31. Gura offers a survey of early-nineteenth-century guitar tutors in a subdivision of his first chapter titled "The American 'Methods.'" Besides focusing on James Ballard's method (1838), Gura briefly touches on books by George Willig (c. 1816), Elias Howe (1846), Richard Culver (1846), and Charles Converse (1855); see Gura, *C. F. Martin*, 24–30. The results of Ferguson's study will appear in 2008 as "American Methods to 1924." I thank him for access to his findings prior to its publication.

20. The citation about notation is taken from Crawford, *America's Musical Life*, 229. See Joseph Horowitz, *Classical Music in America* (New York: Norton, 2005), especially chapter 1, for a recent

examination of John Sullivan Dwight's attitudes and influence. Representative works by these all-but-unknown guitarist/composers (as well as brief biographical sketches) appear in Danner, *The Guitar in America*.

21. For tours and performances by Huerta, Dorn and Coupa, see Douglas Back, "Guitar on the New York Concert Stage, 1816–1890 as chronicled by George C. D. Odell and George Templeton Strong," *Soundboard* 25/4 (1999): 11–18. For biographies of Huerta and Dorn, see Philip J. Bone, *The Guitar and Mandolin: Biographies of Celebrated Players and Composers* (1914, 1954; rpt. London: Schott, 1972), 171–73 and 99–101. Longworth, 2, and Gura, *C. F. Martin*, 67–68 and 74–78, offer discussions of the business relationship between Martin and Coupa. Based on archival documentation, Gura suggests that Coupa probably died in 1850; Gura, *C. F. Martin*, 79.

22. See Shearer, "A Review . . . ," 25, and Tanno, 31, who lists six different American editions of Carcassi, beginning with a "New and Improved Method," edited by Charles de Janon (Boston: Oliver Ditson, 1859) and concluding with an edition by G. C. Santisteban (Bryn Mawr, PA: Theodore Presser, 1926). Tanno intended his list to be comprehensive, but numerous editions of Carcassi other than those he cited were published in both the nineteenth and twentieth centuries. For example, Philip Gura documents an early edition by Leopold Meignen (New York: Wm. Hall & Son, 1847); see Gura, *C. F. Martin*, 26–27; and the author of this study owns a bilingual "Student Edition" ([Philadelphia]: W. F. Shaw, 1884), not listed by Tanno. Robert Ferguson's forthcoming article about American guitar tutors includes approximately fifteen American editions of Carcassi from 1847 to 1925.

23. Author's introduction, *Holland's Comprehensive Method* [n.p.] Among his sources are Fernando Sor, Mateo Carcassi, Mauro Giuliani, and J. K. Mertz. For Ballard's method see Peter Danner, "A Noteworthy . . ." For Holland, see Justin Holland, *Holland's Comprehensive Method for the Guitar . . . Also A Choice Collection of Music . . .* (New York: J. L. Peters, 1874, 1876). See also Barbara Clemenson, "Justin Holland: African-American Guitarist of the 19th Century," *Soundboard* 21/2 (1994): 13–20. Shearer, "A Review . . . ," discusses Holland's *Method* at some length, calling it "far superior to any other early American publication" of this sort. Also see Gura, *C. F. Martin*, 160–67, for a discussion of Holland, especially his business relationship with Martin.

24. Lopes, [3].

25. See Nicholas E. Tawa, *High-Minded and Low-Down: Music in the Lives of Americans, 1800–1861* (Boston: Northeastern University Press, 2000), 68ff., for an examination of how Americans learned music in this period. Although Tawa allows for oral instruction, the bulk of his examples involve the transmission of musical instruction and works via printed sheet music. See Crawford, *America's Musical Life*, 221ff., for a discussion of the dissemination of popular music across America in print and its relation to performance. He distinguishes between the oral transmission of "traditional" music and the loosely structured interpretation and performance of popular, printed music. For the late introduction of the guitar to rural string bands, see, for example Bob Carlin, *String Bands in the North Carolina Piedmont* (Jefferson, NC: McFarland, 2004). Carlin observes that "Although the guitar had been in the Piedmont [North Carolina] since the 1850s, it didn't enter the picture as a part of the string bands until early in the twentieth century," 9. Neil V. Rosenberg makes a similar observation in *Bluegrass: A History* (Urbana: University of Illinois Press, 1985), 21.

Modern studies of America's nineteenth-century guitar repertoire confirm the preponderance of standard notation. See, for example, Shearer, "A Review . . . ," and John C. Tanno, "American

Guitar Methods . . ." for American guitar methods in standard notation. In his count of guitar music in the 1870 Board of Trade Catalog, Peter Danner tallies "over a thousand pieces for solo guitar (plus an even larger number of songs with guitar accompaniment)"; see "Foreword," Lopes, iii.

26. Danner, "The Guitar in 19th-Century America," and Back, "The Guitar in New York," describe the guitar's waning popularity in the private and public spheres respectively. A decline in the use of the guitar, as well as the harp, in home music-making in England has been credited in part to popular music's increasing chromaticism in the mid-nineteenth century; see Derek Scott, *The Singing Bourgeois: Songs of the Victorian Drawing Room and Parlour* (Milton Keynes, UK: Open University Press, 1989), 50. But the most popular American songs of the same era—Stephen Foster's plantation melodies, for example—displayed little in the way of unplayable chromaticism. See note 19 above, for a description of Robert Ferguson's recent study of American guitar tutors.

27. The author devotes an entire section to the piano in the United States in Arthur Loesser, *Men, Women and Pianos: A Social History* (New York: Simon and Schuster, 1954). For the citation from the *Atlantic Monthly* as well as Joseph Hale's story, see "A Whole is Made of the Parts" and "Pianos and Stencils—For 'The People,'" 520–31. Other book-length studies documenting aspects of the piano's nineteenth-century history include Rosamond E. M. Harding, *The Piano-forte: Its History Traced to the Great Exhibition of 1851* (1933; rpt. New York: Da Capo, 1973); David S. Grover, *The Piano: Its Story from Zither to Grand* (New York: Scribner's, 1976); and Edwin M. Good, *Giraffes, Black Dragons, and Other Pianos* (Stanford, CA: Stanford University Press, 2001).

28. Dale Cockerell, "Nineteenth-century popular music" in *The Cambridge History of American Music*, ed. David Nicholls (Cambridge: Cambridge University Press, 1998), 159.

29. For the development of the banjo, see Phillip Gura and James F. Bollman, *America's Instrument: The Banjo in the Nineteenth Century* (Chapel Hill: University of North Carolina Press, 1999); Karen Linn, *That Half-Barbaric Twang: The Banjo in American Popular Culture* (Urbana & Chicago: University of Illinois Press, 1994); and Cecelia Conway, *African Banjo Echoes in Appalachia: A Study of Folk Traditions* (Knoxville: University of Tennessee Press, 1997). The minstrel show has been the subject of many studies, especially in the last decades of the twentieth century, and all touch on the banjo to one degree or another. Significant book-length studies include William J. Mahar, *Behind the Burnt Cork Mask: Early Blackface Minstrelsy and Antebellum American Popular Culture* (Urbana: University of Illinois Press, 1999); Dale Cockrell, *Demons of Disorder: The Early Blackface Minstrels and their World* (New York: Cambridge University Press, 1997); Annemarie Bean, James V. Hatch, and Brooks McNamara, eds., *Inside the Minstrel Mask: Readings in Nineteenth-Century Blackface Minstrelsy* (Hanover, NH: Wesleyan University Press. 1996); and Eric Lott, *Love and Theft: Blackface Minstrelsy and the American Working Class* (New York: Oxford University Press, 1995). For an early consideration of the minstrel show, see Carl F. Wittke, *Tambo and Bones: A History of the American Minstrel Stage* (Durham, NC: Duke University Press, 1930).

30. *Dwight's Journal of Music* 4 (January 28, 1854): 133. The citation about art songs and the banjo is drawn from Gura and Bollman, *America's Instrument*, 76. See Linn, 7 for citations about the "elevated banjoist." She devotes an entire chapter to the elevation of the banjo. For a discussion of the appeal of the minstrel show to the middle class, see Russell Sanjek, *American Popular Music and Its Business: The First Four Hundred Years*, 3 vols. (New York: Oxford University Press, 1988), 2: 174.

31. See, for example, *Stewart's* 2/12 (October-November 1884): 2.

32. Gura and Bollman, *America's Instrument*, 75–90.

33. *Stewart's* 2/11 (August-September 1884): 3. Tablature exists in a variety of forms but the most common depicts the strings of the banjo or guitar. Numbers or letters on these strings indicate left-hand fretting patterns. Significant amounts of Renaissance and Baroque music for lute and five-course guitar exist in tablature formats, but by the early nineteenth century guitar music was more generally transmitted in standard musical notation.

34. Charles Burney, "Guittarra," in *The Cyclopedia; or Universal Dictionary of Arts, Sciences, and Literature*, ed. Abraham Rees (London: Longman, Hurst, Rees, Orme & Brown, 1819).

35. *Stewart's* 5/2 (June-July 1888): 9. For a succinct discussion of the transition from stroke playing to "guitar-style," see Robert Lloyd Webb, *Ring the Banjar! The Banjo in America from Folklore to Factory* (Cambridge, MA: The MIT Museum, 1984), 13.

CHAPTER 2. INTERLUDE: THE GUITAR IN THE BMG MOVEMENT—THE SOURCES

1. Several serious studies of the mandolin and banjo offer important information about the organological development, playing techniques, and cultural significance of these instruments, some considering the association of the three instruments in the late nineteenth century. While many studies of the banjo and mandolin deal principally with their construction, physical development, and production, the following delve into the social and musical contexts of the two instruments and remain the best sources for mandolin and banjo in Victorian America. For the banjo, see Gura and Bollman, *America's Instrument*, and Linn. For the mandolin, see Scott Hambly, "Mandolins in the United States Since 1880: An Industrial and Sociological History of Form," Ph.D. diss., University of Pennsylvania, 1977 (Ann Arbor, MI: UMI, 1977). A more recent study of the mandolin, while more circumscribed than Hambly's, provides a helpful introduction to the mandolin orchestra: Paul Ruppa, *The Mandolin in America After 1880 and The History of Mandolin Orchestras in Milwaukee, Wisconsin* (M.Mus. thesis, University of Wisconsin-Milwaukee, 1988).

2. For an overview of nineteenth-century American musical magazines, see my survey in chapter 2 of "The Guitar in America As Reflected in Topical Periodicals, 1882–1933" (Ph.D. diss., Washington University in St. Louis, 2004). For a broader discussion see *The New Grove Dictionary of American Music*, 1986, s.v. "periodical," by Imogene Fellinger and John Shepard. The most thorough studies of American musical periodicals are Vera S. Flandorf, "Music Periodicals in the United States: A Survey of their History and Content" (M.A. thesis, University of Chicago, 1952); Charles Edward Wunderlich, "A History and Bibliography of Early American Musical Periodicals, 1782–1852" (Ph.D. diss., University of Michigan, 1962); and Mary Veronica Davison, "American Music Periodicals: 1853–1899" (Ph.D. diss., University of Minnesota, 1973).

3. Peter Danner, "The Guitar in America as Mirrored in Cadenza (1894–1924)," *Soundboard* 18/3(1991): 10–19.

4. Richard Ohmann, *Politics of Letters* (Middletown, CT: Wesleyan, 1987), 149–50.

5. Gura and Bollman, *America's Instrument*, 138.

6. Philip Gura has produced two important studies of the operations of nineteenth-century plucked-string manufacturing operations. "Manufacturing Guitars for the American Parlor: James Ashborn's Wolcottville, Connecticut Factory, 1851–1856," *Proceedings of the American Antiquarian*

Society 104/1 (1994): 117–55, documents the operations of the Connecticut factory that produced thousands of instruments for the New York music retailers William Hall & Son and Firth, Pond & Co. His more recent *C. F. Martin and His Guitars* offers a detailed examination of the famed Martin operation up to the 1870s, including business arrangements between the Martin Company and numerous partners and representatives. Such manufacturing and business arrangements, though earlier in the century, were not unique to Ashborn or Martin and persisted well into the twentieth century.

7. Citations are from Ellen Gruber Garvey, *The Adman in the Parlor: Magazines and the Gendering of Consumer Culture, 1880s to 1910s* (New York and Oxford: Oxford University Press, 1996), 3–4. See Susan Porter Benson, *Counter Cultures: Saleswomen, Managers and Customers in American Department Stores, 1890–1940* (Urbana and Chicago: University of Illinois Press, 1986), especially chapter 1, "The New Kind of Store," for a concise evaluation of the many changes that occurred in promotion and sales in the 1890s. See also, Neil Harris, *Cultural Excursions: Marketing Appetites and Cultural Tastes in Modern America* (Chicago and London: University of Chicago Press, 1990), 184–85.

8. See, for example, J. J. Derwin's speech in *Cadenza* 16/11 (May 1910): 12, and an editorial, probably by Walter Jacobs, in *Cadenza* 18/10 (April 1912): 33.

9. Ohmann, 15.

10. "In the nineteenth century, the old conception of separate but complementary 'spheres' of work for men and women in preindustrial economies was incorporated into a new kind of domesticity, one in which women became the guardians of the finer human feelings as well as the administrators of the household. In this vision of appropriate domestic life, 'home' became not the resource for minimum subsistence but the space for psychological refuge from the rigors of economic life as well as the proper site for expression of familial love and guidance." Katherine C. Grier, *Culture & Comfort: Parlor Making and Middle-Class Identity, 1850–1930* (Washington and London: Smithsonian Institution Press, 1988), 5.

11. "Is the Banjo Musical?" *Cadenza* 17/6 (December 1910): 9–10. For other examples, see *Stewart's* 13/2 (June-July 1896): 1; "The Banjo World," *Stewart's* 13/3 (August-September 1896): 5; *Stewart's* 14/4 (October-November 1897): 2; and *Gatcomb's* 9/11 (July 1896): 4. *Crescendo's* guitar columnist recommended that musicians pursue a hobby or fad, listing antique or stamp collecting, photography, basketry, and, especially, the sciences (!) of physiognomy, phrenology, astrology, and psalmistry. See, Ethel Lucretia Olcott, "The Guitarists Round Table—'Hobbies' and 'Fads,' " *Crescendo* 6/2 (August 1913): 21.

12. *Gatcomb's* 1/3 (January 1888): 2.

13. *Cadenza* 21/4 (October 1914): 9, featured a portrait and description of H. A. Webber's Juvenile Orchestra of Portland, Oregon.

14. See *Stewart's* 9/6 (February-March 1893): 1; *Cadenza* 5/1 (September-October 1898): 17; and James P. Downs, "Beauty and the Beast," *Cadenza* 13/3 (November 1906): 15.

15. *Stewart's* 14/5 (December 1897–January 1898): 2. For a slightly more complete biography of Stewart, see *The New Grove*, 2001 ed., s.v. "Stewart, S(amuel) S(wain) [*sic*]," by Jay Scott Odell. Gura and Bollman, *America's Instrument*, devote an entire chapter to Stewart's role in the development of the banjo. As early as 1885 Stewart featured a full-page advertisement depicting his employees at their posts, each working on several banjos at specific work stations; see *Stewart's* 3/2 (February-March 1885): 16.

16. *Stewart's* 8/6 (February-March 1892): 1. See also, *Stewart's* 2/9 (April-May 1884): 1, and 8/4 (October-November 1891): 1.

17. Gura and Bollman, *America's Instrument*, 138.

18. Chapter 4 of Gura and Bollman, *America's Instrument*, identifies and examines Stewart's principal competitors, especially Fairbanks and Cole.

19. Gatcomb's biography to approximately 1895 appears in *Cadenza* 2/1 (September-October 1895): 2. Also see *Cadenza* 6/2 (November-December 1899): 21 for information on Gatcomb's business. The quote about Galeucia appears in *Gatcomb's* 1/1 (September 1887): 4.

20. See Gura and Bollman, *America's Instrument*, 107ff., for a detailed account of the Dobson banjo dynasty and its contributions to the history of the instrument. Unless noted otherwise, biographical data on the Dobson brothers derives from this source. A blurb about the *Era's* success notes that "Our circulation is steadily increasing. We are respected. Ours is the only publication ever edited by a Dobson that can say this"; *New York Musical Era* 1/4 (July 1890): 4. Of the five brothers, George C., who abandoned New York for Boston in 1869, remains the best known, primarily because of his widely used banjo tutor. He was the only banjoist to appear in F. O. Jones, *A Handbook of American Music and Musicians* (1886; rpt. New York: Da Capo Press, 1971), 49.

21. *New York Musical Era* 1/2 (May 1890): 3. Dobson's hyperbolic biography ran in *New York Musical Era* 2/1 (January 1891): 1. The comment about Dobson posters in New York is cited in Gura and Bollman, *America's Instrument*, 109.

22. Dobson's obituary ran in *Cadenza* 16/8 (February 1910): 10. The citation about Dobson's studio appeared as a news blurb in *Cadenza* 6/1 (September-October 1899): 23.

23. No significant biographical information about Henning appeared in his own magazines, but between 1885 and 1890 *Stewart's* detailed many of Henning's musical accomplishments; see *Stewart's* 3/2 (February-March 1885): 1–3 and 3/12 (October-November 1886): 4.

24. For listings of The Henning Music Company in Chicago, see Theodore Winton Thorson, "A History of Music Publishing in Chicago 1850–1960" (Ph.D. diss., Northwestern University, 1961), 172, 195ff., and 317. For a typical Henning advertisement see *Chicago Trio* 1/1 (October-November 1897): 21. Henning's arrangement to market instruments built by others was not uncommon, especially in the upper Midwest, where large-scale instrument companies flourished. See James P. Kraft, "Manufacturing" in *The Electric Guitar: A History of an American Icon*, André Millard, ed. (Baltimore: The Johns Hopkins University Press, 2004), 63–87, for an excellent overview of development of musical instrument production in the early twentieth century.

25. Letter from H. J. Isbell, *Cadenza* 1/4 (March-April 1895): 9. See Partee's editorial in *Cadenza* 1/5 (May-June 1895): 9. Partee did introduce a line of mandolins (which he called "American lutes") in the very early years of the twentieth century, but they appear to have met with little success. In all likelihood, the rapid success of the Gibson Mandolin-Guitar Company and its violin-inspired line of mandolins overpowered Partee's more traditional Venetian-style instruments.

26. Partee first appeared in *Stewart's* 4/7 (December 1887–January 1888): 4. Notices about Partee and his brother Charles appeared regularly through the 1880s and early 1890s, including Charles Partee's endorsement of the Stewart banjo in *Stewart's* 6/5 (December 1889–January 1890): 6. By 1896, Stewart had begun his attacks on Partee and *Cadenza*. See *Stewart's* 13/1 (April-May 1896): 4; 13/6 (February-March 1897): 4, 7; 14/1 (April-May 1897): 6; 14/2 (June-July 1897): 3; and 14/3 (August-September 1897): 5. After Stewart's death, Partee once again advertised in *Stewart's Journal* and participated in its pages in the discussion about establishing the American Guild of Banjoist, Mandolinists and Guitarists. See *Stewart's* 18/5 (April 1901): 7.

27. Partee announced the magazine's move in "Editorial," *Cadenza* 6/4 (March–April 1900): 10.

28. Partee's retirement was credited to ill health, though he lived another ten years after he gave up *Cadenza*. See *Cadenza* 21/11 (May 1915): 16, for Partee's obituary. The quote about Jacobs's catalog is from *Stewart's* 12/4 (October-November 1895): 9. Much of this extended biographical sketch of Jacobs was duplicated in a similar sketch in *Cadenza* 15/1 (July 1908): 20–21. Jacobs first appeared in *Stewart's* 11/3 (August-September 1894): 12. Jacobs's other music periodicals were *Jacobs' Orchestral Monthly* (Boston, 1910–41); *Jacobs' Band Monthly* (Boston, 1916–41); and *Melody* (Boston, 1917–30).

29. The cover of *Cadenza* carried several subtitles through the years, including the early "An Educational Magazine devoted to the interests of the Banjo, Mandolin, Guitar and kindred instruments" and the later "An Educational Monthly Magazine Devoted to the Literature and Music of the Violin, Mandolin, Guitar, Banjo, Zither, Harp and Piano." When *Cadenza* became the "Official Organ" for the American Guild of Banjoists, Mandolinists and Guitarists, its subtitle emphatically read, "Issued in the Exclusive Interests of the Mandolin, Banjo and Guitar." When Walter Jacobs later expanded its subject matter, the subtitle grew accordingly: "A Monthly Music Magazine for the Musical Home and the Professional Pianist."

30. *FOG* 4/1 (November-December 1903): 21.

31. *Cadenza* 6/5 (May-June 1900): 45. Details of Gutman's life were gleaned from a brief biography in *Cadenza* 4/3 (January-February 1898): 12. See Samuel Adlestein, "The Bandurria and the Spanish Students," *Cadenza* 6/5 (May-June 1900): 4–5, for a contemporary account of the Spanish Students and the *bandurria*. *FOG* offered a similar article, "Some Interesting Facts About the Mandolin," by R. M. Tyrrell in *FOG* 4/3 ([March-April 1904]): 2–3. See Hambly, 55ff., and Ruppa, 21–29, for discussions of the original Spanish Students as well as imitators. Hambly, relying on the *Cadenza* biography, assumes that Gutman studied with members of the original Spanish Students, but the evidence appears inconclusive. For a notice about Gutman's instruments see "Trade Notes," *Cadenza* 4/3 (January-February 1898): 17. See page 13 of the same issue for a photo of The Ladies Euterpean Club, led by Gutman. See *FOG* 3/4 (May-June 1903): 2, 5, for a brief blurb and photo of The Sicilian Club of Cleveland, another of Gutman's women's ensembles.

32. See *FOG* 2/1 (November-December 1901): 32, for Gutman's promotion of a national BMG organization.

33. See *Cadenza* 1/6 (July-August 1895): 4, for Partee's first call for an association or union for banjoist, mandolinists, and guitarists. See *Cadenza* 6/5 (May-June 1900): 10 for Partee's first endorsement of the newly created Guild.

34. The final issue of *FOG* was 4/3 ([March-April 1904]). The earliest extant number of *American Music Journal* includes Gutman's plans for his organization; see "League Matters," *AMJ* 5/2 (September 1905): 23.

35. *Crescendo* 8/4 (October 1915): 6.

36. "Guild Bulletin," *Crescendo* 1/1 (July 1908): 6–7.

37. See "I. H. Odell," *Crescendo* 2/3 (September 1909): 7.

38. Lewis A. Williams, "What's The Use?" *Crescendo* 1/1 (July 1908): 4. Biographical information for H. F. Odell has been taken from this article as well as from "Prominent Players and Teachers—Herbert Forrest Odell (1872–1926)," *Crescendo* 18/10 (April 1926): 9, and "Herbert Forrest Odell, 1872–1926," *Crescendo* 25/10 (October 1933): 1.

39. See Bone, *Guitar and Mandolin*, 282, for a brief biographical sketch of the father and son bearing this name. Bone offers dates for neither, indicating only that they were active in Paris and

London "during the end of the nineteenth and commencement of the twentieth centuries." Given the sparse information, it remains impossible to identify with which of these mandolinists Odell studied.

40. See, for example, "Guild Bulletin," *Crescendo* 1/1 (July 1908): 6–7 for a report on the interminable debates at the Guild convention about C and A banjo notation, or D. E. Hartnett, "The Issue of the Hour," *Crescendo* 1/2 (August 1908): 5, about the same subject. Advocates for the non-transposing C-notation won this battle; see "Fretted Instrument Progress of Twenty-five Years," *Crescendo* 25/10 (October 1933): 3. Universal Notation employed the treble clef alone, allowing a player to negotiate all instruments with command on only one clef. *Crescendo* 4/3 (September 1911) includes accounts of the hot debates about Universal Notation at the 1911 Guild convention. See also, "Clef Question," *Crescendo* 5/8 (February 1913): 10, 24.

41. Bauer offers an overview of the mandolin's popularity in America as well as some details of his biography in "The Mandolin in America" in Robert Carl Hartman, *Guitars and Mandolins in America* (Hoffman Estates, IL: Maurer, 1984): 9–10. See also "Walter Bauer, 97; Renowned as a Musician and Composer," *Hartford Courant* (January 21, 1997): B7.

CHAPTER 3. THE GUITAR IN THE BMG MOVEMENT, 1880–1900

1. Charles Morris, "En Passant," *Stewart's* 15/6 (February-March 1899): 10. The first citation is from *Stewart's* 10/2 (June-July 1893): 10.

2. *Stewart's* 3/1 (December-January 1885): 4. The comments about the society ladies appeared on page 1 of the same issue. The citation comparing the banjo and guitar is from *Stewart's* 6/1 (April-May 1889): 3.

3. See "Guitar Items," *Stewart's* 3/3 (April-May 1885): 1; "U.S. LEADS ALL," C. S. Patty, *Stewart's* 16/2 (June-July 1899): 3; and *Stewart's* 15/2 (June-July 1898): 10.

4. *Stewart's* 8/2 (June-July 1891): 2.

5. *Stewart's* 12/5 (December 1895–January 1896): 10.

6. *Gatcomb's* 1/1 (September 1887): 1.

7. P. H. Coombs, "Question of Raised Frets. Are They Designed to Advance the Banjo to a Higher Standard?" *Gatcomb's* 1/4 (March 1888): [1].

8. *Gatcomb's* 1/1 (September 1887): 1.

9. A number of mid-century American guitar methods indicated that their purpose was to teach song accompaniment. For example, in the Preface to his to *New Method for the Guitar*, Charles Converse observes that "I find that by far the greater number of Guitar players have studied it on account of its charming quality for accompaniment to the Voice; and for such purpose I have treated it, and endeavored, by the simplest and most direct route, to lead the student to a mastery of its resources in this respect."

10. *New York Musical Era* 1/1 (April 1890): 1–2 and 1/2 (May 1890): 8.

11. *Elite Banjoist* 1/1 (October-November 1890): 13.

12. *Chicago Trio* 1/1 (October-November 1897): 3–4.

13. For Henning's biography of his late father-in-law, see *Elite Banjoist* 1/2 (January–February 1891): 2–3, and *Chicago Trio* 1, no. 4 (April-May 1898): 14. Ferranti's biography appeared on pages 2–3 of the former. This detailed account of Ferranti's career reads very much like the entry for him

in Philip Bone's encyclopedic *The Guitar and Mandolin* published almost twenty-five years later. Emma Miller's father, J. M. Miller, apparently contributed material to Bone's project that may, in fact, have included this same letter. That such a significant historical document would first appear in a short-lived regional periodical suggests we reconsider Henning's role in the BMG world. My thanks to Brian Torosian for suggesting this connection between Bone and Miller. This same letter appears as an unascribed typescript in the Foden Collection in the Missouri Historical Society Library, St. Louis, Mo. Thanks to Robert Ferguson for this information.

14. For example, C. F. E. Fiset, replying to a correspondent, notes in a letter dated July 29, 1898, "Bischoff's arr. I do not care for." Quoted in "The Correspondence of C.F.E. Fiset to Mr. Sheppard," compiled and annotated by Ronald C. Purcell, *Soundboard* 16/4 (1989–90): 20. Despite Henning's claims, Bischoff does not appear in Bone's *Guitar and Mandolin* or in histories of music in Chicago.

15. I utilize the late-twentieth-century classical guitar nomenclature for the right hand: p=thumb, i=index, m=middle, and a=ring or third finger.

16. For a detailed examination of late-century guitar techniques in America, see chapter 4 in Noonan, "The Guitar . . ."

17. George W. Gregory, "A Few Observations On Guitar Fingering," *Stewart's* 12/3 (August-September 1895): 9.

18. Letter from A. L. Camp in *FOG* 4/1 (November-December 1903): 3.

19. For *Stewart's* attack on the Carcassi sitting position, see *Stewart's* 3/1 (December-January 1885): 1. See Gura and Bollman, *America's Instrument*, for numerous illustrations from the nineteenth century of banjoists sitting both cross-legged and flat-footed. A famous example of *Stewart's* no-holds-barred attacks on unrefined technique are the back-to-back illustrations of an unkempt, ill-mannered blacked-up minstrel player and the refined Alfred Farland and his sister sitting in a proper Victorian parlor, he holding a Stewart banjo, she at an upright piano. Stewart titled these illustrations, respectively, "The Banjo As It Used To Be" and "A Chaste Picture—The Banjo of 1894." *Stewart's* 10/5 (December 1893–January 1894): 14–15. See Linn, 19–21, for a discussion of this comparison, including reproductions of the pages from *Stewart's*. For an overview of nineteenth-century interpretations of body language, see Kenneth Ames, *Death in the Dining Room and Other Tales of Victorian Culture* (Philadelphia: Temple University Press, 1992), especially his chapter entitled "Posture and Power," 185–232.

20. *Stewart's* 12/1 (April-May 1895): 6.

21. J. W. Freeman, "How to Hold the Guitar," *Cadenza* 2/5 (May-June 1896): 4–5.

22. C. L. Partee, "A Few Remarks and Other Things," *Cadenza* 6/3 (January-February 1900): 2–3.

23. Ronald C. Purcell, "Letters From the Past: Segovia Perceived: The American Reaction of Segovia's Arrival," *Soundboard* 20/3 (1994): 21. Articles on this topic in the magazines spilled into the third decade of the new century. See R. M. Tyrrell, "Some Suggestions as to a Proper Method of Studying the Guitar," *Cadenza* 3/1 (September-October 1896): 12–13; Agnes S. Gramm, "Some Reasons Why," *Cadenza* 8/7 (March 1902): 12–14; William Foden, "The Guitarist," *Cadenza* 18/6 (December 1911): 40; Vahdah Olcott-Bickford, "The Guitarist," *Cadenza* 26/7 (July 1919): 22, and 27/2 (February 1920): 38; and William Foden, "Guitarists Round Table—Holding the Guitar by George C. Krick," *Crescendo* 14/11 (May 1922): 22.

24. Peter Danner has suggested that steel strings entered the United States as a result of the Mexican War of 1846, citing an 1888 guitar tutor, but *Stewart's Journal* ran advertisements for steel

strings at least five years earlier. See Danner, "The Guitar in Nineteenth Century America," 294, and *Stewart's* 2/1 (May 1883): 4. The editorial comments about gut and steel are from *Gatcomb's*, 1/3 (January 1888): 3. Tim Brookes alerted me to a description of women winding steel guitar strings in a Connecticut string factory in the 1860s; Virginia Penny, *The Employments of Women: A Cyclopaedia of Woman's Work* (Boston: Walker, Wise, 1863), 463–64.

25. See, for example, S. H. Voyles's letter that offers a point-by-point argument for using steel strings, *Stewart's* 9/4 (October-November 1892): 8.

26. *Stewart's* 14/1 (April-May 1897): 30.

27. For example, Thomas J. Armstrong, "Banjo Orchestra Music. A Few Hints to Arrangers and Leaders of Banjo Clubs, Chapter III," *Stewart's* 7/5 (December 1890–January 1891): 2.

28. These observations appeared in a serial column devoted to the guitar: "Guitar Notes," *Stewart's* 9/1 (April-May 1892): 3, and "Guitar Notes," *Stewart's* 9/4 (October-November 1892): 8.

29. *Chicago Trio* 1/1 (October-November 1897): 21.

30. *Stewart's* 2/11 (August-September 1884): 12.

31. "The Banjo vs. Guitar, as a 'Ladies' Instrument,'" *Stewart's* 3/1 (December-January 1885): 1.

32. See, for example, *Stewart's* 4/8 (February-March 1888): 5. Lynch's "The Enterprise Waltz" appears in *Stewart's* 12/4 (October-November 1895): 16–17.

33. See Hambly, especially chapter 9, which documents many of these hybrid and exaggerated instruments. More than thirty years after Stewart's "Six-String Banjo" appeared, the Vega Banjo Company promoted its version of the guitar-banjo, observing, "By the way, do you know that one guitar banjo is equal to about six guitars in an orchestra . . . ?" See "Vega News—To Mandolin Orchestra Leaders," *Crescendo* 11/6 (December 1918): 1.

34. R. S. Chase, "The Guitar and its Teaching," *Cadenza* 1/1 (September-October 1894): 3. See Bone, *Guitar and Mandolin*, 195, for a biography of Kreutzer (1780–1849) and 320–22 for an account of the father-son guitarists, both named Leonard Schulz. Curiously, Chase omitted Johann Mertz from this list of esteemed European guitarists.

35. Alfred Chenet, "The Guitar and Its Progress in America," *Cadenza* 1/2 (November-December 1894): 3–4.

36. For a contemporaneous biographical sketch, see "R. M. Tyrrell," *Cadenza* 5/1 (September-October 1898): 10–11. His articles for *Cadenza* include "The Guitar. The Reason Why It Should Be Strung with Gut Strings," *Cadenza* 2/4 (March-April 1896): 9–10; "Some Suggestions as to a Proper Method of Studying the Guitar," *Cadenza* 3/1 (September-October 1896): 12–13; "System vs. Inspiration in the Construction of Melodies," *Cadenza* 3/3 (January-February 1897): 12, and *Cadenza* 3/4, (March-April 1897): 10–11; "Classic vs. Popular Songs," *Cadenza* 8/3 (November 1901): 12–13; and "A Good Ear for Music—What It Implies," *Cadenza* 6/4 (March-April 1900): 14.

37. Pelzer's article was "The Guitar as a Solo Instrument," *Cadenza* 6/2 (November-December 1899): 5–6. See Bone, *Mandolin and Guitar*, 286–87, for a biography of Pelzer's more famous older sister, Mme. Sidney Pratten. Bone offers no information on Giulia Pelzer, but *Cadenza* 6/3 (January-February 1900): 19–20, prints an overblown biography from *The Gentlewoman's Court Review*. Another biography from London's *Amusement* magazine appeared in *Cadenza* 11/7 (March 1905): 32–33. Pelzer achieved considerable recognition as a teacher in London, being appointed "Professor of the guitar and mandolin at the Guildhall School of Music" in the early 1890s. She appeared again in *Cadenza* with "The Guitar As An Accompaniment to the Voice," *Cadenza* 6/3 (January-February 1900): 4–5. Kitchener's article spanned March to August 1899: "The History and

Development of the Guitar," *Cadenza* 5/4 (March-April 1899): 7–9; *Cadenza* 5/5 (May-June 1899): 5–7; and *Cadenza* 5/6 (July-August 1899): 5–7.

38. Partee's variations appeared in *Cadenza* 3/6 (July-August 1897): 20–22.

39. Stickles's version of "Confidence, Song Without Words No. 4" appeared in *New York Musical Era* 2/1 (January 1891): 7, and "Consolation, Song Without Words No. 9" appeared the following month in *New York Musical Era* 2/2 (February 1891): 6. This second piece also appeared in *Cadenza* 16/5 (November 1909): 22, in an arrangement by R. E. Hildreth. C. H. Stickles, a guitarist based in New York City, contributed articles and music regularly to C. Edgar Dobson's *New York Musical Era*. Fiset's transcriptions appeared in *Stewart's* in 1898 and 1899: J. S. Bach's "Gavotte. 6th Cello Suite" in 14/6 (February-March 1898): [14–15]; Frederick Chopin's "Nocturne, Op. 37, no. 1" in 15/4 (October-November 1898): [20–21]; Edvard Grieg's "Anitra's Tanz" in 15/5 (December 1898–January 1899): [13–14]; Pietro Mascagni's "Intermezzo from Cavalleria Rusticana" in 15/2 (June-July 1898): [18–19]; and Franz Schubert's "Hark! Hark The Lark" in 16/2 (June-July 1899): [18–19]. In addition to the pieces published in *Stewart's*, Fiset set other works by Pergolesi, Schubert, and Beethoven. See advertisements for his editions in *Stewart's* 15/4 (October-November 1898): 25, and *Stewart's* 15/5 (December 1898–January 1899): cover, 31. For more detailed descriptions of these solos by Stickles and Fiset, see Noonan, "The Guitar . . . ," chapter 7.

40. Thomas J. Armstrong, a banjoist active in Philadelphia during Stewart's heyday, discussed the importance of Stewart's banjeaurine in "Banjoists Round Table—A Banjeaurine Revival," *Crescendo* 14/12 (June 1922): 24. See Gura and Bollman, *America's Instrument*, 177–82 for a discussion of Stewart's sized banjos and their impact within the banjo-playing community. For an introduction to the Boston Ideals, see Ruppa, 29–31.

CHAPTER 4. INTERLUDE: A NEW GENERATION OF GUITARISTS

1. Holland wrote two methods, the better-known titled *Holland's Comprehensive Method for the Guitar* (New York: J. L. Peters, 1874, 1876). This tutor remained in active use into the twentieth century, its last edition dated 1903. See James M. Trotter, *Music and Some Highly Musical People . . . [with] Sketches of the Lives of Remarkable Musicians of the Colored Race. With Portraits, and an Appendix Containing Copies of Music Composed by Colored Men* (Boston: Lee & Shephard and New York: C. T. Dillingham, 1885), 114–30 for a biography as well as a short guitar solo by Holland in the musical appendix. Holland was one of a handful of American guitarists to appear in Bone's *The Guitar and Mandolin*, 167–68. Holland's music has been reproduced numerous times in *Soundboard* and he has been the subject of one article in that magazine by Barbara Clemenson. A brief biography and one of his pieces appear in Danner, *The Guitar in America*. More recently, Philip Gura examined Holland's business dealings with guitar manufacturer C. F. Martin; see Gura, *C. F. Martin*, 163–67.

2. See Bone, *Guitar and Mandolin*, 300–301, for a biography of Romero. The guitarist was featured in nearly every issue of *Stewart's* in 1891; see, *Stewart's* 8/1 (April-May 1891): 5; 8/2 (June-July 1891): 2; 8/4 (October-November 1891): 4; 8/6 (February-March 1892): 7; and especially 8/5 (December 1891–January 1892): 2–3, which contains several reviews of Romero performances.

3. See Bone, *Guitar and Mandolin*, 117–19. For Romero being compared to Tárrega, see Vahdah Olcott-Bickford, "The Guitarist—Appreciative Audiences," *Cadenza* 24/5 (May 1917): 10–11.

Stewart described Romero as one of the original Spanish Students in *Stewart's* 8/5 (December 1891–January 1892): 2. Romero corrected the mistake in *Stewart's* 8/6 (February-March 1892): 6.

4. See Bone, *Guitar and Mandolin*, 182–83, for de Janon's biography. For other comments on de Janon and/or his compositions, see Alfred Chenet, "The Guitar and Its Progress in America," *Cadenza* 1/2 (November-December 1894): 3–4; R. M. Tyrrell, "The Guitar and Its Music," *FOG* 4/1 (November-December 1903): 2; Thos. C. B. Tyler, "Chas. De Janon," *Crescendo* 6/9 (March 1914): 7; Vahdah Olcott-Bickford, "The Guitarist," *Cadenza* 24/8 (August 1917): 12–13; and William Foden, "The Guitarists Round Table," *Crescendo* 15/2 (August 1922): 22. An obituary for de Janon appeared in "News," *Crescendo* 4/1 (July 1911): 22. The Guild's "Standards of Attainment" for all three plectral instruments ran in *Cadenza* 20/7 (January 1914): 13–14.

5. Henning's Conservatory is listed in Thorson, 317. For Stewart's screed against the guitar see "The Banjo vs. Guitar, as a 'Ladies' Instrument,'" *Stewart's* 3/1 (December-January 1885): 1. The report of Bischoff and Henning's first joint recital appears in "The Banjo World," *Stewart's* 3/9 (April-May 1886): 3, and her biography and portrait appear on 12–13. Notices of the Hennings' joint performances following their marriage appeared in *Stewart's* 3/10 (August-September 1886): 5, 9, and "The Banjo World," *Stewart's* 3/12 (October-November 1886): 4–5. For other reports on Bischoff-Henning's activities, see *Stewart's* 6/3 (October-November 1889): 5, and *Elite Banjoist* 1/2 (January-February 1891): 3.

6. The few available details of Lynch's biography are drawn from "Dominga I. Lynch," *Stewart's* 11/5 (December 1894–January 1895): 2. Lynch's articles are "Hints to Guitar Students," *Stewart's* 11/6 (February-March 1895): 5, and "Mandolin and Guitar Notes," *Stewart's* 12/2 (June-July 1895): 9.

7. A typical example of the disparity in recognition given men and women was the sketch of Mr. and Mrs. Fred Turner, *Cadenza* 4/1 (September-October 1897): 1. See Paula Gillett, *Musical Women in England, 1870–1914: "encroaching on all men's privileges"* (New York: St. Martin's Press, 2000), 9ff., for a brief consideration of the Victorian female music teacher.

8. "New Notes," *Cadenza* 3/6 (July-August 1897): 12, 14.

9. Tooker's first notice appeared in "News Notes," *Cadenza* 5/2 (November-December 1898): 14. Her photograph and biographical sketch appear in *Cadenza* 5/6 (July-August 1899): 1–2. Tooker's mother, Mrs. S. E. (Carrie) Tooker, made several appearances in *Stewart's*. Elsie Tooker's later magazine notices were in "Club Notes," *Cadenza* 18/9 (March 1912): 41, and "News," *Crescendo* 4/9 (March 1912): 22. I thank Elsie Tooker's family, especially Lesley Howard Hobbs, for access to their collection of Tooker's letters, photographs, press notices, radio logs, and recording.

10. Durkee's first biographical sketch was "Jennie Durkee," *Cadenza* 6/4 (March-April 1900): 12. The last was "Jennie Durkee," *Crescendo* 10/5 (November 1917): 7. *Cadenza* credited George Durkee with inventing and designing "the Washburn instruments, and also the new Lyon & Healy harp" in "Miss Jennie M. Durkee," *Cadenza* 15/5 (November 1908): 35–36. He published numerous articles in the BMG magazines about instrument design or instruments in the guitar family. Her ukulele method was published as *The American Way of Playing Ukulele Solos* (Chicago: Jennie M. Durkee, 1917). For her ukulele activities, see *Cadenza* 25/7 (July 1918): 37 ,and 29/6 (June 1922): 10, as well as an advertisement titled "The Ukulele Rejuvenated," *Crescendo* 11/1 (July 1918): 22. Her final notice was from "News," *Crescendo* 18/1 (July 1925): 8.

11. Several biographical sketches of Miller appeared in the BMG magazines; see "Gertrude Miller," *Cadenza* 6/2 (November-December 1899): 1; Elsie Tooker and Edna May Sanders, "The Ladies of the Banjo, Mandolin and Guitar Realm," *Stewart's* 18/6 (May 1901): 2; and *The American*

Music Journal 5/9 (April 1906): 19, 28. For the Miller family's connection to Mertz and Ferranti, see *Elite Banjoist* 1/2 (January-February 1891): 2–3, and the introduction to Josephine Mertz, "Life of the Late J.K. Mertz, Guitar Virtuoso," *Cadenza* 1/3 (January-February 1895): 4. Miller's activity with The American Guitar Society was documented in Gertrude Miller, "The American Guitar Society," *The American Music Journal* 5/5 (December 1905): 16, and Gertrude Miller, "The American Guitar Society," *Cadenza* 12/3 (November 1905): 12–13. Miller's short-lived organization, centered in the upper Midwest, should not be confused with Vahdah Olcott-Bickford's later West Coast society. For Olcott-Bickford's views of Miller, see Ethel Lucretia Olcott, "Guitarists Round Table—Answers by Walter Francis Vreeland, Carl W. F. Jansen, Gertrude Miller Strong," *Crescendo* 8/4 (October 1915): 19, and Vahdah Olcott-Bickford, "The Guitar in America," *Guitar Review* 23 (June 1959): 18.

12. "The Guitar and Its Progress in America," *Cadenza* 1/2 (November-December 1894): 3–4. An early biography of Chenet with a portrait ran in *Cadenza* 3/2 (November-December 1896): 2.

13. Vreeland's biography and photograph appeared as "A Concert Artist," *Cadenza* 21/9 (March 1915): 11–12. The account of his work with Hawaiian instruments appeared in "Prominent Boston Teachers," *Cadenza* 24/4 (April 1917): 6, 45. *Crescendo* published similar notices of Vreeland and his performances; his obituary ran in *Crescendo* 19/8 (February 1927): 8, and in Bill Smith, "Fretitorials," *Frets* 2/11 (February 1927): 7. His letterpress contributions to the BMG literature include "The Guitar Accompanist," which ran in three successive issues beginning with *Cadenza* 16/1 (July 1909): 13–14, and "The Guitar Superior for Personal Pleasure," which ran for two issues beginning in *Cadenza* 18/2 (August 1911): 8–10. Although he endorsed the techniques of the European masters, Vreeland apparently experimented with a thumb pick; see "Personal Notes," *Crescendo* 3/8 (February 1911): 22.

14. Fiset first appeared in *Stewart's* 14/5 (December 1897–January 1898): 30. See *Stewart's* 15/2 (June-July 1898): 5, for an extended sketch of Fiset's career to that date. This biography did not mention Fiset's American upbringing, perhaps an attempt to enhance his image as an exotic foreign musician. Purcell offers a thorough biography of Fiset in "Letters from the Past," reporting that Fiset eventually abandoned music for a successful career in dentistry.

15. This review from the *Minneapolis Journal* (December 6, 1897) was cited in *Stewart's* 15/1 (April-May 1898): 22. A biographical sketch listed among Fiset's repertoire not only Bach's "Sixth Cello Suite" but also his "Fugue in G Minor"; *Stewart's* 15/2 (June-July 1898): 5. Fiset's comments appeared in "Mandolin and Guitar Notes," *Stewart's* 14/5 (December 1897–January 1898): 30, and 14/6 (February-March 1898): 14–15.

16. Fiset focused on left-hand technique in "A System of Technique for the Guitar, Article III," *Stewart's* 16/3 (August-September 1899): 5–6, with musical examples on 13–16. His articles about left-hand technique appeared in "A System of Technique for the Guitar, Article IV," *Stewart's* 16/5 (December 1899–January 1900): 7–9, and "A System of Technique for the Guitar, Article V," *Stewart's* 16/6 (February-March 1900): 5–6.

17. See "A Guitarist of European Training," *Cadenza* 5/1 (September-October 1898): 14, for a biography of Schettler. See Danner, "The Guitar in America as Mirrored in *Cadenza*," 13, for a summary of Schettler's career. Another biography and portrait of Schettler appeared in *Cadenza* 5/5 (May-June 1899): 18. Schettler's series on technique ran for three consecutive issues, beginning with "The Art of Guitar Performing," *Cadenza* 7/1 (September 1900): 13. His other contributions include "Reflections of a Guitarist," *Cadenza* 5/2 (November-December 1898): 7, and "A Few Remarks on Artistic Performing," *Cadenza* 5/4 (March-April 1899): 4.

18. Danner's comments about Schettler are from "The Guitar in America as Mirrored in *Cadenza*," 13. Tyrrell's review of the 1904 Guild concert ran as "The Grand Mandolin, Banjo and Guitar concert given at Carnegie Hall, New York City.—A full, complete and critical report," *FOG* 4/2 (January-February 1904): 2–3.

19. Several biographies of Jansen appeared in the BMG magazines. See *FOG* 4/2 (January-February 1904): 2; "C. W. F. Jansen," *Cadenza* 15/11 (May 1909): 10, and "Carl W. F. Jansen," *Crescendo* 23/7 (March 1931): 15. A photo of Jansen with a mandolin quartet promoted his performance of Giuliani's Op. 103 Quintet for strings and terz guitar; *Crescendo*, 4/9 (March 1912): 5. The journal listings indicate that most of his performing occurred in Chicago, Wisconsin, and Michigan, but he appeared at Guild Conventions concerts in 1903 (Philadelphia) and 1912 (Chicago). His contributions to the magazines include "Crescendo Scrap Book—The Harp-Guitar," *Crescendo* 10/9 (March 1918): 7, as well as the guitar solo "At Dusk" in *Crescendo* 6/4 (October 1913).

20. Beginning in the late 1890s, Bane was an almost monthly presence in the magazines, usually in notices or recital programs documenting recent performances. A full-page advertisement for Bane and his Saxton System ran in *Cadenza* 7/1 (September 1900): 38. By and large, the leading guitarists of the day resoundingly rejected open tunings like Bane's to be impractical and unsophisticated. For example, see "Questions and Answers," *FOG* 2/3 (March-April 1902): 7, and Danner, "The Guitar in America," 14, for a brief discussion of Bane's Saxton System. See Danner's introduction to Henry Worrall's arrangement of "The Spanish Fandango" in *The Guitar in America: A Historical Collection*, 9, and Paul Cox's commentary about Worrall's "Sebastopol" in "Return With Us Now," *Soundboard* 2/2 (May 1975): 26. A late biography of Bane observed that he had performed "about eighty high and grammar school recitals in New York City and New Jersey" when he was in his early sixties. See "Johnson Bane. Guitarist," *Crescendo* 16/4 (October 1923): 9.

CHAPTER 5. TRANSITIONS: FROM THE PARLOR TO THE CONCERT HALL

1. The arrival of the original Spaniards was reported in "The Spanish Student Troupe: They Reach New York after a Voyage of Twenty-Two Days," *New York Times* (2 January 1880): 8 (Hambly, 57, quotes the entire article). For a discussion of their instruments and the connection to the mandolin, see Samuel Adlestein, "The Bandurria and the Spanish Students," *Cadenza* 6/5 (May-June 1900): 4–5, and R. M. Tyrrell, "Some Interesting Facts About the Mandolin," *FOG* 4/3 ([March-April 1904]): 2–3. Hambly, 55ff., and Ruppa, 21–29, offer discussions of the original Spanish Students as well as imitators. Hambly, 81ff., documents the adoption of the mandolin by immigrant violinists, especially Italians in New York City, in the 1880s.

2. While Latin-flavored music and costuming remained popular, BMG ensembles also regularly used music and costuming from America's minstrel shows. Although most BMG ensembles discontinued costuming, vaudeville performers, on the other hand, regularly played up ethnic associations with elaborate and fanciful costumes. See illustrations pages 79 and 122, for example.

3. See Bauer, "The Mandolin in America", 9–10, for a reminiscence of these early ensembles. Bauer attributes the transition from "club" to "orchestra" to the invention and marketing of the tenor mandola and the mando-cello.

4. A. H. M'Connell, "The Coming of the New Orchestra," *Cadenza* 14/2 (October 1907): 10–11. Some BMG apologists called on composers and arrangers to rethink the traditional string

orchestra, incorporating banjos, mandolins, and guitars into their works. See, for example, L. A. Bidee, "Orchestral Uses of the Mandolin, Banjo and Guitar," *Cadenza* 2/3 (January-February 1896): 8–10. Citing Hector Berlioz as a model for contemporary musicians, one BMG enthusiast intimated that the French composer would have looked kindly on banjos, mandolins, and guitars in modern orchestras: "What the musical world requires to-day is a modern Berlioz—a genius of nature, untrammeled by the stereotyped traditions and dry as dust antiquated school of instrumentation." Philip Bone, *Cadenza* 11/3 (November 1904): 17.

5. *Cadenza* 1/6 (July-August 1895): 4.

6. "Practical Hints on Guitar Playing" first appeared in *Cadenza* 4/1 (September-October 1897): 2–3. It ran through *Cadenza* 5/2 (November-December 1898) and was eventually collected in a book (with the same title) published by Partee.

7. "Popular Illusions Concerning the Guitar and Mandolin," *Cadenza* 7/9 (May 1901): 3–6.

8. *Cadenza* 7/10 (June 1901): 5. C. D. Schettler offered a similar justification for America's perceived preeminence in the BMG world; see "A Guitarist of European Training," *Cadenza* 5/1 (September-October 1898): 14.

9. Besides a biographical sketch in Bone, *Guitar and Mandolin*, 120–21, these studies include John F. Greene, "William Foden: American Guitarist and Composer" (Ph.D. diss., University of Missouri-Kansas City, 1988); Peter Danner, "William Foden in His Own Words. Annotated by Peter Danner," *Soundboard* 22/4 (Spring 1996): 31–37, and *Soundboard* 23/1 (Summer 1996): 35–42; Douglas Back, "A Forgotten Community: Classical Guitar in St. Louis 1870–1900," *Soundboard* 17/2 (Summer 1990): 27–33; Arthur Hoskins, "William Foden," *Guitar Review* 23 (1959): 21–22; George C. Krick, "Reminiscences of William Foden," *Guitar Review* 23 (1959): 27; Giuseppe Pettine, "Foden as I Knew Him, *Guitar Review* 23 (1959): 23; George C. Krick, "William Foden," *The Etude* 57/2 (November 1939): 750–51. Foden's series of autobiographical sketches in *Crescendo*, "Looking Backward," serve as the basis for many of these secondary sources. The first of these sketches ran in *Crescendo* 9/9 (March 1917): 19; the last appeared over two years later in *Crescendo* 12/2 (August 1919): 2.

10. Foden's comments about Fernando Sor are illustrative. Although Foden expressed a very real admiration for the Spaniard, his comments almost always begin or end with technique. "Many of [Sor's] compositions are very difficult of accomplishment in more ways than one. . . . His knowledge of harmony, counterpoint and composition, as applied to guitar music is masterly; his harmonic progressions and melodic successions are refined and, in general, closely conform to the rules governing these points. . . . Sor's two Grand Sonatas, Op. 22 and 25, are to the guitar what the works of Beethoven, Mozart, Haydn, Schumann and others of the musical giants are to the piano. In these two numbers of Sor are incorporated form, movement and all that is necessary to contribute to the grand sonata. His Fantasies, Salon music and Etudes, all written with the greatest care, are musical models whereby all may profit and from which all may draw inspiration." *Cadenza* 19/2 (August 1912): 34. Later the same year, Foden offered a column about Ferranti which recognized the Italian's innovations, but reduced them to a lengthy discussion of left-hand technique; see *Cadenza* 19/5 (November 1912): 34.

11. While notices of Olcott's performances ran as early as 1904 in *Cadenza*, she did not appear as a contributor to that magazine until November 1916, when "The Guitarist" column commenced. Olcott's earliest articles appeared in *American Music Journal* in 1906–7. See "In the Sphere of the Guitar," *AMJ* 6/1 (August 1906): 24; "Personal Reminiscences of the Late M.Y. Ferrer," *AMJ* 6/5

(December 1906): 32, 34, 36; and "Guitar Repertoire," *AMJ* 6/9 (April 1907): 31–32, and 6/10 (May 1907): 21–22. Her first article for *Crescendo*, "Guitar Repertoire," *Crescendo* 1/11 (May 1909): 4, was a nearly identical reproduction of her earlier *AMJ* article with the same title.

12. Ethel Lucretia Olcott, "Anent Commercialism Among Teachers of Guitar, Banjo & Mandolin," *Crescendo* 3/12 (June 1911): 21. Over fifteen years later, as Vahdah Olcott-Bickford, she sounded the same theme even more strongly: "Man would still be in the ape stage of civilization if all in the past had advocated 'business' and money-getting as the highest ideal to aim for. We would have had no Beethovens, Bachs or Schuberts, no Sir Isaac Newtons, no really great men in any time, if these men followed the advice that is given so glibly by some of the fretted instrument propagandists of today of being 'twenty-five per cent musician and seventy-five per cent business.'" Vahdah Olcott-Bickford, "Business or Profession?" *Crescendo* 19/9 (March 1927): 6.

13. Ethel Lucretia Olcott, "Guitar Repertoire," *Crescendo* 1/11 (May 1909): 4. Olcott's other early *Crescendo* articles on this subject are "The Guitar and its Music," *Crescendo* 3/3 (September 1910): 6, and "Repertoire Hints for Two Guitars," *Crescendo* 4/6 (December 1911): 7.

14. "A Splendid Musical Investment," *Cadenza* 24/4 (April 1917): 10.

15. *Cadenza* 20/7 (January 1914): 14. The pieces (in order) are:

"Fantasie Americaine" and "Rigoletto Fantasie" (Romero)
"Valse Caprice, 'The Wizard'" (Foden)
"L'Adieu" (Sor)
"Ernani" Op. 18, no. 14 and "Le Gondolier," Op. 65, no. 3 (Mertz)
"Fantasie sur une Melodie Russe," Op. 32 (Pettoletti)
"Caprice," Op. 20, no. 2 and "Caprice," Op. 20, no. 9 (Legnani)
"Divertisement on 3 English Airs" and "Caprice, 'Loin du Toi' " (Ferranti)
"Valse Poetique" and "Chopin's Nocturne," Op. 9, no. 2 (de Janon)
"Capricho Arabe, Serenade" (Tárrega)
"Fantasie 'Lucrezia Borgia'" and "El Jasmine, Valse" (Ferrer)

16. For a comprehensive list of such works culled from articles, programs, and reviews, see *Appendix B: Professional and Semi-professional Guitar Repertoire from the BMG Periodicals* in Noonan, "The Guitar . . ."

17. Thomas C. B. Tyler, "Some Compositions by Mertz," *Cadenza* 3/8 (February 1911): 7. Mertz's Op. 65, a tripartite set published within a year of the composer's death in 1856, had been considered for over one hundred years to have been his winning entry in a guitar competition held in Brussels that same year. Astrid Stempnik argues persuasively that while this Op. 65 set was entered in Nikolai Pertrovich Makaroff's guitar competition, a concertino by Mertz actually took first prize. While Stempnik has set the chronological record straight, Op. 65's reputation as "Mertz's last work" has contributed to its romantic cachet and its continued popularity well into the twentieth century. See Astrid Stempnik, "Concertino or Trois Morceaux?" *Soundboard* 9/1 (1982): 35–37. Stempnik expanded this article in her dissertation; see "Der Gitarrenwettbewerb," 369–92, in Astrid Stempnik, *Caspar Joseph Mertz, Leben und Werk desletzten Gitarristen im österreichischen Biedermeier: eine Studie über den Niedergang der Gitarre in Wein un 1850* (Frankfurt am Main: P. Lang, 1990). For a more succinct discussion of this work in English, see Simon Wynberg's "Introduction" to *Johann Kaspar Mertz (1806–1856) Guitar Works, Vol. IX, Trois Morceaus Op. 65*, Simon Wynberg, ed. (Heidelberg: Chanterelle Verlag, 1985, 1999).

18. For a comparison of Foden's compositional approach to Mozart's, see Greene, *William Foden*, 82–83. See Stempnik, *Caspar Joseph Mertz*, 203ff., for an analysis of Mertz's approach to theme and variations.

19. "The Grand Concert," *Cadenza* 10/6 (February 1904): 24. A biographical sketch from 1933 lists his "Alice" variations among Foden's "better known" pieces, while his "Lucia" setting is not even listed; "William Foden," *Crescendo* 25/8 (June 1933): 1.

20. Richard Crawford has proposed that the balancing act between compositional authority and performing accessibility has played a significant role in America's musical history. See his *American Musical Landscape*, 85–107, where he applies these terms to a variety of American musical styles. Foden himself equated musical or expressive playing with a performer's strict adherence to a composer's dynamic and expression markings; see William Foden, "Guitarists Round Table—Noise Versus Music," *Crescendo* 11/12 (June 1919): 19.

21. "Editorial," *Crescendo* 11/8 (February 1919): 8, 17, and 24.

22. See, for example, F. O. Gutman's description of the responsibilities of the teacher as a businessman, "Editorial," *FOG* 2/3 (March-April 1902): 4–5.

23. For nearly twenty years, S. S. Stewart stood at the vanguard of this movement while he not only invented, manufactured, and retailed the banjeaurine but also published solo and ensemble works for it. The Gibson Mandolin-Guitar Company aggressively followed Stewart's lead in its production and promotion of mandolins, banjos, and plectrum guitars as well as music for these instruments. Gibson's advertisements in the BMG magazines regularly took sides in debates about notation for and use of the plectral instruments, especially the mandolin. Additionally, Gibson developed training programs for teachers and music store owners, offering them promotion, sales, and management techniques all focused on making students and customers "Gibsonites."

24. For an example of a BMG apologist rhapsodizing about the benefits and powers of music, see Thomas J. Armstrong, "Music, The Civilizer," *Crescendo* 10/3 (September 1917): 4.

25. See [Herbert F. Odell,] "Editorial," *Crescendo* 18/7 (January 1926): 10, for a description of balanced programming: "To the average mind, there are two kinds of music, high-brow and low-brow, but it seems to us there might be another classification of some of our music called good-brow. High-brow music, in the popular mind, means the extreme classics, and many people like that kind of music. Today we have a supersufficiency [*sic*] of low-brow music. . . . Dance hall habitués seem to prefer mostly low-brow music. On the other hand, Symphony Hall audiences prefer the high-brow music, but the great masses of the American public want good-brow music. . . . There are some popular tunes, even well-known songs, that have been written in foxtrot time for dancing purposes that are just as good in their way as any of the high-brow music. . . . It is our belief that in making up programs some high-brow music should be used, more good-brow music and mighty little low-brow. . . . As variety is the spice of life, so it should be with a concert program. The heavier numbers, shall we say the high-brow music, should come at the beginning of the program as a general rule. A large part of the program should consist of good-brow music, and if it must be used, a little low-brow toward the end of the program."

26. [Herbert F. Odell], "Editorial," *Crescendo* 15/3 (September 1922): 10. A full-page advertisement from the Gibson Mandolin-Guitar Company featuring the headline "Mandolin Club or Mandolin Orchestra?" argues for the use of "orchestra" based on the newly developed Gibson mandola, mando-cello, and mando-bass. *Crescendo* 14/4 (October 1921): 19. A decade later, the same magazine's last editor, Walter Kaye Bauer, encouraged a return to more classically oriented

programming, citing the examples of contemporary symphonic conductors, Arturo Toscanini, Serge Koussevitzky, and Eugene Ormandy among them. See, [Walter Kaye Bauer,] "What Constitutes a Good Program?" *Crescendo* 23/9 (May 1931): 5.

27. In his examination of early jazz, Paul Lopes describes how professional musicians raised the status of American popular music by notating it. See *The Rise of a Jazz Art World* (Cambridge and New York: Cambridge University Press, 2002).

28. This figure does not include guitar duets, nor does it include ensemble pieces that do not involve the guitar. These other works include banjo duets and trios and mandolin duets, trios, and quartets, as well as large mixed ensembles in which the piano replaced the guitar.

29. Among the BMG works in which guitar appears, over 500 are in G major, slightly over 300 in D major, over 250 in C major, nearly that many in A major or A minor, and approximately 40 in E major. F major and Bb major are represented by about 40 and fewer than ten pieces, respectively.

30. Barre chords require that a player's index finger of the left hand depress all six strings while other fingers are set on frets above it. Some beginning guitarists can manage such configurations, but most become adept only after several years of playing. See *Cadenza* 6/5 (May–June 1900): 13, or [Herbert F. Odell], "Editorial," *Crescendo* 15/3 (September 1922): 10, for descriptions of ensemble pieces and the simple guitar parts.

31. Hayden's compositions for guitar, numbering nearly a thousand, ran regularly in the principal BMG magazines. Despite his drowning death in 1886 (see *Stewart's* 3/12 [October–November 1886]: 2), solos and duos by Hayden and his daughter, Carrie, ran through the 1920s. His "Elsie Waltzes" appeared in *Crescendo* 25/5 (March 1933).

32. Folwell, a native of Camden, New Jersey, began teaching banjo and guitar in his teens and contributed more than twenty guitar solos to *Cadenza* and *Crescendo* between 1904 and 1926. See *Cadenza* 14/4 (December 1907): 33, for a biographical sketch. William Stahl Music of Milwaukee published a collection of Folwell's guitar works in 1929; see *Crescendo* 22/6 (December 1929): 17.

33. Of nearly 500 solos published in the extant BMG magazines, 131 have "waltz" in their title. 57 dances are called one-steps or marches while polkas number 25, mazurkas 25, gavottes 29, schottisches 23, barcaroles 9, and minuets only 3. Approximately 75 pieces are identified as serenades, reveries, idylls, or songs without words. The balance of the guitar solos are songs, variations, or unspecified dance forms.

34. See Jon W. Finson, *The Voices That Are Gone: Themes in 19th-Century American Popular Song* (New York: Oxford University Press, 1994), 67ff., for a discussion of the "covert association [of the waltz] with the more titillating aspects of courtship." Foden's waltz appeared twice in *Crescendo*, first in 13/12 (June 1921): 16–17, and again in 23/7 (March 1931): 6–7. The waltzes by Bone and Weidt ran in *Cadenza* 19/5 (November 1912): 24–25, and *Cadenza* 24/1 (January 1917): 32, respectively.

35. In a typical column reflecting such interests, Vahdah Olcott-Bickford fielded eight questions in February 1918. Four were requests about arrangements and she answered a fifth with a list of solo arrangements; *Cadenza* 25/2 (February 1918): 5. The earliest guitar solos to appear in a BMG magazine was a set of untitled "Operatic Selections" arranged by Charles H. Loag; *Stewart's* 2/1 (May 1883): 3. Two of the last guitar solos published in *Crescendo* were settings by Sophocles Papas of "Long, Long Ago" and "Old Black Joe"; *Crescendo* 25/6 (April 1933): 5.

36. These variations sets are: Clarence Partee's solo "Fantasia on 'Believe Me If All Those Endearing Young Charms,'" *Cadenza* 3/6 (July-August 1893): 20–22; E. H. Frey's divisions on

Stephen Foster's "My Old Kentucky Home," *Cadenza* 4/1 (September–October 1897): 24–25; Walter Burke's variations on "Long, Long Ago," *Cadenza* 16/1 (July 1909): 24–25; Vahdah Olcott-Bickford's "Fantasie" on James Bland's "Carry Me Back to Old Virginny," *Crescendo* 19/7 (January 1927): 11–12, 17–18; C. W. F. Jansen's variations on "Yankee Doodle," *Crescendo* 23/6 (February 1931): 7; and P. W. Newton's "Annie Laurie Variations," *Crescendo* 24/12 (October 1932): 6–7. Burke's variations ran a second time in *Crescendo* 25/10 (October 1933): 8–9.

CHAPTER 6. INTERLUDE: THE GUITAR AS ICON

1. Recent literature about the guitar includes numerous examples. See Waksman for a consideration of the meanings of the electric guitar and its sounds. *Guitar Cultures*, Andy Bennett and Kevin Dawe, eds. (Oxford and New York: Berg, 2001) ranges from Spain to Brazil and from the American rural south to the Indian subcontinent in its examination of the meaning of the guitar. In a catalog for a recent museum show, the title alone—*Dangerous Curves: The Art of the Guitar* (Boston: MFA Publications, 2000)—implies a cultural interpretation for the guitar.

2. This advertisement ran several times in the *Chicago Trio*, usually on the back cover. For an especially good example of a history that elides the lute and the guitar, see Vahdah Olcott-Bickford, "The Guitar in the History of Chamber Music," *Crescendo* 20/10 (April 1928): 7, 24; *Crescendo* 20/11 (May 1928): 7–8; and *Crescendo* 21/1 (July 1928): 10, 28.

3. C. F. W., "Fame-Art-Love. (A Musician's Choice)," *Cadenza*, 2/1 (September-October 1895): 6. In an editorial, John Henning observed that "those who can give a little time to the study of an instrument demand the quickest results possible. The piano or instruments of the violin class are generally out of the question owing to the great amount of time required to achieve satisfactory results." He noted that many respected men—doctors, attorneys, ministers, and businessmen—had taken up the plectral instruments. See *Chicago Trio* 1/1 (October–November 1897): 4.

4. For the citations about Victorian medieval mythology, see T. J. Jackson Lears, *No Place of Grace: Antimodernism and the Transformation of American Culture 1880–1920* (New York: Pantheon Books, 1981), 142, 163. The BMG advertisement ran as "Story of the Troubadours," *Cadenza* 6/4 (March-April 1900): 36. See also, Giulia Pelzer, "The Guitar As An Accompaniment to the Voice," *Cadenza* 6/3 (January-February 1900): 4–5, for an ecstatic encomium to the guitar as an evocation of "knights, druids, cavaliers, crusaders, troubadours, hidalgos, and Spanish paisanos."

5. "In part, the perception of medieval vitality stemmed from a liberal Protestant assumption that Catholic practices bred undisciplined emotion. In the dominant view, the immoderation of excitable Catholics immersed in pointless piety was another childlike trait inherited from the medieval past." Lears, *No Place of Grace*, 161.

6. W. Sanders, "Our Instruments," *Cadenza* 15/2 (August 1908): 16–17.

7. Quoted in Levine, *Highbrow*, 219.

8. *Dwight's* 8 (October 6, 1855): 6.

9. "Guitar Items," *Stewart's* 3/3 (April–May 1885): 1. While Stewart never claimed that the banjo could play counterpoint, he often compared it to the violin: "The violin would have remained to this day, an undeveloped musical instrument, had it not been for the genius and laborious practice of Paganini and his school of artists. The banjo, in the hands of Horace Weston and other musical geniuses, develops a power of expression and compass, far beyond that of its so-called 'first cousin,'

the guitar, and, moreover, the unfretted banjo is capable of producing all the grades of musical tone, that are possible to the violin." *Stewart's* 6/6 (February-March 1890): 2. Alfred Farland's performances of Beethoven's violin sonatas and Mendelssohn's violin concerto on the banjo reinforced Stewart's comparison. Farland's accomplishments appeared regularly in the *Journal* beginning with *Stewart's* 9/5 (December 1892–January 1893): 3.

10. *Stewart's* 15/2 (June-July 1898): 10. The poem "U.S. LEADS ALL," by C. S. Patty, appeared in *Stewart's* 16/2 (June-July 1899): 3. Patty appeared frequently in the pages of the *Journal*, contributing poems, a history of musical instruments (culminating in the perfection of Stewart's banjos), and the occasional composition. A year earlier, a tongue-in-cheek poem from *Cadenza* attributed President McKinley's decision to declare war on Spain to an inept guitarist, whose playing drove the president to distraction. When McKinley learned that the piece being played so badly was "The Spanish Fandango," he could take no more and declared war. See Horace Huron, "The Last Straw," *Cadenza* 4/5 (May-June 1898): 2. "The Spanish Fandango," an American creation, was a favorite guitar solo of self-taught amateurs but regarded by many BMG apologists as hackwork unworthy of trained musicians. Huron's humorous comments took aim at both the piece's Spanish connection and its low musical quality. For another comic commentary on the piece see E. R. Day, *Cadenza* 17/9 (March 1911): 26–27, and for a typical critique of the piece see Vahdah Olcott-Bickford, "The Guitarist—'Do You Play the Spanish Fandango?'" *Cadenza* 26/9 (September 1919): 24–25.

11. Albert Baur, "Reminiscences of a Banjo Player," *Stewart's* 10/3 (August-September 1893): 5. Contributors to the BMG magazines often linked Latin musicians to the "original Spanish Students," generally as verification of the authenticity of a player. More often than not, these ascriptions were incorrect.

12. Philip J. Bone, "The Guitar in Spain," *Cadenza* 9/7 (March 1903): 15–17. This article continued in *Cadenza* 11/4 (December 1904): 21, 41. See also James P. Downs, "La Guitarra En Espana. (The Guitar in Spain)," *Cadenza* 11/3 (November 1904): 12–16.

13. The first installment of "Evangeline and Her Mandolin" appeared in *Cadenza* 5/1 (September-October 1898): 17; "Sancho and His Banjo" first ran in *Cadenza* 6/5 (May-June 1900): 14–18.

14. C. E. Pomeroy, "Carrara and His Guitarra," *Cadenza* 5/6 (July-August 1899): 15–16.

15. Such characterizations were not limited to fictional accounts. A report about a music competition sponsored by an Italian club in New York observed that "Foreign-born soloists usually are looked upon as better musically equipped than our native-born, and not without good reason"; *Cadenza* 23/5 (November 1916): 3. The musical activities of Andres Segovia and other Spaniards and Italians in the late 1920s and early 1930s drew a number of observations about race and culture. See, for example, Walter Kaye Bauer, "Editorial," *Crescendo* 22/6 (December 1929): 1.

16. *Cadenza* 13/7 (March 1907): 11, 14. *Cadenza* reported the *Chicago Tribune* to be the story's source. This story echoes the narrative of Charles K. Harris's late-century hit "After the Ball," but with a happy ending. In recounting the story of "After the Ball," Harris noted the importance of the "sentimental" in creating a best-selling song. See Charles K. Harris, *After the Ball* (New York), 57, 62.

17. James Whitcomb Riley, "The Old Guitar," *Cadenza* 7/5 (January 1901): 2.

18. See, for example, *Cadenza*: Samuel Minturn Peck, "The Old Guitar," *Cadenza* 2/2 (November-December 1895): 13; M. E. Wardwell, "My Sweetheart," *Cadenza* 6/1 (September-October 1899): 2; Frank Colbourn, "Inspiration," *Cadenza* 7/1 (September 1900): 1; Joshua Roberts, "The Dying Minstrel to His Guitar," *Cadenza* 7/6 (February 1901): 12; and "To My Guitar," *Cadenza* 7/11 (July 1901): 1. *Crescendo* offered: W. S. Marsh, "An Old Guitar," *Crescendo* 5/11 (May 1913): 6;

W. B. G. Keller, "My Guitar," *Crescendo* 6/2 (August 1913): 21; and Susan Wilbur Smith, "My Old Guitar," *Crescendo* 6/9 (March 1914): 21.

19. Linda Phyllis Austern, "'My Mother Musicke': Music and Early Modern Fantasies of Embodiment," in *Maternal Measures: Figuring Caregiving in the Early Modern Period*, Naomi J. Miller and Naomi Yavneh, eds. (Aldershot, UK and Burlington, VT: Ashgate, 2000), 239–81.

20. Giulia Pelzer, "The Guitar as a Solo Instrument," *Cadenza* 6/2 (November-December 1899): 5.

21. Linda Phyllis Austern, "Music and the English Renaissance Controversy over Women," in *Cecilia Reclaimed: Feminist Perspectives on Gender and Music*, Susan C. Cook and Judy S. Tsou, eds. (Urbana and Chicago: University of Illinois Press, 1994), 52.

22. See Austern, "Music and the English Renaissance Controversy," 54–56, for a discussion of the Renaissance conceit of both music and women as representations and inspirations of love.

23. James P. Downs, "Beauty and the Beast," *Cadenza* 13/3 (November 1906): 15.

24. Austern, "My Mother Musicke," 241.

25. Ibid., 254ff., for a discussion the lute's regular association with the maternal womb.

26. See Carolyn Kitch, *The Girl on the Magazine Cover: The Origins of Visual Stereotypes in American Mass Media* (Chapel Hill and London: University of North Carolina Press, 2001). Kitch traces these images from late-nineteenth-century images in *Ladies Home Journal* to less wholesome depictions in the 1920s and 1930s. For succinct biographies as well as examples of their "Girls," see Catherine A. Hastedt, "Charles Dana Gibson," and Katherine Kominis, "Howard Chandler Christy," in *Dictionary of Literary Biography: American Book and Magazine Illustrators to 1920*, vol. 188, Steven E. Smith et al., eds. (Detroit, Washington, and London: Gale Research, 1998).

27. Besides Gibson and Christy, Harrison Fisher and James Montgomery Flagg are recognized as "America Beauty illustrators." See James J. Best, *American Popular Illustration: A Reference Guide* (Westport, CT: Greenwood Press, 1984), 9. Best's opening chapter, "A Historical Overview," 3–20, offers an excellent survey of the field.

28. Kitch, 44–45, observes that the restraint of the self-possessed, unapproachable Gibson Girl usually melted quickly when she was pictured near or in water.

29. Partee announced the magazine's move in "Editorial," *Cadenza* 6/4 (March-April 1900): 10. The first of W. L. Hudson's covers appeared on the cover of *Cadenza* 7/9 (May 1901); the last appeared in September 1905. Two artists active in the late nineteenth and early twentieth centuries bore the name of Will or William Hudson. The more likely candidate, Will L. Hudson, has been identified as a painter active in New York City between 1890 and 1905. Aside from several exhibition credits, no other biographical data is available for him. See Peter Hastings Falk, ed., *Who Was Who in American Art 1564–1975: 400 Years of Artists in America* (Madison, CT: Soundview Press, 1999), 1650.

30. Kominis, 51.

31. Ibid.

32. Kitch, 48.

CHAPTER 7. A NEW INSTRUMENT

1. For an authoritative and comprehensive examination of Torres, see José L. Romanillos, *Antonio de Torres: Guitar Maker—His Life & Work* (Shaftsbury, UK: Element Books, 1987, rev. 1995).

See also John Huber, *The Development of the Modern Guitar* (Westport, CT: Bold Strummer, 1991), especially his chapter titled "From Torres to Segovia: How We Got Where We Are Today," 9–21. For a graphic demonstration of the development of the European classical guitar from the late eighteenth century through the first half of the twentieth, see *La Guitarra Española/ The Spanish Guitar* (Madrid: Opera Tres, 1993), the lavishly illustrated exhibition catalog from the Museo Municipal in Madrid and New York's Metropolitan Museum of Art. An idiosyncratic look at the Ramirez dynasty and tradition might be found in Jose Ramirez III, *Things About the Guitar* (Madrid: Soneto, 1993).

2. Hartman, 5.

3. James Oliver Robertson, *American Myth, American Reality* (New York: Hill & Wang, 1980), 288. For a discussion of America's late-nineteenth-century industrial growth and its links to the theories of Darwin and Spenser, see Vincent P. DeSantis, *The Shaping of Modern America: 1877–1920* (Arlington Heights, IL: Forum Press, 1989), 8ff. A concise overview of the era that considers the social, economic, and political activities of the period can be found in the opening chapters of Steven J. Diner, *A Very Different Age: Americans of the Progressive Era* (New York: Hill & Wang, 1998).

4. For a detailed examination of Gibson's design and marketing ideas, see Hambly, especially Chapter 11, "Gibson Mandolins." Also see his chapter 9 for an overview of many of these hybrid and exaggerated instruments of the mandolin family.

5. The first citation is from Odell's serialized article "The Mandolin Orchestra," *Crescendo* 1/12 (June 1909): 4. The later article appeared with the same title in *Crescendo* 2/ 2 (August 1909). Unfortunately, Odell failed to indicate whether the music his ensemble played was above or below the grade of music preferred by the harpist. Odell's earliest argument for the mandolin orchestra appeared as "About the Guild," *Crescendo* 1/2 (August 1908): 6–7. "The Mandolin Orchestra" began in *Crescendo* 1/7 (January 1909): 4, and ran sporadically to 3/7 (January 1911): 20; "Mandolin Orchestra Instrumentation and Orchestration" first appeared in *Crescendo* 5/2 (August 1912): 7, and extended through 5/9 (March 1913): 7. The final citation is from *The 1921 Gibson Catalog*, William Ivey, ed. (Nashville, TN: Country Music Association Press, 1973), 6. A Gibson advertisement from the same year makes the same argument; see "Mandolin Club or Mandolin Orchestra?" *Crescendo* 14/4 (October 1921): 19.

6. [Walter Kaye Bauer,] "The New Era of Instrumentation Part Three—The Tenor Guitar," *Crescendo* 23/4 (December 1930): 1–2.

7. Ethel Lucretia Olcott, "Guitarists Roundtable—Shall the Guitar Be Eliminated From the Mandolin Orchestras of the Future?" *Crescendo* 5/6 (December 1912): 23. See Ruppa, 16–23 and 176, for a summary (with seating charts) of suggested forces for mandolin ensembles ranging from ten to one hundred players. While the harp-guitar figures in all, the six-string guitar appears in none of these ensembles. Ruppa assembled his data from William Place Jr.'s *The Organization, Direction and Maintenance of the Mandolin Orchestra* published by the Gibson Mandolin-Guitar Company in 1917.

8. While early notices reveled in a player's multi-instrumental skills, later BMG apologists encouraged specialization, especially on the guitar. Ethel Lucretia Olcott encouraged specialization well before it became popular. See Ethel Lucretia Olcott, "Anent Commercialism Among Teachers of Guitar, Banjo & Mandolin," *Crescendo* 3/12 (June 1911): 6, 21. A later notice on the same subject, probably by Walter Kaye Bauer, appeared as "Editorial," *Crescendo* 22/12 (July-August 1930): 1, 6.

9. Lucas's reminiscence appears in *The Guitar in Jazz: An Anthology*, James Sallis, ed. (Lincoln, NE, and London: University of Nebraska Press, 1996), 12–19.

10. In recent years, Lang's short career and accomplishments have received much deserved attention. A short biography can be found in Maurice J. Summerfield's *The Jazz Guitar: Its Evolution, Players and Personalities Since 1900* (Newcastle on Tyne, UK: Ashley Mark Publishing, 1998), 213. Lang's style and influence are considered in more detail in Pete Welding's contribution to Allan Kozinn, Pete Welding, Dan Forte, and Gene Santoro, *The Guitar: The History, The Music, The Players* (New York: William Morrow & Co., 1984), 92–95, and in Sallis, 20–32.

11. A quick perusal of the biographies of early jazz guitarists in Summerfield confirms that nearly all of the white guitarists of the 1920s and 1930s played mandolin and/or tenor banjo before they committed to the guitar full-time.

12. Vahdah Olcott-Bickford, "The Guitarist," *Cadenza* 29/1 (January 1922): 42–43. Lang and Lucas appeared together in an advertisement for the *Mastertone Guitar Method* on the inside cover of *Crescendo* 21/12 (June 1929). The same magazine identified Lucas as "the most prominent guitarist making records" in "News," *Crescendo* 18/4 (October 1925): 8. When Lang died *Crescendo* published "Obituary—Eddie Lang," *Crescendo* 25/7 (May 1933): 13.

13. "The Guitarist—A Plea for More Concerts," *Cadenza* 26/1 (January 1919): 22–23.

14. For example, F. L. Littig, "The Hawaiian Steel Guitar and Ukulele," *Crescendo* 7/12 (June 1915): 4; S. de Vekey, "The Steel Guitar," *Cadenza* 28/9 (September 1921): 10–11; Myron Bickford, "The Problem Prober," *Cadenza* 28/11 (November 1921): 37; L. M. Gill, "The Steel Guitar," *Cadenza* 29/10 (October 1922): 12, 44; and James F. Roach, "What is the Future of the Steel Guitar?" *Cadenza* 30/8 (August 1923): 8–9. In October 1916 *Crescendo* began a regular column, "Hawaiian Round Table," offering technical advice and answering readers' questions about the steel guitar and ukulele. Despite her objections, Olcott-Bickford performed a ukulele and steel guitar duet in 1915; "Programs of Concerts and Recitals," *Crescendo* 10/5 (November 1917): 17.

For a contemporary survey of the Hawaiian guitar's development, see George T. Noe and Daniel L. Most, *Chris J. Knutsen: From Harp Guitars to the New Hawaiian Family—History and Development of the Hawaiian Steel Guitar* (Everett, WA: Noe Enterprises, 1999). Noe and Most date the Hawaiian craze to Seattle's 1909 Alaska-Yukon-Pacific Exposition, which featured a Hawaiian Building with performing musicians. Charles de Lano, a BMG teacher from Los Angeles, became one of the strongest proponents for the Hawaiian instruments, incorporating them into performances by his mandolin orchestra as early as 1912. Jim Beloff's *The Ukulele: A Visual History* (San Francisco: Miller Freeman, 1997) offers a concise and entertaining overview of the instrument's history.

Several companies promoted devices or kits to convert a standard guitar to a Hawaiian setup. See *Crescendo* 7/5 (November 1914): 6, for an advertisement promoting the "Johnstone Steel Guitar Adjustor" and *Crescendo* 10/8 (February 1918): 21, for a promotion of the "Kamiki Guitar Readjustor."

15. *Cadenza* 15/8 (February 1909): 43. Olcott-Bickford strenuously objected to the harp-guitar as a solo instrument, citing its bulk and undampered basses as major impediments; "Guitarists Round Table—The Guitar vs. the Harp-Guitar As a *Solo* Instrument," *Crescendo* 9/5 (November 1916): 19, 21, and *Crescendo* 9/6 (December 1916): 19. She did not appear to object to its use in accompaniments, especially in mandolin orchestras.

16. Walter A. Boehm, "The Harp Guitar," *Crescendo* 1/1 (July 1908): 5. Boehm's first prose offering about the instrument—"The Harp Guitar," *American Music Journal* 6/6 (January 1907): 44–46—was

followed by this *Crescendo* article and, two years later, by "The Modern Harp-Guitar," *Cadenza* 17/2 (August 1910): 12–13. He contributed harp-guitar solos as well as a bombastic serial article, "Harp-Guitar Ideality," to *Crescendo* for several years in the teens. Boehm also hosted the 1909 convention of the American Guild of Banjoists, Mandolinists and Guitarists in Buffalo, New York, where he featured exhibitions and recitals involving the harp-guitar.

Despite Boehm's claims, articles and advertisements had described the harp-guitar as early as 1897 when a short announcement in *Cadenza* noted the production of a harp-guitar by Biehl: "Trade Notes," *Cadenza* 4/2 (November-December 1897): 18. Noe and Most document an extant nine-string guitar (perhaps a prototype) by Chris J. Knutsen of Portland, Oregon, dated 1898 as well numerous sophisticated harp-guitars by Knutsen from 1900 on. The earliest extended article about the harp-guitar in a BMG journal is Lewis A. Williams, "The Harp-Guitar," *American Music Journal* 5/9 (April 1906): 34, 36–37, 40, apparently a reprint from a publication from the Gibson Mandolin-Guitar Company. J. Hopkins Flinn was another early experimenter with less woodworking finesse: he devised a primitive harp-guitar by nailing a block of wood to his six-string guitar; "Prominent Teachers and Players—J. Hopkins Flinn," *Crescendo* 10/2 (August 1917): 7.

In the introduction to *Johann Kaspar Mertz, Guitar Works*, vol. 1 (Heidelberg: Chanterelle Verlag, 1985), editor Simon Wynberg documents a number of extended guitars in Europe in the mid-nineteenth century. Johann Kaspar Mertz played a ten-string guitar, Giulio Regondi and Luigi Legnani eight-string guitars, Napoleon Coste a seven-string, and Fernando Carulli a ten-string instrument called the Decachorde. See also Joscelyn [sic] Godwin, "Eccentric Forms of the Guitar, 1770–1850," *Journal of the Lute Society of America* 7 (1974): 90–102. Bone, *The Guitar and Mandolin*, 28, credits S. Ritter von Beniezki with the invention of the harp-guitar in the first half of the nineteenth century. BMG contributors regularly stated that Fernando Sor and Mauro Giuliani played extended guitars, but neither of their recent biographies documents either of them doing so. See, for example, Carl Jansen, "Crescendo Scrap Book—The Harp Guitar," *Crescendo* 10/9 (March 1918): 7.

17. Only one American BMG writer, William Foden, noted the parallels between the modern harp-guitar and the Baroque theorbo and archlute; "Guitarists Round Table—Brief History of the Guitar," *Crescendo* 9/7 (January 1917): 19. A later German contributor noted the same connection in his article about the lute; see Alfred Sprissler, "The Lute Today," *Crescendo* 25/1 (November 1932): 3.

18. *Cadenza* 24/9 (September 1917): 16, and *Crescendo* 2/10 (April 1910): 1.

19. See the advertisement for J. A. Witter's *Book of Solos for the Harp-Guitar* in *Crescendo* 11/5 (November 1918): 7, as well as an editorial endorsement of the anthology on the following page. For an example of a harp-guitar piece with simple doubling of a bass line, see Walter Boehm's arrangement of "Absence Makes The Heart Grow Fonder" and his accompanying article explaining the harp-guitar techniques utilized therein; "Harp-Guitar Ideality," *Crescendo* 8/11 (May 1916): 4, 7. Among the top-flight soloists in the BMG movement, only Chicago-based C. W. F. Jansen regularly played a harp-guitar as a solo instrument, endorsing its solo use in "Crescendo Scrap Book—The Harp Guitar," *Crescendo* 10/9 (March 1918): 7.

20. *Cadenza* 16/4 (October 1909): 9–10.

21. See, for example, the Gibson ad in *Cadenza* 15/1 (July 1908): 10. For brief biographies of W. J. Dyer and Wm. C. Stahl, see Hartman, 20.

22. See "Convention Cozy Corner," *Cadenza* 18/9 (March 1912): 10, for a promotional article about Jansen's performance. The issue also includes a photograph of Jansen with his

accompanying ensemble of mandolinists. For Olcott-Bickford's comments about the terz guitar, see "The Guitarist," *Cadenza* 28/1 (January 1921): 43–44, and "The Guitarist—Concerning Strings," *Cadenza* 26/4 (April 1919): 25–26. Olcott-Bickford recognized Jansen's daughter, Elsa, as well as Durkee as important American players of the terz guitar; "Guitarists Round Table—Some Facts about the Evolution of the Guitar," *Crescendo* 8/3 (September 1915): 19. For Jennie Durkee's use of the terz guitar, see "Jennie M. Durkee," *Cadenza* 11/9 (May 1905): 31, and George B. Durkee, "A Practical Treatise on the Guitar and Kindred Instruments," *Crescendo* 2/10 (April 1910): 21. A biographical sketch of Jennie Durkee features an illustration of her elaborately decorated terz guitar: *Cadenza* 15/5 (November 1908): 35–36.

23. Wood's guitar was described in "The Orchestral Guitar," *Cadenza* 12/9 (May 1906): 18–19. The earlier citations are from *Cadenza* 12/6 (February 1906) and *Cadenza* 12/7 (March 1906): 16. Wood's instrument had been reported nine years earlier than these notices in a news article from the *Philadelphia Times* (June 16, 1897). See "A Musical Wonder. The Remarkable Combination Instrument Made by an Indiana Professor," *Cadenza* 3/6 (July-August 1897): 19. Peter Danner offers commentary about Woods and his instrument in "The Most Remarkable Instrument We Have Ever Seen," *Soundboard* 26/2 (1999): 55. Another experiment to appear in the late teens was the Tonaharp Guitar, a Hawaiian auto-harp, played like a steel or Hawaiian guitar but also fitted with push-button chording device. See the Tonaharp advertisement in *Crescendo* 10/9 (March 1918): 22, as well as an editorial blurb about it *Crescendo* 10/10 (April 1918): 8.

24. Lloyd Loar, revered as the visionary behind many of the Gibson Company's innovations, became an advocate for the electric amplification of the plectral instruments. Loar, a mandolinist, left Gibson in the mid-1920s to pursue his ideas about amplification with his own company, Vivi-tone. The Vivi-tone vision was promoted on the pages of *Crescendo* in a series of articles beginning with L. A. Williams, "The Theory of Electrically Energized String Instruments," *Crescendo* 25/4 (February 1933): 4.

25. William Foden, "Guitarists Round Table—Eccentric Shapes in Guitars," *Crescendo* 11/5 (November 1918): 19, and *Crescendo* 11/6 (December 1918): 19.

CHAPTER 8. INTERLUDE: THE WIZARD AND THE GRAND LADY

1. Foden's biographical columns first appeared in early 1917 and ran well into 1919; see "Guitarists Round Table—Looking Backward," *Crescendo* 8/9 (March 1917): 19.

2. For an early reference to Foden, see *Stewart's* 3/10 (August-September 1886): 5. For the poem comparing Foden to famous violinists and pianists, see C. F. W., "Fame-Art-Love. (A Musician's Choice)," *Cadenza* 2/1 (September-October 1895): 6.

3. R. M. Tyrrell, "The Grand Mandolin, Banjo and Guitar concert given at Carnegie Hall, New York City.—a full, complete and critical report," *FOG* 4/2 (January-February 1904): 2–3, 5. Another review appeared in *Cadenza* 10/6 (February 1904): 22–24.

4. In 1917 Foden appeared as featured soloist in Boston's Festival Mandolin Concert, playing the allegro movement from Fernando Sor's "Sonata, Op. 22." See "News" and "Programs of Recitals and Concerts," in *Crescendo* 9/11 (May 1917): 4, 6, 17.

5. The edition, while running to ten pages, has no actual instructional guidelines. Foden apparently considered (or at least promoted) the work itself to be instructive, probably owing to the

extensive right- and left-hand fingerings, position markings, and detailed expressive, dynamic, and tempo indications. Other solo editions by Foden in this same collection range in price from 40¢ to $1.25. Foden published his "Lucia" variations in 1913 and advertisements for it ran frequently in *Cadenza* and *Crescendo*. See *Cadenza* 20/7 (January 1914): 46, for an early notice.

6. William Foden, "Guitarists Round Table—Resignation of William Foden," *Crescendo* 19/9 (March 1927): 22. See also in the same number, "Editorial—Mr. William Foden," 10.

7. Greene, 95. For a discussion of the late-nineteenth-century language of technology and science, see Jackson Lears, *Fables of Abundance: A Cultural History of Advertising in America* (New York: Basic Books, 1994), especially 82–88.

8. Foden's comment about right-hand technique appeared in "Guitarists Round Table—Right-Hand Manipulation," *Crescendo* 16/4 (October 1923): 22–23, a response to a reader's inquiry from "Guitarists Round Table," *Crescendo* 16/3 (September 1923): 22, 26–27. Other *Crescendo* columns by Foden dealing with the subject include "Guitarists Round Table—Touch and Tone," *Crescendo* 12/8 (February 1920): 19, and *Crescendo* 12/9 (March 1920): 19. For earlier columns see "The Guitarist," *Cadenza* 18/9 (March 1912): 36–37; *Cadenza* 18/10 (April 1912): 36–37; *Cadenza* 18/11 (May 1912): 49–50; and *Cadenza* 18/12 (June 1912): 37.

9. For Foden's response to the *apoyando* stroke, see "Guitarists Round Table," *Crescendo* 18/4 (October 1925): 22.

10. Olcott's first notice was "Program of Ethel Lucretia Olcott, guitar virtuoso," *Cadenza* 10/12 (August 1904): 35. In addition to her biography in Bone, *The Guitar and Mandolin*, 37–38, several biographical sketches appeared in *Cadenza* 13/2 (October 1906): 31; *Cadenza* 15/9 (March 1909): 11–12; and *Cadenza* 24/1 (January 1917): 15, 34. She offered some biographical information in a column in *Cadenza* 27/6 (June 1920): 35–38. The 1917 biographical sketch notes that she "spent a season with the late Manuel Y. Ferrer." Ronald Purcell writes that she "spent a year in San Francisco as a student of the Mexican guitarist Manuel Y. Ferrer," in "The Early Vahdah," *Soundboard* 25/1 (Summer 1998): 20. A succinct account of Olcott-Bickford's life may be found at the web site for International Guitar Research Archive at California State University-Northridge: <http://library.csun.edu/igra/vob.html>.

11. For a program of Olcott's trio see *Cadenza* 13/5 (January 1907): 30. The *New Grove* entry for "Recital" credits Andres Segovia with introducing the guitar as a "recital instrument" in 1908, certainly a late date given that numerous American guitarists like Olcott-Bickford, Johnson Bane, and others had been offering similar solo recitals since the late 1890s.

12. *Cadenza* 24/1 (January 1917): 15. Olcott-Bickford's first recital listed in *Cadenza* included a reading, but the remainder consisted of guitar solos including works by Schumann, Verdi, and Flowtow arranged by Ferrer, Mertz, Olcott herself, and others. Original compositions were by Olcott, the American guitarist C. V. Hayden, and Luis T. Romero. See *Cadenza* 10/12 (August 1904): 35, for the program, which Olcott performed in Los Angeles in May 1904. See Danner, "The Guitar in America as Mirrored in Cadenza," 16, for a discussion of Olcott-Bickford's performing career as documented in the magazine. *Cadenza* 11/10 (June 1905): 33, reports her performance of Sor's "Variations on a Theme of Mozart," Op. 9 in 1905. Tárrega's "Capricho Arabe" first appeared on a Bickford-Olcott recital in *Cadenza* 20/1 (July 1913): 43–44. She regularly performed this work, as well as his arrangements of Chopin piano works. Olcott-Bickford offered some guidelines on creating suitably varied programs in a later column, "Program Building," *Cadenza* 28/8 (August 1919): 7, 22.

13. Olcott-Bickford protested that her astrological interests were "amateurish," but she lectured and taught classes on the topic in addition to offering predictions and charts to members of the BMG community; "Mrs. Vahdah Olcott-Bickford," *Cadenza* 24/1 (January 1917): 15, 34. See Ronald C. Purcell, "In Memoriam: Vahdah Olcott Bickford Revere," *Soundboard* 7/3 (1980): 120, for some details of her astrological interests. Although she performed and published under several names throughout her career (Ethel Lucretia Olcott, Mrs. Olcott-Bickford, and Ethel Olcott-Bickford) and remarried after Myron Bickford's death, she remains best known as Vahdah Olcott-Bickford or VOB.

14. Olcott-Bickford's first BMG article, "In the Sphere of the Guitar," ran in *American Music Journal* 6/1 (August 1906): 24. She published several articles in *Crescendo* beginning in 1909, before becoming its regular guitar columnist in 1912. In 1916 Olcott-Bickford and William Foden switched allegiances, she resuming his column in *Cadenza* and he replacing her in *Crescendo*. For the Shakespeare photograph see "News," *Crescendo* 9/1 (July 1916): 21. For her Vanderbilt connection, see "News," *Crescendo* 13/1 (July 1920): 6. A later notice listed the program of a concert Olcott-Bickford directed at the Vanderbilt home the next May; *Cadenza* 28/7 (July 1921): 42.

15. For her endorsement of earlier music see Vahdah Olcott-Bickford, "When Does a Musician Become an 'Old Timer'?" *Cadenza* 24/2 (February 1917): 10. Although long out of print, copies of her method can still be found; Vahdah Olcott-Bickford, *The Olcott-Bickford Guitar Method*, Op. 85 (Boston: Oliver Ditson Company, 1921). Bickford's "Concerto Romantico" never found a commercial publisher, but the Bickfords self-published and sold it by subscription. Bone, *Guitar and Mandolin*, 38, identified this work as "the first guitar concerto to be published in America."

16. These citations are from "The Guitarist—A Splendid Musical Investment," *Cadenza* 24/4 (April 1917): 10–11. For other comments on this topic see "The Guitarist—Musicianship Versus Technic," *Cadenza* 25/9 (September 1918): 22–25. For some of her columns specifically about technique, see Olcott-Bickford's two-issue discussion of right-hand position in *Cadenza* 25/7 (July 1918): 41–43 ,and 25/8 (August 1918): 7, 26, or her column titled "A Few General Rules for Guitar Fingering," *Cadenza* 27/3 (March 1920): 40–42.

17. "The Problem Prober," *Cadenza* 25/3 (March 1918): 37.

18. Olcott-Bickford's performance at the 1922 Guild convention of a movement from Giuliani's Op. 36 Concerto received considerable press in both *Crescendo* and *Cadenza*. See "Editorial—Guild Convention/New York City, April 23–26," *Crescendo* 14/9 (March 1922): 10; and Zarh Myron Bickford, "The President's Corner," *Cadenza* 29/3 (March 1922): 6. Her performance of a Paganini quintet and a duo for guitar and piano by Diabelli was noted in S. Franklin Harvey, "Echoes of the Convention," *Cadenza* 29/8 (August 1922): 9–12.

19. She addressed the elfin nature of some pieces (including works by J. K. Mertz and her husband, Zarh Myron Bickford) in "Fairy Music for Guitar," *Crescendo* 19/8 (February 1927): 6. Her attacks on business ran in "Crescendo Scrap Book," *Crescendo* 19/8 (February 1927): 26, and "Business or Profession?" *Crescendo* 19/9 (March 1927): 6, 28.

20. The first notice for the American Guitar Society appeared with a photograph in *Crescendo* 17/6 (December 1924): 5. Zarh Myron Bickford documented her role in the founding and development of the AGS in "A Brief History of the American Guitar Society," *Guitar Review* 23 (June 1959): 20. The Carulli program was reported in "Programs of Concert and Recitals," *Crescendo* 21/3 (September 1928): 26. For the de Call program, see "Life and Works of De Call Presented at Guitar Society Lecture-Recital," *Crescendo* 20/7 (January 1928): 8. Programs featuring Bathioli

and Calegari appeared in "News," *Crescendo* 18/10 (April 1926): 8, and "The American Guitar Society Presents a Lecture Recital," *Crescendo* 20/1 (July 1927): 20. Olcott-Bickford undoubtedly based her presentations on Philip Bone's biographies in *Guitar and Mandolin*, a book published with her active support. The AGS program featuring works of Heinrich Albert (1870–1950) was first announced in late 1930; see "Guitar Society will Feature All Albert Program," *Crescendo* 23/4 (December 1930): 4. The program was finally presented in late 1931; see "American Guitar Society Lecture Recital," *Crescendo* 24/4 (December 1931): 16.

21. Vahdah Olcott-Bickford, "The Guitar in the History of Chamber Music," *Crescendo* 20/10 (April 1928): 7, 24; *Crescendo* 20/11 (May 1928): 7–8; and *Crescendo* 21/1 (July 1928): 10, 28. Her earlier article on chamber music was "The Guitar in Ensemble," *Crescendo* 18/7 (January 1926): 6, 25. For a notice of reviews of her chamber music performances, see "Editorial," *Crescendo* 16/10 (April 1924): 10, 26.

22. Later players and luthiers often jokingly call this hybrid a "lutar" or "gui-lute." A visitor to Europe in 1924 reported that "during the summer months, when the German students wander out into the woods or mountains on their vacation trips, one hardly sees them without their guitar or *laute* hanging over their shoulder, to help cheer them on their way"; George C. Krick, "The Mandolin and Guitar in Europe," *Crescendo* 17/6 (December 1924): 6. A later article from Germany recommends this instrument for home use and identifies it as a "lute-guitar"; Helene Wuelfing, "Foreign News—The Mandolin, Guitar & Lute As House & Orchestra Instruments, Theodore Ritter, Dortmund, Germany," *Crescendo* 24/7 (March 1932): 3. Another writer observed that "today lutes are being played all over Germany by school boys and girls! Because the lute of today only looks like one! It is only a lute-shaped instrument strung and played exactly like a guitar, and to the handful of lute players in the world today it is anathema and a whited sepulchre"; Alfred Sprissler, "The Lute Today," *Crescendo* 25/1 (November 1932): 3. Olcott-Bickford's lute activities were documented in "Shakespearean Lute in Concert," *Crescendo* 21/3 (September 1928): 22; "News Notes in Brief," *Crescendo* 22/11 (June 1930): 3; and "Vahdah Olcott Bickford, America's Only Lute Exponent," *Crescendo* 23/4 (December 1930): 4.

23. See Vahdah Olcott-Bickford, "American Guitar Society Doings," the *Serenader* 1/6 (September 1932): 6–9, for the announcement of the AGS association with the magazine. See Olcott-Bickford's "The Mail Bag" and "Fingers versus the Pick for the Guitar," the *Serenader* 1/7–8 (October-November 1932): 3, 6–7, 9, for her comments about jazz and hybrid instruments. Her report about the Bickfords' activities in Los Angeles in 1927 come from a letter to a student; see Ronald Purcell, "Vahdah the Letter Writer," *Soundboard* 25/1 (1998): 23–26.

24. Olcott-Bickford insisted, however, that technically proficient women guitarists outnumbered the competent men who played the guitar in this country: "I cannot explain *why* there are more men guitarists than lady guitarists, for the simple reason that there *aren't*! I am referring to guitarists who are technically equipped to play the masterpieces for the instrument, and who have given years to its study. I can pick out today in the United States more good feminine soloists on our instrument, who can play a given masterpiece creditably, than men who can do the same thing." Vahdah Olcott-Bickford, "The Guitarist—Question and Answers," *Cadenza* 26/3 (March 1919): 25.

25. *Cadenza* 23/5 (November 1916): 4.

26. See Vahdah Olcott-Bickford, "Fairy Music for Guitar," *Crescendo* 19/8 (February 1927): 6. A biographical sketch noted that for medical reasons young Olcott-Bickford's "guitar study was discontinued for a time, but she was allowed and encouraged to go on with the study of elocution and

dramatics . . . and there arose a question as to whether she would become an impersonator, actress or musician"; "Mrs. Vahdah Olcott-Bickford," *Cadenza* 24/1 (January 1917): 15.

27. A violinist who worked with Olcott-Bickford described her many years later: "In her youth, her appearance was utterly charming—a doll, in present day vernacular. I am sure the audience was very impressed and delighted . . ." Guy Horn, "January 8th, 1928: The Moment of Truth for the Classic Guitar in the United States," *Soundboard* 20/3 (1994): 17.

CHAPTER 9. THE OLD WORLD RECLAIMS ITS INSTRUMENT

1. See, for example, "Editorial," *Crescendo* 22/12 (July-August 1930): 1, 6.

2. "Personal Notes," *Crescendo* 1/2 (August 1908): 13. Santos's program is listed on pages 10–11.

3. *Cadenza* 19/5 (November 1912): 16.

4. "News," *Crescendo* 5/5 (November 1912): 22.

5. A notice of this concert, including a clipping from a *Philadelphia Record* review, appeared as part of Ethel Lucretia Olcott's "Guitarists Round Table," *Crescendo* 5/7 (January 1913): 21, 24. While this report on the concert appears under Olcott's byline, it is unlikely that she actually attended the concert and wrote the report. Although she definitely traveled east later in 1913, notices of her performances through 1912 and into early 1913 place her in California.

6. George C. Krick, "Miguel Llobet (1878–1938)," *Etude* 56 (November 1938): 762.

7. See Ethel Lucretia Olcott, "The Guitarists Round Table—On Giving Modern Composers and Arrangers a Place on Guitarist's [*sic*] Programs and in their Repertoire," *Crescendo* 6/1 (July 1913): 21. In the same issue, see "Programs of Concerts and Recitals," 19, for performances by Olcott in Los Angeles and Cleveland, Ohio.

8. Ethel Lucretia Olcott, "The Guitarists Round Table—The Highest Points to be Attained in Music," *Crescendo* 7/1 (July 1914): 19, 23.

9. Julian Arcas was a noted touring performer and composer of "national dances." See Bone, *The Guitar and Mandolin*, 11–12, for a biography of Arcas. Bobrowicz, a student of Mauro Giuliani, spent his youth in Vienna and his later years in Leipzig. He appears to have been at least as well known for his literary work as for his playing and composing. See Bone, *The Guitar and Mandolin*, 44–46, for Bobrowicz's biography.

10. George C. Krick, "The Mandolin and Guitar in Europe," *Crescendo* 17/6 (December 1924): 27. Luigi Mozzani, trained as an oboist, apparently took up the guitar after meeting and hearing William Foden in St. Louis following an ill-fated orchestra tour of America. A luthier and composer as well as a performer, Mozzani became a well-established pedagogue in Bologna, Italy. See, George C. Krick, "Luigi Mozzani," *Etude* 57 (April 1939). Despite his apparent fame in Europe at the time, Mozzani does not have an entry in Bone. For a biographical sketch of Krick through 1931, see "Our New Guitar Editor," *Crescendo* 23/11–12 (July-August 1931): 3.

11. See Messina's advertisement in *Crescendo* 20/4 (October 1927): 24. Messina's advertisements began running with Krick's in *Crescendo* 18/1 (July 1925). See *Crescendo* 17/8 (February 1925): 22, for one of Krick's early ads.

12. See George C. Krick, "Foreign Department," *Crescendo* 18/6 (December 1925): 8, for a biographical sketch and evaluation of Llobet. See also Graham Wade and Gerard Garno, *A New*

Look at Segovia: His Life, His Music, 2 vols. (Pacific, MO: Mel Bay Publications, 1997), 1: 57–59. Wade discusses Segovia's career in the mid-1920s on these pages, citing Fritz Buek's 1926 *Die Gitarre und ihre Meister* to suggest that Llobet "had already prepared the way for other guitarists [including Segovia] to follow."

13. Vahdah Olcott-Bickford, "Guitarists Round Table—Why is the Guitar More Popular in Europe than in America?" *Crescendo* 19/10 (April 1927): 22. Her desire to expand her American Guitar Society had to wait until 1931; See "American Guitar Society Announces Its First Branch Society," *Crescendo* 23/7 (March 1931): 2. For more information on the American Guitar Society and Olcott-Bickford's role in it, see Zarh Myron Bickford.

14. "Why Is Not the Guitar More Universally Studied?" *Crescendo* 20/2 (August 1927): 5.

15. "Spain and the Guitar," *Crescendo* 20/2 (August 1927): 5, 28.

16. "Andres Segovia, Celebrated Guitarist," *Crescendo* 20/8 (February 1928): 5–6. For an overview of the critical response to Segovia's debut see Horn and Peter Danner, "Segovia: A Postscript," *Soundboard* 20/3 (Winter 1994): 19.

17. See, for example, Vahdah Olcott-Bickford, "Guitarists Round Table," *Crescendo* 21/1 (July 1928): 25, 27; and *Crescendo* 21/2 (August 1928): 25, 27–28. For publication references using Segovia's name and repertoire, see "Messina Catalog Issued," *Crescendo* 21/2 (August 1928): 20, and a quarter-page box ad for Columbia Music promoting "all the numbers played by Andres Segovia" in *Crescendo* 21/4 (October 1928): 8.

18. Walter Kaye Bauer, "Guild Talks," *Crescendo* 21/10 (April 1929): 23. For the official report on the award ceremony, see "Andres Segovia Presented with First Honorary Membership to the Guild," in the same issue, 5, 7.

19. Walter Kaye Bauer, "The Publisher's Greatest Need," *Crescendo* 21/2 (August 1928): 5–6. For an example of his enthusiastic endorsement of Segovia, see "Segovia Gives Brilliant Recital," *Crescendo* 22/8 (February 1930): 16, 18. Despite his enthusiasm for Segovia's programming of Bach and nineteenth-century works, on more than one occasion Bauer critiqued Segovia's "modernistic" repertoire: "The modern works of Torroba and Turina while exquisitely played do not show Segovia up to the best advantage. True—these works are unusual, but they are at the same time too futuristic for our American audiences and seem to leave one more puzzled than pleased"; Walter Kaye Bauer, "Guild Talks," *Crescendo* 21/10 (April 1929): 23.

20. Walter Kaye Bauer, "Editorial," *Crescendo* 22/6 (December 1929): 1. Pasquale Taraffo, an Italian harp-guitarist, created quite a splash in his American debut in early 1929, but disappeared from *Crescendo*'s pages within about a year. His first notice in *Crescendo* cites a *New York Times* review; see "Italian Guitarist Makes American Debut," *Crescendo* 21/9 (March 1929): 21. For a less enthusiastic critique see [Sophocles Papas,] "The Advisory Board," *Crescendo* 22/11 (June 1930): 4, which includes George C. Krick's generally dismissive evaluation of Taraffo and his unique instrument.

21. See Wade and Garno, especially the chapters devoted to Segovia's career and repertoire from 1922 to 1934. Wade notes that Segovia had little patience for tracking down old manuscript or print sources in libraries, while Emilio Pujol's research and transcription efforts remain a cornerstone for much historical research into the vihuela, lute, and guitar literatures. For Foden's early response to Segovia, see Robert Ferguson, "Foden, Segovia, Oyanguren: Crosscurrents and Confluence in the Changing Traditions of the Guitar in America," *Soundboard* 29/3 (Winter 2003): 7–17. Ferguson examines a recently discovered letter in which Foden criticized Segovia's playing and programming, principally because neither appeared to be sufficiently virtuosic.

22. Vahdah Olcott-Bickford, "The Guitarists Round Table," *Crescendo* 21/2 (August 1928): 27.

23. *Crescendo* twice cited Lawrence Gilman's review from the *New York Herald*: "[Segovia] has made the guitar a thing to be spoken of in the same breath with the harpsichord of Landowska, the cello of Casals, the violin of Heifetz, the piano of Gieseking." See "Andres Segovia—Celebrated Guitarist," *Crescendo* 20/8 (February 1928), 5–6, and "Andres Segovia to Return for American Tour, January 4th," *Crescendo* 21/5 (November 1928), 22. Segovia was compared to violinist Fritz Kriesler in the first article cited, as well as in "Fretitorials" on page 9 of the same issue. Later authors have offered evaluations of Segovia's repertoire, especially the new works composed for him. Among the best are Harvey Turnbull, *The Guitar from the Renaissance to the Present Day* (Westport, CT: Bold Strummer, 1991), 111–15; Graham Wade, *Traditions of the Classical Guitar* (London: John Calder, 1980), 152–200; and Kozinn et al., 33–37.

24. His appointment was first promoted in "Announcing," *Crescendo* 21/8 (February 1929): 7. This announcement also indicated that Papas's column would expand to consider not just the guitar but also the Hawaiian guitar, an instrument Papas played and taught. Papas's first column ran the next month in *Crescendo* 21/9 (March 1929): 19, 23.

25. A brief biographical sketch of Papas appeared in *Crescendo* in anticipation of his appearance as a soloist at the 1928 Guild convention in Hartford, Connecticut. See "Prominent Soloists at Convention," *Crescendo* 20/12 (June 1928): 28–29. Papas's second notice in *Crescendo* made note of "over 50 radio concerts"; "News," *Crescendo* 19/4 (October 1926): 8. A photograph of "The Sophocles Papas Mandolin Orchestra" decked out in gypsy costumes appeared on the cover of *Crescendo* 24/8 (April 1932). The most detailed account of Papas is Elisabeth Papas Smith, *Sophocles Papas: The Guitar, His Life* (Chapel Hill, NC: Columbia Music, 1998). This book contains a wealth of information about the author's father, much of it gleaned from his personal papers, including numerous letters from Andres Segovia to Papas. This biography is clearly a work of love but not necessarily of incisive scholarship, and the author's comments about American music, performers, sources of music, guitar technique, etc., should be vetted before being cited. A more concise survey of Papas's long career may be found in an affectionate testimonial by a former student; Larry Snitzler, "Sophocles Papas 1893–1986," *Guitar Review* 65 (Spring 1986): 24–25.

26. Sophocles Papas, "Segovia and I," Appendix H, in Smith, 206.

27. Sophocles Papas, "The Guitar and Steel Guitar Round Table," *Crescendo* 21/9 (March 1929): 19, 23.

28. Papas's close personal relationship with Segovia allowed him direct access to Segovia's technical and musical ideas. "After the debut, Segovia invited Papas to come to New York as often as he could, to sit and listen while [Segovia] practiced from 3 to 6 p.m. Segovia even encouraged him to interrupt to ask questions, and he called Papas 'The Detective' because of his detailed observations and questions. . . . The relationship between them was based on Papas's eagerness to learn and Segovia's ability and interest in teaching"; Smith, 25–26.

29. Sophocles Papas, "The Hawaiian Guitar," *Crescendo* 22/3 (September 1929): 16, 18.

30. Sophocles Papas, "The Guitar and Steel Guitar Round Table," *Crescendo* 22/2 (August 1929): 15.

31. By early 1930 *Crescendo* had consolidated its various advice columns into one, "The Advisory Board," restricting subject matter to readers' questions. While Papas could no longer promote Segovia in *Crescendo*, that same year he published his most important article to date in *Etude*, one of America's most popular and widely distributed music journals. "The Romance of the Guitar," a four-part series based on interviews of Segovia, ran from April to July 1930. In these columns, Papas traced the guitar's history through Segovia's eyes. The first installment appeared in *Etude* 48 (April 1930): 252, 300.

32. See "Vahdah Olcott-Bickford, America's Only Lute Exponent," *Crescendo* 23/4 (December 1930): 4. While Olcott-Bickford had no competition from Spain's guitarists in this area, the Aguilar Lute Quartet created a sensation in the United States at this time. See, for example, "They Came –We Heard –They Conquered!" *Crescendo* 22/6 (December 1929): 2, a review of their American debut; and Sophocles Papas, "The Anguilar [sic] Lute Quartet," *Crescendo* 22/8 (February 1930): 4, 16.

33. William Sewell Marsh, "What Do You Most Desire?" *Crescendo* 23/9 (May 1931): 3.

34. George C. Krick, "The Guitar 1831–1931," *Crescendo* 24/1 (September 1931): 14.

35. See Ferguson, "Foden, Segovia, Oyanguren," who not only documents Foden's early negative response to Segovia but also convincingly demonstrates Foden's eventual change of heart.

36. Segovia even shied away from honorary associations. For example, in homage to their hero, the Washington [D.C.] Classical Guitar Society renamed itself "The Segovia Society" in the late 1930s or early 1940s. Although he had dealings with this group through his close friend and disciple Sophocles Papas, Segovia himself requested that his name be dropped by the organization in the 1950s. See Smith, 29.

CHAPTER 10. SUMMARY AND CONCLUSIONS

1. The first of the articles on amplification appeared in February 1933; L. A. Williams, "The Theory of Electrically Energized String Instruments," *Crescendo* 25/4 (February 1933): 4. A plectrum guitar solo had appeared in the magazine in 1932, but the only piece from the magazine identified as a blues ran in June 1933; Walter Kaye Bauer, "Big Boy Blues," *Crescendo* 25/8 (June 1933): 11. For Lang's obituary see *Crescendo* 25/7 (May 1933): 13. Foden's biography ran as "William Foden," *Crescendo* 25/8 (June 1933): 1, while the Segovia appreciation was G. Jean Aubry, "The Spell of the Guitar," *Crescendo* 25/6 (April 1933): 2–3. Olcott-Bickford reported her activities in "American Guitar Society News," *Crescendo* 25/7 (May 1933): 15. Concert announcements for Walker and Segovia can be found in "Luise Walker, Guitar Virtuoso," *Crescendo* 25/3 (January 1933): 15, and "Segovia to Tour United States Again," *Crescendo* 25/10 (October 1933): 6. See also George C. Krick, "Luise Walker's Debut. Guitar Recital by Luise Walker at Town Hall, New York City On the Evening of February Second," *Crescendo* 25/4 (February 1933): 15.

2. The Editor [Walter Kaye Bauer], "Fingers and Picks," *Crescendo* 25/9 (September 1933): 1–2.While most articles about this topic in the BMG magazines seldom compared the two styles head to head, George Krick did so in a later article for *Etude* magazine. He observed that the plectrum guitar might provide a player with a livelihood in dance bands, but not even the best of these players "can be compared from a purely musical standpoint, with any of the modern exponents of classic guitar playing." See George C. Krick, "The Guitar—Fingers or Plectrum," *Etude* 57/8 (August 1939): 540.

3. William Sewall Marsh, "Da Capo Al Segno 1933," *Crescendo* 25/10 (October 1933): 2–3; and "Fretted Instrument Progress For Twenty-five Years," *Crescendo* 25/10 (October 1933): 3.

4. Two American periodicals prominent in the second half of the twentieth century focused exclusively on the classical guitar. Especially in its early years, the older *Guitar Review* (1948–) was both a promotional tool for Albert Augustine's revolutionary nylon guitar strings and an ongoing paean to Segovia. The more recent *Soundboard* (1974–), published by the Guitar Foundation of America, has affected a more disinterested academic stance, offering a wider range of topics while never forgetting the debt of America's classical guitar community to Segovia.

5. Charlie Christian, "Guitarmen, Wake Up and Pluck: Wire for Sound; Let 'Em Hear You Play," *Down Beat* (December 1, 1939). This article has been reprinted in various sources, most recently in *Down Beat* 72/1 (January 2005): 94. Some commentators have remarked that this article was probably ghostwritten. If so, one might surmise that the Gibson Company ad department had a hand in its writing. Christian played Gibson guitars and the article reads very much like promotions for Gibson instruments that appeared in the BMG magazines.

6. The periodical most attuned to the BMG movement was the *Serenader*, subtitled "A National Journal for Teachers, Players and Dealers of Banjo, Mandolin and Guitar." Published initially out of Sioux City, Iowa, and later from York, Pennsylvania, the *Serenader* featured Zarh Myron Bickford and Vahdah Olcott-Bickford as regular columnists. For promotions and accounts of the Guild conventions see George C. Krick, "Fun with Fretted Instruments," *Etude* 55/11 (November 1937): 756; "The Future of Fretted Instruments," *Etude* 59/11 (November 1941): 791, 793; and "Personal Glimpses," *Etude* 60/6 (June 1942): 425, 427. Walter Kaye Bauer founded and directed Bauer's Banjo Big Band in the 1950s; see "Walter Bauer, 97; Renowned as a Musician and Composer," *Hartford Courant* (January 21, 1997): B7. Ruppa, 51–70, traces Milwaukee's Bonne Amie Musical Circle from its founding in 1900 through various incarnations into the 1960s. The ensemble was reconstituted in 1982 as the Milwaukee Mandolin Orchestra, and remains an active ensemble in that city.

7. George C. Krick, "The Guitar and Modern Music," *Etude* 57/9 (September 1939): 610. He sounds the same theme in "The Guitar—Fingers or Plectrum," *Etude* 57/8 (August 1939): 540.

8. See, for example, George C. Krick, "World Artists on the Classic Guitar," *Etude* 58/7 (July 1940): 495, 497, 499.

9. Krick had always considered and promoted Llobet as Tárrega's direct heir and at least Segovia's equal as a player and pioneer for the modern classical guitar. He dedicated an entire column in *Etude* to Llobet's obituary; see George C. Krick, "Miguel Llobet 1878–1938," *Etude* 56/11 (November 1938): 762.

10. Jazz guitarist Charlie Byrd (1925–1999), studied with Segovia in the late 1940s, eventually adapting a classical technique to "finger-style" jazz on a nylon-string classical guitar. Although he often featured classical guitar solos in his performances, his classical playing was not considered his strongest asset, especially by classical guitarists. Chet Atkins (1924–2001), recognized as "Mr. Guitar" on Nashville's Music Row, often performed on a nylon-strung classical guitar. He recounted a meeting with Segovia at which the Spaniard dismissed Atkins because of his electric guitar work and an unorthodox technical approach to the classical instrument. For some of Segovia's pointed comments on popular music, jazz, and amplification see Graham Wade, *Maestro Segovia* (London: Robson Books, 1986), 31, 76–78.

11. See, for example, Sonneck's paper "The Bibliography of American Music" (1904–5), and his survey of histories and bibliographies of American music at the conclusion of "The Musical Life of America from the Standpoint of Musical Topography" (1909). These papers are collected in *Oscar Sonneck and American Music*, 18–30 and 89ff., respectively. See also "Music in Our Libraries" (1917), collected in O. G. Sonneck, *Miscellaneous Studies in the History of Music* (1921; rpt. New York: Da Capo, 1968), 287–95.

12. "The Musical Life of America from the Standpoint of Musical Topography" (1909), in *Oscar Sonneck and American Music*, 76–78, 85.

13. Ibid., 86.

14. Ibid.

-<- WORKS CITED ->-

Ames, Kenneth. *Death in the Dining Room and Other Tales of Victorian Culture*. Philadelphia: Temple University Press, 1992.

Austern, Linda Phyllis. "Music and the English Renaissance Controversy over Women." In *Cecilia Reclaimed: Feminist Perspectives on Gender and Music*, Susan C. Cook and Judy S. Tsou, eds., 51–69. Urbana and Chicago: University of Illinois Press, 1994.

———. "'My Mother Musicke': Music and Early Modern Fantasies of Embodiment." In *Maternal Measures: Figuring caregiving in the early modern period*, Naomi J. Miller and Naomi Yavneh, eds., 239–281. Aldershot, UK, and Burlington, VT: Ashgate, 2000.

Back, Douglas. "A Forgotten Community: Classical Guitar in St. Louis 1870–1900." *Soundboard* 17/2 (1990): 31–32.

———. "The Guitar on the New York Concert Stage, 1816–1890 as chronicled by George C. D. Odell and George Templeton Strong." *Soundboard* 25/4 (1999): 11–18.

Bauer, Walter. "The Mandolin in America." In Robert Carl Hartman, *Guitars and Mandolins In America* (Hoffman Estates, IL: Maurer & Co., 1984).

Bean, Annemarie, James V. Hatch, and Brooks McNamara, eds. *Inside the Minstrel Mask: Readings in Nineteenth-Century Blackface Minstrelsy*. Hanover, NH: Wesleyan University Press. 1996.

Beloff, Jim. *The Ukulele: A Visual History*. San Francisco: Miller Freeman, 1997.

Bennett, Andy, and Kevin Dawe, eds. *Guitar Cultures*. Oxford and New York: Berg, 2001.

Benson, Susan Porter. *Counter Cultures: Saleswomen, Managers and Customers in American Department Stores, 1890–1940*. Urbana and Chicago: University of Illinois Press, 1986.

Best, James J. *American Popular Illustration: A Reference Guide*. Westport, CT: Greenwood Press, 1984.

Bickford, Zarh Myron. "A Brief History of the American Guitar Society." *Guitar Review* 23 (1959): 20.

Board of Music Trade of the United States of America. *Complete Catalog of Sheet Music and Musical Works 1870*. 1871. Reprint, New York: Da Capo, 1973.

Bone, Philip J. *The Guitar and Mandolin: Biographies of Celebrated Players and Composers*. 1914, 1954. Reprint, London: Schott & Co., 1972.

Brookes, Timothy. *Guitar: An American Life*. New York: Grove Press, 2005.

———. "Martin's Millionth Guitar Is a Flash of Its Future." *Philadelphia Inquirer* (December 21, 2003).

Broyles, Michael. "Art Music from 1860–1920." In *The Cambridge History of American Music*, David Nicholls, ed. 214–54. Cambridge: Cambridge University Press, 1998.

———. "Music and Class Structure in Antebellum Boston." *Journal of the American Musicological Society* 44 (Fall 1991): 451–93.

Burney, Charles. "Guittarra," in *The Cyclopedia; or Universal Dictionary of Arts, Sciences, and Literature*. ed. Abraham Rees. London: Longman, Hurst, Rees, Orme & Brown, 1819.

Carcassi, Matteo. *Method for Guitar*, Leopold Meignen, ed. New York: Wm. Hall & Son, 1847. Cited in Philip Gura, *C. F. Martin and His Guitars, 1796–1873* (Chapel Hill and London: University of North Carolina Press, 2003), 26–27.

———. *Method for Guitar*, G. C. Santisteban, ed. Bryn Mawr, PA: Theodore Presser, 1926.

———. *Method for Guitar. Student Edition*. [Philadelphia]: W. F. Shaw, 1884.

———. *New and Improved Method*, Charles de Janon, ed. Boston: Oliver Ditson, 1859.

Carlin, Bob. *String Bands in the North Carolina Piedmont*. Jefferson, NC: McFarland, 2004.

Carter, Walter. "Happy 100th, Gibson Company." *The GIBSON & Baldwin Player* 1/2 (October 2002): n.p.

———. *The Martin Book: A Complete History of Martin Guitars*. San Francisco: Miller Freeman Books, 1995.

Christian, Charlie. "Guitarmen, Wake Up and Pluck: Wire for Sound; Let 'Em Hear You Play." *Down Beat* (December 1, 1939). Rpt., *Down Beat* 72/1 (January 2005): 94.

Clemenson, Barbara. "Justin Holland: African-American Guitarist of the 19th Century," *Soundboard* 21/2 (1994): 13–20.

Cockrell, Dale. *Demons of Disorder: The Early Blackface Minstrels and their World*. New York: Cambridge University Press, 1997.

———. "Nineteenth-century popular music." In *The Cambridge History of American Music*, David Nicholls, ed., 158–85. Cambridge and New York: Cambridge University Press, 1998.

Coggins, P. "'This easy and agreeable instrument': A History of the English Guittar." *Early Music* 15 (1987): 204–18.

Converse, Charles. *New Method for the Guitar, containing Elementary Instructions in Music, designed for those who study without a master* . . . New York: William Hall & Son, 1855.

Conway, Cecelia. *African Banjo Echoes in Appalachia: A Study of Folk Traditions*. Knoxville: University of Tennessee Press, 1997.

Cox, Paul. "Classic Guitar Technique and Its Evolution as Reflected in the Method Books ca. 1770–1850." Ph.D. diss., Indiana University, 1978.

———. "Return With Us Now." *Soundboard* 2/2 (May 1975): 26.

Crawford, Richard. *The American Musical Landscape. The Business of Musicianship from Billings to Gershwin*. Berkeley: University of California Press, 1993.

———. *America's Musical Life*. New York and London: W. W. Norton, 2001.

Dangerous Curves: The Art of the Guitar. Boston: MFA Publications, 2000.

Danner, Peter, ed. *The Guitar in America. A Historical Collection of Classical Guitar Music in Facsimile*. Melville, NY: Belwin Mills, 1978.

———. "The Guitar in 19th-century America: A Lost Social Tradition." *Soundboard* 12/3 (1985): 292–98.

———. "The Guitar in America as Mirrored in Cadenza (1894–1924)." *Soundboard* 18/3 (1991): 10–19.

———. "The Meaning of American Parlor Music." Unpublished paper, 1996.

———. "The Most Remarkable Instrument We Have Ever Seen." *Soundboard* 26/2 (1999): 55.

———. "Notes on Some Early American Guitar Concerts." *Soundboard* 4/1 (1977): 8–9, 21.

———. "A Noteworthy Early American Guitar Treatise: James Ballard's 'Elements' of 1838." *Soundboard* 8/4 (1981): 270–76.

———. "Return With Us Now." *Soundboard* 11/2 (Summer 1984): 141.

———. "Segovia: A Postscript." *Soundboard* 20, no. 3 (1994): 19.

———. "William Foden in His Own Words. Annotated by Peter Danner." *Soundboard* 22/4 (Spring 1996): 31–37, and *Soundboard* 23/1 (Summer 1996): 35–42.

Davison, Mary Veronica. "American Music Periodicals: 1853–1899." Ph.D. diss., University of Minnesota, 1973. Ann Arbor, MI: UMI, 1974.

DeSantis, Vincent P. *The Shaping of Modern America: 1877–1920*. Arlington Heights, IL: Forum Press, 1989.

Diner, Steven J. *A Very Different Age: Americans of the Progressive Era*. New York: Hill & Wang, 1998.

Durkee, Jennie M. *The American Way of Playing Ukulele Solos*. Chicago: Jennie M. Durkee, 1917.

Evans, Tom, and Mary Anne Evans. *Guitars: Music, History, Construction and Players From the Renaissance to Rock*. New York: Paddington Press, 1977.

Falk, Peter Hastings, ed. *Who Was Who in American Art 1564–1975: 400 Years of Artists in America*. Madison, CT: Soundview Press, 1999.

Ferguson, Robert. "American Guitar Methods to 1924." (forthcoming).

———. "Foden, Segovia, Oyanguren: Crosscurrents and Confluence in the Changing Traditions of the Guitar in America." *Soundboard* 29/3 (Winter 2003): 7–17.

Finson, Jon W. *The Voices That Are Gone: Themes in 19th-Century American Popular Song*. New York: Oxford University Press, 1994.

Flandorf, Vera S. "Music periodicals in the United States; a survey of their history and content." M.A. thesis, University of Chicago, 1952.

Foden, William. *Foden's Grand Method for Guitar, Book I*. New York: Wm. J. Smith Music, 1920.

Foster, Stephen Collins. *The Music of Stephen Foster*, 2 vols. Steven Saunders and Deane L. Root, eds. Washington and London: Smithsonian Institution Press, 1990.

Garvey, Ellen Gruber. *The Adman in the Parlor. Magazines and the Gendering of Consumer Culture, 1880s to 1910s*. New York and Oxford: Oxford University Press, 1996.

Gillett, Paula. *Musical Women in England, 1870–1914: "encroaching on all men's Privileges."* New York: St. Martin's Press, 2000.

Godwin, Joscelyn. "Eccentric Forms of the Guitar, 1770–1850." *Journal of the Lute Society of America* 7 (1974): 90–102.

Good, Edwin M. *Giraffes, Black Dragons, and Other Pianos: A Technological History From Cristofori to the Modern Concert Grand*. Stanford, CA: Stanford University Press, 2001.

Greene, John F. "William Foden: American Guitarist and Composer." D.M.A. diss., University of Missouri-Kansas City, 1988. Ann Arbor, MI: UMI, 2001.

Grier, Katherine C. *Culture & Comfort: Parlor Making and Middle-class Identity, 1850–1930*. Washington and London: Smithsonian Institution Press, 1988.

Grover, David S. *The Piano: Its Story from Zither to Grand*. New York: Scribner's, 1976.

Grunfeld, Frederic V. *The Art and Times of the Guitar: An Illustrated History of Guitars and Guitarists*. New York: Collier Books, 1969.

Gura, Philip F. *C. F. Martin and His Guitars, 1796–1873*. Chapel Hill and London: University of North Carolina Press, 2003.

———. "Manufacturing Guitars for the American Parlor: James Ashborn's Wolcottville, Connecticut Factory, 1851–1856." *Proceedings of the American Antiquarian Society* 104/1 (1994): 117–55.

Gura, Phillip, and James F. Bollman. *America's Instrument: The Banjo in the Nineteenth Century*. Chapel Hill: University of North Carolina Press, 1999.

Hambly, Scott. "Mandolins in the United States Since 1880: An Industrial and Sociological History of Form." Ph.D. diss., University of Pennsylvania, 1977. Ann Arbor, MI: UMI, 1977.

Harding, Rosamond E. M. *The Piano-forte: Its History Traced to the Great Exhibition of 1851*. 1933. Reprint, New York: Da Capo, 1973.

Harris, Charles K. *After the Ball: Forty Years of Melody*. New York: 1926.

Harris, Neil. *Cultural Excursions: Marketing Appetites and Cultural Tastes in Modern America*. Chicago and London: University of Chicago Press, 1990.

Hartman, Robert Carl. *Guitars and Mandolins in America. Featuring the Larsons' Creations*. Hoffman Estates, IL: Maurer, 1984.

Hastedt, Catherine A. "Charles Dana Gibson." In *Dictionary of Literary Biography: American Book and Magazine Illustrators to 1920*, vol. 188. Steven E. Smith, Catherine A. Hastedt, and Donald A. Dyal, eds. Detroit, Washington, and London: Gale Research, 1998.

Heck, Thomas F. "The birth of the classic guitar and its cultivation in Vienna, reflected in the career and compositions of Mauro Giuliani (d. 1829)." Ph.D. diss., Yale University, 1970.

———. *Mauro Giuliani: Virtuoso Guitarist and Composer*. Columbus, OH: Editions Orphee, 1995.

Hitchcock, H. Wiley, and Stanley Sadie, eds. *The New Grove Dictionary of American Music*. London: Macmillan Press, 1984.

Holland, Justin. *Holland's Comprehensive Method for the Guitar . . . Also A Choice Collection of Music . . .* New York: J. L. Peters, 1874, 1876.

Horn, Guy. "January 8th, 1928: The Moment of Truth for the Classic Guitar in the United States." *Soundboard* 20/3 (1994): 17–19.

Horowitz, Joseph. *Classical Music in America*. New York: W. W. Norton, 2005.

Hoskins, Arthur. "William Foden." *Guitar Review* 23 (1959): 21–22.

Housewright, Wiley L. *A History of Music and Dance in Florida, 1565–1865*. Tuscaloosa: University of Alabama Press, 1991.

Huber, John. *The Development of the Modern Guitar*. Westport, CT: Bold Strummer, 1991.

Ivey, William, ed. *The 1921 Gibson Catalog*. Nashville, TN: Country Music Association Press, 1973.

Jones, F. O. *A Handbook of American Music and Musicians*. 1886. Reprint, New York: Da Capo Press, 1971.

Kitch, Carolyn. *The Girl on the Magazine Cover: The Origins of Visual Stereotypes in American Mass Media*. Chapel Hill and London: University of North Carolina Press, 2001.

Kominis, Katherine. "Howard Chandler Christy." In *Dictionary of Literary Biography: American Book and Magazine Illustrators to 1920*, vol. 188. Steven E. Smith, Catherine A. Hastedt, and Donald A. Dyal, eds. Detroit, Washington, and London: Gale Research, 1998.

Koskoff, Ellen, ed. *Garland Encyclopedia of World Music*. New York and London: Garland Publishing, 2001.

Kozinn, Allan, Pete Welding, Dan Forte, and Gene Santoro. *The Guitar: The History, The Music, The Players*. New York: William Morrow, 1984.

Kraft, James P. "Manufacturing" in *The Electric Guitar: A History of an American Icon*. André Millard, ed. Baltimore: The Johns Hopkins University Press, 2004.

Krick, George C. "Fun with Fretted Instrument." *Etude* 55/11 (November 1937): 756.

———. "The Future of Fretted Instruments." *Etude* 59/11 (November 1941): 791, 793.

———. "The Guitar and Modern Music." *Etude* 57/9 (September 1939): 610.

———. "The Guitar—Fingers or Plectrum." *Etude* 57/8 (August 1939): 540.

———. "Luigi Mozzani." *Etude* 57/4 (April 1939): 280.

———. "Miguel Llobet, 1878–1938." *Etude* 56/11 (November 1938): 762.

———. "Personal Glimpses." *Etude* 60/6 (June 1942): 425, 427.

———. "Reminiscences of William Foden." *Guitar Review* 23 (1959): 27.

———. "William Foden." *Etude* 57/2 (November 1939): 750–51.

———. "World Class Artists on the Classic Guitar." *Etude* 58/7 (July 1940): 495, 497, and 499.

La Guitarra Española/The Spanish Guitar. Madrid: Opera Tres, 1993.

Lears, T. J. Jackson. *Fables of Abundance: A Cultural History of Advertising in America*. New York: Basic Books, 1994.

———. "From Salvation to Self-Realization: Advertising and the Therapeutic Roots of the Consumer Culture, 1880–1930." In *The Culture of Consumption: Critical Essays in American History 1880–1980*, Richard Wrightman Fox and T. J. Jackson Lears, eds., 1–38. New York: Pantheon, 1983.

———. *No Place of Grace: Antimodernism and the Transformation of American Culture 1880–1920*. New York: Pantheon, 1981.

Levine, Lawrence W. *Highbrow Lowbrow: The Emergence of Cultural Hierarchy in America*. Cambridge, MA: Harvard University Press, 1988.

Linn, Karen. *That Half-Barbaric Twang: The Banjo in American Popular Culture*. Urbana and Chicago: University of Illinois Press, 1994.

Locke, Ralph P. "Music Lovers, Patrons and the 'Sacralization' of Culture in America." *19th-Century Music* 17 (Fall 1993): 149–73.

Loesser, Arthur. *Men, Women and Pianos: A Social History*. New York: Simon and Schuster, 1954.

Longworth, Mike. *Martin Guitars: A History*. Cedar Knolls, NJ: Colonial Press, 1975.

Lopes, Antonio. *Instruction for the Guitar*. 1884. Reprint, Menlo Park, CA: Instrumenta Antiqua, 1983.

Lopes, Paul. *The Rise of a Jazz Art World*. Cambridge and New York: Cambridge University Press, 2002.

Lott, Eric. *Love and Theft: Blackface Minstrelsy and the American Working Class*. New York: Oxford University Press, 1995.

Mahar, William J. *Behind the Burnt Cork Mask: Early Blackface Minstrelsy and Antebellum American Popular Culture*. Urbana: University of Illinois Press, 1999.

Mortimer, Frank. "Music for the Funeral Services for George Washington." *Guitar Review* 23 (June 1959): 14–15.

Mott, Frank Luther. *A History of American Magazines, 1741–1885,* 5 vols. Cambridge, MA: Harvard University Press, 1957.

Mussulman, Joseph A. *Music in the Cultured Generation: A Social History of Music in America, 1870–1900.* Evanston, IL: Northwestern University Press, 1971.

Noe, George T., and Daniel L. Most. *Chris J. Knutsen: From Harp Guitars to the New Hawaiian Family—History and Development of the Hawaiian Steel Guitar.* Everett, WA: Noe Enterprises, 1999.

Noonan, Jeffrey J. "A Desirable and Fashionable Instrument." *NYlon Review* 2/1 (Fall 2004). <http://www.nylonreview.com/>

———. "The Guitar in America As Reflected in Topical Periodicals, 1882–1933." Ph.D. diss., Washington University in St. Louis, 2004.

———. "The Guitar in America's BMG Movement: Culture, Commerce, and Aesthetics in Late 19th-century America," *Soundboard* 31/1 (2005): 47–53.

Ohmann, Richard. *Politics of Letters.* Middletown, CT: Wesleyan, 1987.

———. *Selling Culture.* London and New York: Verso, 1996.

Olcott-Bickford, Vahdah. "The Guitar in America." *Guitar Review* 23 (June 1959): 17–19.

———. *The Olcott-Bickford Guitar Method, Op. 85.* Boston: Oliver Ditson Company. 1921.

Papas, Sophocles. "The Romance of the Guitar." *Etude* 48/4 (April 1930): 252, 300.

Penny, Virginia. *The Employments of Women: A Cyclopaedia of Woman's Work.* Boston: Walker, Wise, 1863.

Pettine, Giuseppe. "Foden as I Knew Him." *Guitar Review* 23 (1959): 23.

Purcell, Ronald. "The Early Vahdah." *Soundboard* 25/1 (Summer 1998): 20–23; *Soundboard* 26/2 (1999): 55.

———. "In Memoriam: Vahdah Olcott Bickford Revere." *Soundboard* 7/3 (1980): 120.

———. "Letters from the Past: The Correspondence of C. F. E. Fiset to Mr. Sheppard." *Soundboard* 16/4 (Winter 1989–90): 18–19.

———. "Letters From the Past: Segovia Perceived: The American Reaction of Segovia's Arrival." *Soundboard* 20/3 (1994): 21.

———. "Vahdah Olcott-Bickford and the 75th Anniversary of the AGS or: Vahdah Olcott-Bickford and the 25th Anniversary of GFA." *Soundboard* 25/1 (1998): 19–20.

———. "Vahdah the Letter Writer." *Soundboard* 25/1 (1998): 23–26.

Ramirez, Jose, III. *Things About the Guitar.* Madrid: Soneto, 1993.

Robertson, James Oliver. *American Myth, American Reality.* New York: Hill & Wang, 1980.

Romanillos, José L. *Antonio de Torres: Guitar Maker—His Life & Work.* Shaftsbury, UK: Element Books, 1987, rev. 1995.

Rosenberg, Neil V. *Bluegrass: A History.* Urbana: University of Illinois Press, 1985.

Rowland, David. *Early Keyboard Instruments: A Practical Guide.* Cambridge: Cambridge University Press, 2001.

Ruppa, Paul. "The Mandolin in America After 1880 and The History of Mandolin Orchestras in Milwaukee, Wisconsin." M.Mus. thesis, University of Wisconsin-Milwaukee, 1988.

Sablosky, Irving. *What They Heard: Music in America, 1852–1881 from Dwight's Journal of Music.* Baton Rouge: Louisiana State University Press, 1986.

Sadie, Stanley, ed. *The New Grove Dictionary of Music and Musicians.* London: Macmillan, 2001.

Sallis, James, ed. *The Guitar in Jazz: An Anthology*. Lincoln, NE, and London: University of Nebraska Press, 1996.

Sanjek, Russell. *American Popular Music and Its Business: The First Four Hundred Years*, 3 vols. New York: Oxford University Press, 1988.

Savino, Richard. "Essential Issues in Performance Practices of the Classical Guitar, 1770–1850." In *Performance on Lute, Guitar, and Vihuela*, Victor A. Coelho, ed. 195–219. Cambridge: Cambridge University Press, 1997.

Schrader, Art. "Guittars and Guitars: A Note on a Musical Fashion." *American Music Research Journal* 1 (2001): 1.

Scott, Derek B. *The Singing Bourgeois: Songs of the Victorian Drawing Room and Parlour*. Milton Keynes: Open University Press, 1989.

Shearer, Aaron. "A Review of Early Methods." *Guitar Review* 23 (June 1959): 24–26.

Simpson, Clinton. "Some Early American Guitarists." *Guitar Review* 23 (June 1959): 16.

Smith, Elisabeth Papas. *Sophocles Papas: The Guitar, His Life*. Chapel Hill, NC: Columbia Music, 1998.

Snitzler, Larry. "Sophocles Papas 1893–1986." *Guitar Review* 65 (Spring 1986): 24–25.

Sonneck, Oscar George Theodore. *Early Concert-Life in America (1731–1800)*. New York: Musurgia Publishers, 1949.

———. *Miscellaneous Studies in the History of Music*. 1921. Reprint, New York: Da Capo, 1968.

———. *Oscar Sonneck and American Music*. William Lichtenwanger, ed. Urbana and Chicago: University of Illinois Press, 1983.

Southern, Eileen. *The Music of Black Americans*. New York: W. W. Norton, 1997.

Stempnik, Astrid. *Caspar Joseph Mertz, Leben und Werk des letzten Gitarristen im öster-reichischen Biedermeier: eine Studie über den Niedergang der Gitarre in Wein un 1850*. Frankfurt am Main: P. Lang, 1990.

———. "Concertino or Trois Morceaux?" *Soundboard* 9/1 (1982): 35–37.

Summerfield, Maurice. *The Jazz Guitar: Its Evolution, Players and Personalities Since 1900*. Newcastle on Tyne, UK: Ashley Mark, 1998.

Tanno, John C. "American Guitar Methods Published from the Turn of the Nineteenth Century to the Present." *Guitar Review* 23 (June 1959): 28–31.

Tawa, Nicholas E. *High-Minded and Low-Down: Music in the Lives of Americans, 1800–1861*. Boston: Northeastern University Press, 2000.

Teagle, John. *Washburn: One Hundred Years of Fine Stringed Instruments*. New York: Music Sales, 1996.

Thorson, Theodore Winton. "A History of Music Publishing in Chicago 1850–1960." Ph.D. diss., Northwestern University, 1961.

Trotter, James M. *Music and Some Highly Musical People . . . [with] Sketches of the Lives of Remarkable Musicians of the Colored Race. With Portraits, and an Appendix Containing Copies of Music Composed by Colored Men*. Boston: Lee & Shephard and New York: C. T. Dillingham, 1885.

Turnbull, Harvey. *The Guitar from the Renaissance to the Present Day*. Westport, CT: Bold Strummer, 1991.

Tyler, James. *The Early Guitar. A History and Handbook*. London: Oxford University Press, 1980.

WORKS CITED

Tyler, James, and Paul Sparks. *The Guitar and Its Music: From the Renaissance to the Classical Era*. New York: Oxford University Press, 2002.

Wade, Graham. *Maestro Segovia*. London: Robson Books, 1986.

———. *Traditions of the Classical Guitar*. London: John Calder, 1980.

Wade, Graham, and Gerard Garno. *A New Look at Segovia: His Life, His Music*. 2 vols. Pacific, MO: Mel Bay Publications, 1997.

Waksman, Steve. *Instruments of Desire: The Electric Guitar and the Shaping of Musical Experience*. Cambridge, MA: Harvard University Press, 1999.

"Walter Bauer, 97; Renowned as a Musician and Composer." Obituary. *Hartford Courant*, January 21, 1997, B7.

Washburn, Jim, and Richard Johnston. *Martin Guitars: An Illustrated Celebration of America's Premier Guitarmaker*. Emmaus, PA: Rodale Press, 1997.

Webb, Robert Lloyd. *Ring the Banjar! The Banjo in America from Folklore to Factory*. Cambridge, MA: The MIT Museum, 1984.

Winner, Septimus. *Winner's New School for the Guitar, in which the instructions are so clearly and simply treated, as to make it unnecessary to require a teacher* . . . Boston: Oliver Ditson & Company, 1870.

———. *Winner's Primary School for the Guitar; a Thorough and Complete Course of Instruction for the Guitar. Written and Arranged for Self-Instruction as well as for Teacher's Use,* . . . Cleveland: S. Brainard's Sons, 1872.

Wittke, Carl F. *Tambo and Bones: A History of the American Minstrel Stage*. Durham, NC: Duke University Press, 1930.

Wunderlich, Charles Edward. "A History and Bibliography of Early American Musical Periodicals, 1782–1852." Ph.D. diss., University of Michigan, 1962. Ann Arbor, MI: UMI, 1964.

Wynberg, Simon, ed. *Johann Kaspar Mertz (1806–1856) Guitar Works*. Heidelberg: Chanterelle Verlag, 1985, 1999.

‑‑ DISCOGRAPHY ‑‑

Contemporary fans of the banjo, Hawaiian guitar, and even ukulele can find LP, cassette, and CD reissues of some of the important players of those instruments from the late 1920s and early 1930s. These recordings feature popular performers like banjoists George van Eps and Vess Ossman and ukulele players like Ukulele Ike (Cliff Edwards). But few guitarists active in the BMG community left audio recordings, and this handful of recordings remains unavailable to the general public at this time. In recent years, however, individuals and ensembles have recreated some of these sounds; their recordings give twenty-first-century listeners an idea of what the BMG movement might have sounded like. The following recordings are available as CDs.

SOLO AND DUO GUITAR

American Pioneers of the Classic Guitar: Parlor Gems and Concert Works of William Foden and Justin Holland, Douglas Back [guitar] (1994: Mentos Press SMM 3023). A selection of some of the best from two of America's greatest nineteenth-century guitarist/composers. Includes Foden's renowned settings of "Sextette from Lucia di Lammermoor" and "Alice Where Art Thou?"

Great American Marches Polkas and Grand Concert Waltzes, Douglas Back [guitar] (1997; out of print) An anthology of compositions and arrangements by William Foden, Charles de Janon, William O. Bateman, and others. Includes arrangements of works by John Philip Sousa and Louis Moreau Gottschalk. Limited availability at <www.douglasback.com>

The Hispanic American Guitar, Douglas Back [guitar] (2003: MelBay MB 97100 BCD). Solo works by Luis T. Romero, Manuel Y. Ferrer, Charles de Janon, J. B. Coupa, and others. The CD accompanies an anthology of print music.

Parlor Guitar at the Patterson Inn, Corning, N.Y., William Groome [guitar] (2003). Bill Groome graciously sent me this self-produced recording as I was beginning work on this book. His live performance features guitar solos by Charles Dorn, P. W. Newton, A. J. Weidt, William Foden, and others. Bill, playing a period guitar by the C. Bruno Company, recreates a parlor performance from the era and demonstrates the charm of so much of the BMG music directed at amateur players.

William Groome–Parlor Guitar: Nature, William Groome [guitar]. This CD available in 2007, features late-Victorian guitar solos inspired by nature. Composers include William Foden,

DISCOGRAPHY

P. W. Newton, Meta Bischoff-Henning, W. L. Hayden, and others. (William Groome, 11 Powderhouse Rd., Corning, NY 14830 or parlourwill@yahoo.com)

American Music for Two Guitars, Phil Mathieu and Giorgia Cavallaro [duo guitars] (2005). This recording features guitar duets of William Foden and the little-known Carrie V. Hayden, daughter of the hyper-prolific Winslow Hayden. The CD includes a "Spanish Carnival (Bolero)," numerous marches, and a charming setting of " 'Tis the Last Rose of Summer," as well as some contemporary works. <http://cdbaby.com/cd/pmgc>

Moonlight Reverie: 19th-Century Music for Guitar, David Raphaelson with Salvatore Salvaggio [guitars] (1998: FMD-1). Playing a Martin & Coupa guitar from the mid-nineteenth century, Raphaelson presents a combination of original guitar works as well as his own arrangements. Composers include Charles Dorn, Antonio Lopes, Justin Holland, and Luis T. Romero.

PLECTRUM ARCH-TOP GUITAR

Tip Toe Through the Tulips, Nick Lucas [guitar & vocals] (2001: ASV Living Era 5329).

Parting the Clouds, Nick Lucas [guitar & vocals] (2001: Soundies SCD 4134). Reissues of Lucas's recordings are generally easy to find, but they focus principally on his singing rather than his guitar work. In addition to the requisite "Tip Toe Through the Tulips" (his most famous composition), be on the lookout for his guitar solos, "Pickin' the Guitar" and "Teasing the Frets."

Stringing the Blues, Eddie Lang and Joe Venuti (2000: Koch Jazz KOC-CD-7888). This is but one of numerous CD reissues of historic recordings of jazz and popular guitarists from the 1920s and 1930s. Released originally in 1962 on LP, these recordings present jazz guitarist Lang with jazz violinist Venuti in a variety of settings from 1927 to 1933.

SMALL ENSEMBLES

The Banjo Goes Highbrow, Douglas Back [classical banjo with piano and guitar] (Belmando Records BMS 3003-2). Includes works by some of the BMG era's most famous banjo soloists, including Alfred Farland and George van Eps. Accompaniment includes guitar and piano. <www.belmando.com>

The Big Trio Reprise, Douglas Back, Richard Walz, and Andrew Zohn [classical banjo, mandolin, and guitar] (Belmando Records BM 53001-2). This modern trio recreates the sound of The Big Trio's historic 1911–12 tour. Comprised of William Foden (guitar), Fred Bacon (banjo), and Giuseppe Pettine (mandolin), The Big Trio ruled as BMG royalty in the early teens. <www.belmando.com>

MANDOLIN ORCHESTRAS

All the Rage: Mandolin Ensemble Music from 1897–1924, Nashville Mandolin Ensemble (1988: New World Records 80544-2). A fourteen-piece ensemble presents large-scale works by Samuel Siegel, H. F. Odell, Walter Jacobs, W. J. Kitchener, and others.

Mandolins in the Moonlight: Music of the American Mandolin Orchestra Era, Milwaukee Mandolin Orchestra (1998: Bonne Amie Music Circle). A charming recording featuring large ensemble works by William Stahl and Thomas S. Allen as well as vocal selections and smaller groups. Director Paul Ruppa reports that their second CD, *The Bonne Amie Music Circle: Unplugged Since 1900*, will be available in May 2007. <www.milmando.org>

Mandoscapes, Louisville Mandolin Orchestra (2000: Louisville Mandolin Orchestra). The most recent recording of this ensemble. While most of the music on this recording does not date to the BMG era, it demonstrates how mandolin ensemble music has developed since the early twentieth century. <www.lmo.org>

The New York Times: American Newspaper Marches for Band, Theater Orchestra, Mandolin Orchestra, and Piano, Louisville Mandolin Orchestra (1998: The Advocate Messenger). The Louisville Mandolin Orchestra joins a turn-of-the-century brass band to play period marches associated with newspapers. (Brass Band CD, c/o The Advocate-Messenger, P.O. Box 149, Danville, KY 40423-0149)

Fine Fretted String Instruments offers a four-part series of CD reissues featuring European mandolin orchestras. *Vol. 1: Classical Mandolin Orchestras and Solos 1904–1938* (G.E. 21); *Vol. 2: Classical Mandolin Orchestras and Solos, 1915–1940* (G.E. 26); *Vol. 3: Classical Mandolin Orchestras and Solos, 1930–1950* (G.E. 37); and *Vol. 4: Classical Mandolin Orchestras and Solos, 1935–1955* (G.E. 50). Clarence Partee admitted that European mandolin orchestras were more refined and more technically adept than most American groups. These period recordings allow a modern listener to hear what Partee was talking about. (randy@finefretted.com)

❯❯ INDEX ❯❯

Page numbers in *italics* indicate illustrations.

Sieling, J., 10

Silverton, Colorado, *81*

simplified notation. *See* tablature

Sioux City, Iowa, 22, 151

six-string banjo. *See* guitar-banjo

Sol, El (newspaper), 160

"Sonatina" (Federico Moreno Tórroba), 165

song, 7, 9, 12, 14, 16, 18–19, 44, 62, 90–91, 93,
95, 151, 176; arrangements, 87–88; Italian
songs and sensuality, 101, 103; troubadour, 99

"Songs without Words" (Felix Mendelssohn), 57

Sonneck, Oscar, 8–9, 177–78

soprano banjo. *See* banjeaurine

Sor, Fernando, 13, 46, 50, 55, 57, 64, 67, 71,
83–84, 86, 140–41, 145–46, 156, 164–65,
167, 196n

Sousa, John Philip, 93, 223

South America, 103

Spain, 8, 9, 19, 42, 44, 55–56, 62–64, 100–4,
117, 148, 159–60, 168–69

"Spanish Fandango," 201n

Spanish guitar, 10–11, 122, 163, 166, 174, 176

Spanish Students, 34, 63, 69, 77–78, 103

Spanish tuning, 52, 75, 143. *See also* Saxton
System

Spanish-American War, 42, 101–2, 201n

special effects (performance), 82, 84, 140–41,
156

sports and guitar, 113

Springfield, Massachusetts, 144

St. Augustine, Florida, 8

St. Louis, Missouri, 67, 69, 73, 138–40, 148

St. Paul, Minnesota, 133

Stahl, William, 133, 225

Standards of Attainment, 64, 86, 197n

status. *See* class

steel guitar. *See* Hawaiian guitar

steel-string guitar, 4, 96, 118, 135, 154–55, 168,
170–71, 175–76

Steinway Hall (Chicago), 65

Stewart, Samuel Swaim, 17–19, 23, 26–29, 27,
31–33, 35, 41–45, 47–48, 51–55, 57, 62–65,
77, 101

Stickles, C. H., 57

Stradivarius, *125*

string band (fiddle band), 4, 14, 124, 173, 183n

string quartet, string quintet, 74, 119–21,
132–34, 149

strings, 4, 11, 18, 42, 46, 51–53, 118, 122, 124,
128, 135, 143, 154–56, 168, 172, 175–76,
190–91n

Studio Journal, The, 22

suffrage movement, 110

"Suite for Lute in C" (Heinrich Albert), 151

"Suite in Olden Style" (Heinrich Albert), 151

Sweden, 73

"Sweet Whispers Waltz" (William Foden), 93

symbol, guitar as. *See* guitar: as icon

symphony, symphonic music, 7, 58, 70, 79, 89,
93, 119–20, 122, 142, 170

Symphony Harp-Guitar, *130*, 133

syncopated music, 90–91. *See also* jazz

tablature, 10, 14, 16–17, 52, 185n

Tannhäusser (Richard Wagner), 134

taro-patch, 173

Tárrega, Francisco, 64, 69, 72, 86, 145, 148,
155–57, 159, 164–65, 169

teachers, 9, 24–25, 29, 34–36, 48, 55–56,
61–63, 67, 69–72, 75–76, 79, 82, 85, 102–3,
128, 131, 139, 141, 146, 148, 150–51, 153,
159–61, 166–71, 172, 177

teaching, as a business, 34–36, 76, 139. *See also*
pedagogy

technique: arch-top guitar, 124–28; left-hand,
18, 71, 82, 92, 94, 125, 141–42, 156, 167;
right-hand, 14, 16–19, 46–48, 52, 70–73, 94,
136, 140–43, 156, 167, 174; sitting position,
17, 42, 46, 48–50, 49–51, 73, 140, 190n;
tenor guitar, 122. *See also* special effects

technology, 4, 10

tenor banjo, 115, 122, 125–28, 136, 166, 175

tenor guitar, 122, 125, 127–28, 135, 173

tenor mandola. *See* mandola

tenor mandolin. *See* mandola

terz guitar, 74, 133–34

Texas, 33

theater, 12, 15, 41

theme and variations, 19, 57, 64, 86–89, 92, 94, 136, 140–42, 165, 167, 199–200n. *See also* arrangements; transcriptions

"Theme and Variations, op. 237" (Luigi Legnani), 64

theory (music), 18, 65, 69–70, 83–84, 92, 101, 141–43, 157

"Three Morceau, Op. 65" (J. K. Mertz), 87

Tooker, Elsie, 66–67, 67–68

Torp, Otto, 10

Torres, Antonio, 117

Tórroba, Federico Moreno, 165, 211n

Town Hall (New York), 165

transcriptions, 70–71, 88–90, 164–65. *See also* arrangements

Traviata, La (Giuseppe Verdi), 87

Travis, Merle, 3, 176

Trotter, James, 62

troubadour, 44, 96–101, 104, 107, 114, 143

trumpet, 175

tunings, 10, 52–53, 75, 83, 143, 160; bass guitar, 139; harp-guitar, 129; tenor banjo, 125–26; tenor guitar, 127–28. *See also* Saxton System; Spanish tuning

Turina, Joaquin, 164, 211n

Turnbull, Harvey, 176

Two-step (dance), 92

Tyrrell, Richard M., 36, 55–56, 73, 81–82, 92, 140, 191n

ukulele, 67, 69, 115, 129, 150, 166, 173

United States Marine Band, 56

Universal Notation, 38, 189n

University of Southern California, 151

Utah, 66, 72

Vallee, Rudy, 172

Van Eps, George, 224

Vanderbilt family, 146

Vanderbilt University Glee, Banjo, Mandolin and Guitar Club, 59

variation. *See* theme and variation

"Variations on a Theme of Mozart" (Fernando Sor), 167

vaudeville, 25, 78–79

Vega guitars, 56

Venetian Troubadours, 69

Venuti, Joe, 224

Verdi, Giuseppe, 90

Vienna, Austria, 8, 72

Villa Lobos, Heitor, 164

Vinton, Iowa, 67

viola, 79, 133, 149

viola da gamba, 151

violin, 5, 17, 27, 31, 33–34, 38, 45, 56, 70–71, 78–79, 85–86, 98, 111, 119, 123–24, 130, 132–33, 138, 157, 165, 173

"Violin Concerto" (Felix Mendelssohn), 71, 119

violincello. *See* cello

Virginia, 61

virtuosity, 73, 81, 84–88, 92, 102, 140–43, 153–54, 156–57, 164–65, 170

Visée, Robert de, 165

vocal music. *See* song

voice, vocal studies, 9, 33–36, 38–39, 66, 85, 181n

Vreeland, Walter Francis, 69–70

Wade, Graham, 164

Wagner, Richard, 79, 134

Waksman, Steve, 4

Walker, Louise, 87

waltz, 54, 90, 92–93, 141

Walz, Richard, 224

Wandervogel movement, 151, 209n

Washburn guitars, 56, 97

Washington, D.C., 166, 169

Washington, George, 10

Waters, Muddy, 176

Weidt, A. J., 76, 93, 223

Whiteman, Paul, 128, 172

women guitarists, 11–12, 33, 47–48, 51, 53, 64–68, 75–76, 81, 87, 106–16, 151–54; in BMG movement, 22, 34, 35, 42, 64–68, 151–54, 177, 209n; magazine images of, 110–16; as musical enchantress or healer, 106–10; Spanish, 103–4; Vahdah Olcott-Bickford's image as, 151–53. *See also* Olcott-Bickford, Vahdah